Praise f[...]

CROSSING THE WATER

"A skilled and careful writer. . . . Robb's adventures and misadventures in *Crossing the Water* provide convincing evidence that effort is sometimes its own reward."

—*The Washington Post*

"A chronicle of brinkmanship; wise, fumbling, and vivid. I read without wanting to stop, and when I did, it peopled my sleep."

—Edward Hoagland

"It's a rare pleasure when a new author shows not only notable talent, but the skill and chutzpah to go where no one else has gone before. Daniel Robb takes a subject that many have considered but few understood—juvenile delinquents—and writes about it with rare insight."

—Amazon.com

"A powerful and profoundly moving book about the greatest challenge some of our boys will ever face: growing safely into manhood."

—Michael Gurian, author of *The Wonder of Boys* and *A Fine Young Man*

"Disturbing, funny, and wise, this memoir charts Robb's eighteen months as a resident teacher working with troubled youth at a small progressive school on a remote, picturesque island near the Massachusetts coast. . . . Robb, with a keen ear for dialogue and an instinct for telling detail, captures the humanity of each boy, thus avoiding

Blackboard Jungle cliches, so the reader sees through the tough facade of the car thief, arsonist, or headbanger to the insecure, lonely kid underneath. . . . This beautifully written, compassionate book should appeal to a wide readership."

—*Publishers Weekly*

"Reflective, spare, and beautiful. . . . This is a book worth reading before forming easy opinions about 'kids today.' "
—Bill McKibben, author of *Long Distance: A Year of Living Strenuously*

"Robb has a wonderful ear for the varied dialects of his characters—the broad New England vowels and clipped hip-hop obscenity let us feel the individuality of each boy and teacher. In a style both lyrical and blunt, Robb writes of his struggle to give the guidance he never had and be the rescuer he so fervently wished for in his youth."
—*Booklist*

"Robb's story may be one that we have heard variations on before, but the scene is very different—in the isolation and beauty the island presents, some young boys who never had hope find their hearts and souls in sand and trees and the quiet understanding of a teacher who truly wants to help."

—Bookreporter.com

"Candidly narrated with a great deal of compassion and thoughtfulness, this profoundly heartrending account is enjoyable to read and hard to put down."
—*Library Journal*

CROSSING
THE WATER

*Eighteen Months on an
Island Working with
Troubled Boys—
A Teacher's Memoir*

DANIEL ROBB

A Touchstone Book
Published by Simon & Schuster
New York   London   Toronto   Sydney   Singapore

TOUCHSTONE
Rockefeller Center
1230 Avenue of the Americas
New York, NY 10020

First Touchstone Edition 2002
TOUCHSTONE and colophon are registered trademarks
of Simon & Schuster, Inc.
For information about special discounts for bulk purchases,
please contact Simon & Schuster Special Sales:
1-800-456-6798 or business@simonandschuster.com
Designed by Karolina Harris
Manufactured in the United States of America
10 9 8 7 6 5 4 3 2 1
Library of Congress Cataloging-in-Publication Data
Robb, Daniel.
Crossing the water : eighteen months on an island working with troubled
boys—a teacher's memoir / Daniel Robb.
p. cm.
1. Penikese Island School (Mass.) 2. Juvenile delinquents—Rehabilitation—
Massachusetts. 3. Juvenile delinquents—Education—Massachusetts.
4. Problem youth—Rehabilitation—Massachusetts. 5. Problem youth—
Education—Massachusetts. 6. Robb, Daniel. 7. Teachers—Massachusetts—
Biography. I. Title
HV9105.M42 P457 2001
362.74'8'092—dc21
[B]
2001020575
ISBN 0-7432-0238-4
       0-7432-0250-3 (Pbk)

Names have been changed throughout this book and in the case of the students and their families who are portrayed in these pages, some identifying
characteristics have also been changed.

For the boys of Penikese,
and those who know 'em.

Acknowledgments

THANKS to John Hough, first-class writer, for first reading the manuscript, tearing it apart, and for saying he thought there might be something in the shreds. Thanks also to Don Mitchell, another first-class writer, for the same.

Thanks to Jim Millinger, Doug Sadler, Margery Sabin, Connie Roosevelt, David Huddle, Michelle Stepto, Robert Stepto, Jack Wixted, Kristen Wixted, Naomi Wax, Tom Funk, and Jeff Sindler for reading the manuscript at subsequent stages, for their notes, and most of all for their encouragement.

Thanks to Jay Allison for allowing my words to reach their first broad audience. Thanks to Rachel Morton.

Thanks to B. J. Robbins, and to Cherie Burns, for considering the manuscript and helping move it along.

Thanks to Alan MacVey, Dan Kirby, Dixie Goswami, Ed Leuders, Jim Maddox, Robert Pack, Carol Knauss, Doug Woodsum, and Nick Siewert, Breadloaf people, all of whom lent some of their energies to the project, perhaps in ways they didn't realize.

Thanks to Robert Kotchen, William Sidney Parker, Elliot Hauser, and Trace Turville, founding members of the Oregon Lab, for listening to me read, and for their big hearts. Thanks also to Positive Bear.

Thanks to Ellen Wixted, Frank Renna, Max and Ms. Alice for their friendship and encouragement. Thanks to Chris Polloni for his maps.

Many thanks to my agent, Jill Kneerim, my editor, Bob Bender, Johanna Li, and Jonathon Brodman for their hard work in taking this book from leaves to bound pages. Thanks also to Stephanie Wilson.

Thanks to Laurie Raymond, Irene Prete, James Gammons, Whit Hanschke, Janet Hoffman, and Tom Quatromoni for your inspiring work.

Thanks of course to George Cadwalader and Dave Masch, who had the imagination, will, and generosity of spirit to build such a marvelous school.

Thanks to all teachers, including Emma Barrow, Sylvia Edwards, Mrs. Perkins, Cindy Zuck, Pat Mormon, Curtis McKee, Robert Pack, Doug Andersen, Richard Romagnoli, Jay Parini, Dick Forman, and especially David English, a substitute, who had the fire in him.

Thanks to Charlotte Brontë, Joseph Conrad, Edward Abbey, James Agee, Athol Fugard, Henry Miller, August Wilson, Gary Snyder, Derek Walcott, John Steinbeck, and to Howell D. Chickering, Jr., for his great translation of *Beowulf*.

Thanks to Ian Bowles for understanding when I needed to leave the campaign.

Thanks to Nick Bennett.

Thanks to Maia Porter, for your friendship and love.

Thanks to my mother, and to my father, for your love of words, and of me.

Thanks to every soul who has worked at Penikese.

Thanks be to the island, for being.

And thanks to every boy whom I knew on Penikese, and those I didn't. May you fly.

But I have observed that profane men living in ships, like the holy men gathered in monasteries, develop traits of profound resemblance. This must be because the service of the men and the service of a temple are both detached from the vanities and errors of a world which follows no severe rule. The men of the sea understand each other very well in this view of earthly things, for simplicity is a good counselor and isolation not a bad educator. A turn of mind composed of innocence and skepticism is common to them all, with the addition of an unexpected insight into motives, as of disinterested lookers on at a game.

—FROM *Chance,* BY JOSEPH CONRAD

An island is but a ship at anchor a little while.

—ANONYMOUS

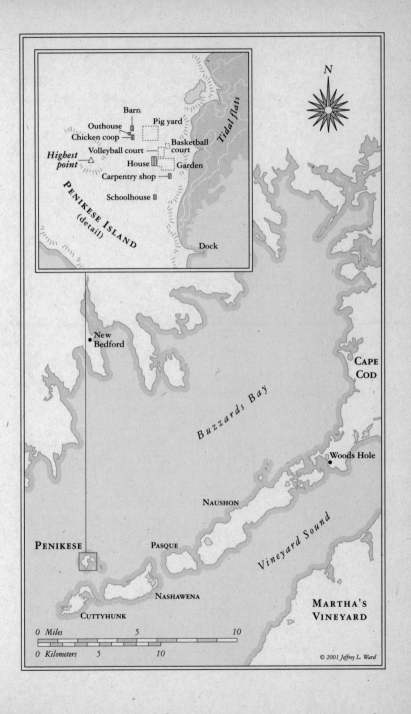

N

Barn

Outhouse
Chicken coop
Volleyball court
House
Carpentry shop

Pig yard

Basketball
court

Garden

*Highest
point*

Schoolhouse

Tidal flats

PENIKESE ISLAND
(detail)

Dock

New
Bedford

CAPE
COD

Buzzards Bay

Woods Hole

NAUSHON

PENIKESE

PASQUE

Vineyard Sound

NASHAWENA

**MARTHA'S
VINEYARD**

CUTTYHUNK

0 Miles   5   10

0 Kilometers   5   10

© 2001 Jeffrey L. Ward

Prologue

L E T me tell you a little about this book. It isn't a manual, and it isn't a minute-by-minute account of teaching at the Penikese Island School. Rather, it is a journal in which I've tried to convey what it *felt* like (looked like, sounded like) to teach the boys of Penikese. It tries to open a window on life at a school for delinquents on a small island a long way from anywhere.

What follows is an account of a school which is less a school than it is a family, or a way of life, a rhythm, a discipline, a music, with many voices of boys competing with mine for ownership of the tale. Here are the words that found their way into my journal over the course of three years. But I hope you see it also as an American coming of age for this boy, who finally figured out what he'd been trying to see all these years, which was how his growing up had affected him, where his angers had their roots, and how to get out from under the weight of his youth, which pinned him still to the field.

We are in trouble here. We all know it. Our children have begun to kill each other, and recently our schools have become the killing fields. Every few months another tragedy leaps from the headlines. Why? How have we failed to bring our young people along? It is a societal failure, and traceable to the lineaments of our country, to the living rooms, with soft lights within, which line any road you care to drive down.

This book is about a small and specific school for juvenile delinquents on a small and specific island off the coast of Cape Cod. It is not about every boy who has lost his way in the great expanse of these United States, but it is about a few of them, and their story is, to some extent, every boy's story. This book is also about my experience of the island and the school, as a staff member, over the course of three years (eighteen months of which are detailed in this book). It is not about what everyone might experience out there, but I believe there is something of me in every American, and the other way too.

Woods Hole, Massachusetts, where the school was born and from which its umbilicus still trails, is a way of seeing the world, a vantage, a scent, a thrust of land out into the currents of the North Atlantic, a warren of people and rocks and streets that somehow holds off the sea. It is home to fishermen, gardeners, merchants, caretakers, wacko artists, barkeeps, waiters, black dogs, teachers, old hippies, catch-as-catch-canners, scientists, and the wealthy who the former crowd have attracted in order to supply themselves with a livelihood. It is a three-sided peninsular end of Cape Cod, well-wooded and possessing a deep harbor, through whose fingers eddy warm waters born in the great Gulf Stream.

We all feel *it*, we who wander the streets here, as if the enormous energies moving just offshore were a pantograph generator flickering possibility in strong lines of power. We sit on the shores and observe the water, or go out even on the currents in boats and suspend ourselves on the ether of the sea, hoping, I think, for transformation. There is the feeling here that *it* might happen, that hopes dimly remembered, of brotherhood and sisterhood, of artistic elopement and self-reliance and ecstatic tolerance and the barn-raising of a community, might just happen.

It is a place where the best-known carpenter, who takes care of the Community Hall and the old schoolhouse—still the spiritual heart of the village—went to Harvard and then found a richer life in a chisel and mallet. There is some hardship in the town, to be sure, some existential angst and the inevitable hard-drinking crew at the Captain Kidd, the local bar. But there is money floating around, money to be made if you want it. Hell, I can get work as a second-rate carpenter at eighteen dollars an hour without a hassle. It is a place that has time to invent a school such as Penikese, to be open to what some would call dilettantism. I'm not saying that the school is a farce—it isn't—just that it wouldn't happen in many places, places where folks don't consider trying to survive on $17,500 (and a boatload of verbal abuse) per year because life is too damned hard to consider working so hard for a pittance. Life isn't that hard in Woods Hole.

Too, there is a remembrance of some of the New Deal, and the Kennedy idealism here, the notion that one should ask what one can do for one's country.

The central question of this book, however, is what makes a boy screw up, turns him toward the belief that he is outside the domain of what would save him, make him whole, safe, valued, loved, integral. When I trace the river to its source, wondering where the lives of the boys and my own have diverged, I come always back to the place, Woods Hole, and its main effects on me, to its green hills giving onto the sea, its eccentric elders wandering its streets, to its hounds, minstrel black dogs with brown eyes watching from the edge of the wood, to its rugged coast strewn with dories, each an advertisement of the easy pull with oars into bay and sudden ocean. More than anything else it was the place that kept me, this once boy, out of the mere.

In winter, a kid, with a six-month sentence and a court order remanding him to Penikese in his pocket, along with four cigarettes and his auntie's phone number, rolling into Woods Hole on a Greyhound bus and seeing for a few torturous minutes the world through my eyes, would see first a little cup of a harbor off to the south, across the highway, down a hill and on the far side of the old rail line, with a line of Coast Guard cutters and buoy tenders along its western edge. Then the bus would pass the white bank building, a one-story affair in white, vaguely Georgian in feature, then the strong-piled stone walls of the small library on the right, then the incongruous Pie In The Sky Bakery, in its '50s stark cube of pillar and glass, where one watches Manny the baker massive-fore-arm-kneading pastry dough behind the counter, and then the post office, in old brick, a room of combination boxes and an open window onto the profane and gustily friendly back room of the postmen, then several smaller stores, and the heart of the village would be glimpsed as the bus hung left and dropped him at the ferry terminal. He would have seen the drawbridge for a moment, the short fat bridge which crosses the channel into Eel Pond, and around which hunker the Community Hall and the old Firehouse and the Fishmonger Cafe and the bar, The Captain Kidd. He would get off the bus and note the expanse of Great Harbor reaching away from the ferry terminal toward the Hebridean Elizabeth Isles, and he would be met by a Penikese staffer and escorted along Luscombe Avenue to a right on Water Street and a left on School Street, where he would pass soon the old four-room school-house looking out over Eel Pond, and then a low place in the road where he could look out again over the pond and see the village crowding its shores, the buildings of the great scientific institutions in brick and cement encircling it halfway, and the wood frame houses circling the other way, with lobster boats and various floating things hunting around on moorings in a fitful southwest breeze. This was where I grew up. This was what saved my ass. And if my childhood hadn't been lived around questions of abandonment and living on the outside of the establishment, I might not have been pulled toward Penikese at all.

My father and mother split in Pittsburgh when I was three, and my mother and I wound up, by the time I was seven, in Woods Hole, in an old and crooked house on the shores of the pond around which the village gathers.

The dream of a day as a boy of seven began with breakfast by the pond in the ancient kitchen (built around the time of the war with Mexico), with my mother trying to warm the porous house with oil or wood, her dishing up eggs and toast or cereal as several cats milled around outside in the warming morning, then my walk of two hundred yards along the eastern edge of the pond, through dank and smelling mud, past carcasses of fish, undisclosed sea beasts, garbage, an occasional bird, under piers, through a litter of old moorings and abandoned marine filigree, to the old schoolhouse, gray, built and opened in 1885, two stories and wood-framed and square, solid, a good-natured building on a low hill overlooking the pond.

In the school there lived (as far as we students were concerned) five teachers—Mrs. Edwards, Mrs. Perkins, Mrs. Eckhardt, Mrs. Zuck, and Mrs. Barrow—whose life's purpose seemed to be to know each of us village kids for five years, to fill us with as much knowledge as they could, and to send us home at three each day never having mentioned the possibility that any of us might be destined to fail. We all lived, within those walls, in a state of mutual admiration and accomplishment, most of the time. It was a cloister in which I learned of how things might be: it was a village school.

Without its large windows and broad-boarded floors, its old bell rung (with a long rope disappearing into the dim belfry) for recess, its lumpy schoolyard lined with old oaks, its calm old rooms, each of which held an entire grade, I might not have made it. There were two other things which contributed, in the main, to my doing all right: the aforementioned town, with its grounding effect, and the steadiness of my mother's home, whose roof never leaked and whose walls offered refuge always.

Without these steadying effects, I might not have loped easily into college and work and teaching, for my father was hardly around, and there was the unmistakable sense in me of having been left behind—which is the lowest common denominator among young men in trouble. They, not knowing where they fit in, and lacking a guide, get angry.

1

SEPTEMBER 1. We were pulling up to the dock. George threw the *Hill* into reverse, bringing us to a gentle stop, and Ned—a taut, tall, feral-looking boy with long brown hair, wearing black jeans and a black leather vest, a silver skull hanging on a thong against his bare chest—jumped on board with a stern line.

"How ah ya, Jawj?" he bawled as George came out of the cabin.

"Fine, Ned. Where are the rest of your clothes? What makes you think I want to see that naked belly of yours?" Ned smiled, showing that he enjoyed the banter, and we clambered up onto the dock. Another kid sauntered down toward us, a broadly-made kid with a strong Italian face and a ponytail of tight black ringlets.

"Sonny, how about giving Dan here a walk around the island?"

"What, this guy?" he said, jabbing a thumb my way and smiling. "This another suckuh who wants to come work out heah? Yeah, I'll give you a friggin' toah. C'mon."

He took me past a massive woodpile of four-foot logs—maybe fifteen cords in all—and along a wagon path which wound through thickets of honeysuckle and sumac, past what looked like an ancient fisherman's shed. From there we headed up a hill to the wood-framed carpentry shop, then past the main house, which he told me was a copy of the oldest home on Nantucket, and further into the buildings and grounds, all built by hand in the past twenty years by the staff and students. We passed the chicken coop, home to forty layers, and the weathered outhouse, crescent moon cut out of the door, a three-holer labeled "chapel," passed the small barn and boat shop, and then headed west, along the upper edge of a hay field. We ambled along an old stone wall there, and I asked him what he thought of the place.

"It's all right, most of the time. Some of the staff are suckuhs, though. I don't know why they fuckin' do it."

"Do what?"

"Work out heah. You gotta be crazy to want to come to a place like this."

I looked out over the island. Behind us, to the southeast, Cuttyhunk and Nashawena lay a mile distant over the water. North, at the base of the field, was the cove, with Tubbs, the peninsula of the island, at the far side, and beyond that Buzzards Bay, stretching away, shimmering in the sun. It was late August, and while the leaves were still on the low sumac trees and virginia creeper and viburnum, the grass was turning blond, losing its juice to the air.

"It's beautiful out here," I said. "I think that's part of it. I mean, it's so quiet, a place where you can think. A lot of people need that."

Sonny looked at me with a combination of disdain and sympathy.

"Christ. If I hear that again I'm gonna puke. What's so beautiful?"

"The whole scene," I said. "You know, it's like a movie. Water, sky, tall grass blowing in the wind."

"Another suckuh. There's nothin' heah. Just a lotta grass and stupid guinea hens and shit. What the fuck izzat?"

He liked shooting holes in my thoughts. We walked on, talking of where he was from.

"Charlestown." He said the word as if "r" were no part of it.

"You like it there?"

"What do you mean do I like it? It's where I'm from. Course I like it. I ain't got a choice."

The path ran north, following that falling-down stone wall which was the western limit of the hay field, and then meandered northwest, past a huge boulder, a glacial erratic, to the low picket rectangle that I knew would mark the final resting place of sixteen lepers, left behind in 1921 when the island was abandoned by the state as a leper colony. I had read about that cemetery, but it was still strange to come upon it. Even Sonny seemed quieter once we were near it.

As we looked, the waves came on in ranks, breaking on the rocky shoreline twenty-five yards from the old settlement, which was abandoned and dynamited in 1921 to keep the disease from spreading.

"That's all the dead lepers," Sonny said with a slight wave of his hand toward the cemetery. "Prisoners just like us." As he said this he rolled his eyes.

I said something like, "At least you get to leave," and he volleyed with, "Yeah, not soon efuckinnough."

"How come you want to leave so bad?"

"Look, I know you're new out here, but don't be stupid. This is a fuckin' jail, with water for bars."

"A lot of people would kill for this view," I said.

"That ain't nothin' I chose."

"Well, at least you aren't a leper, right?"

I had left myself open for the kill.

"Oh, yeah. Thank you God. I'm just in jail. At least I don't have a terminal disease. I am sooo thankful."

He was enjoying himself. He took me further, showing me the crumbling foundations of the lepers' cottages. We stood on the edges of the old walls, built with rounded beach stone and cement, kicking pebbles and shards of mortar down into the grass and twisted bed frames in their cellar holes, open to the sky. The wind moved with a chirr through the tall grass which grew all around, and which was littered with old lobster-pot buoys and scraps of wood from long-ago sundered boats. In the five-mile distance the hills of South Dartmouth and Pada-naram stood out dark against the bay. I imagined the fine wooden yawls and ketches of the Concordia boat works lying lithe at their moorings in the harbor over there, lean and sexy with their narrow white hulls.

We headed back, through the grass and up the hill again to regain the spine of that stone wall. My thought was of the feel of the place—beautiful desolation and isolation. Sonny had managed to be both surly and charming at once. We made small talk. I asked him what did he like about the place, and he said,

"The weekends, coffee and a smoke on the deck—I mean a cup of some of the strong black stuff Gail makes—and some of the staff, and cooking breakfast for myself on Sunday mornings, and that's about it. I'm out in three months."

"What are you in for?" I ventured, hesitant to broach a sensitive subject.

"Grand theft auto."

He wore the words like a badge.

"I took one too many," he said, with the emphasis on "one." "I can take anything. I have taken anything. Fifteen seconds with a screwdriver, I'm gone."

"What was the best you ever took?"

"Cream Mercedes 580 something. Turbo diesel. They're tough 'cause you gotta have glow plugs firin' to start a diesel, so you gotta hot that relay, too. Gotta know that shit, Jim. Fifteen extra seconds while they heat up, you're sweatin'. I took that one clean, though. Drove it straight to Lawrence."

"Who's he?"

"It's a town, where the chop shops are."

"Oh." Visions swam through my head: Sonny tossing the keys of a soon-to-be-dismembered Mercedes to a greasy me-

chanic in a parking lot on the outskirts of a dying Massachusetts mill town, the grubby envelope of bills handed over, and
the woman down the street in the liquor store refusing to sell
Sonny a six-pack. "You're just a kid," she'd say.

We walked back. The land, stretching away and giving onto
the sea, was a constant presence. We stopped in the house. It
was rough-hewn within, with huge knees taken from ancient
boats wrecked on the island's coast used as beams and sup-
ports. A massive wood-burning cook stove and chimney stood
in the center, with a kitchen and dining area on one side, a living space on the other; homemade couches gathered around
another big woodstove there, and books lined the walls. This
was home.

We walked back to the boat. I thanked Sonny, climbed
aboard the *Hill*, and George backed her down, eased her out
into the cove. Ned was with us, going to have his eyes checked.

"Lemme drive, Jawj. I know the way. I just leave that can to
stahbud."

"Okay, Ned, but leave it to port."

"Nuh-uh. It's stahbud."

"Ned, we leave that one to port. Leave it to port."

"No way, Jawj. What you want to do, get us fuckin' killed?"

AT the end of the summer, I had sent George Cadwalader a
résumé of teaching experience and called him a few days later
to ask if he had any need of a teacher. His voice came back on
the phone with the direct tone of the marine he'd been.

"Well, I might need a teacher, and I might need a punching
bag for the boys. Which might you be?"

But he was encouraging, and we arranged that I'd accompany him on a trip to the island on the last day of August.

I met him at the boat that day, docked at a slip in Woods
Hole. It was just he and I, headed out to bring a kid in for a
medical appointment. He stood there, on the dock, an older
version of the man who had bought our house years before,

about six feet tall, dressed in battered work pants and a sweat-shirt, with a worn engineer's cap over gray hair cut short. His hands were those of a lobsterman (a third or fourth vocation), which is to say large and work-hardened. As I'd grown up, I'd been intimidated by him when I'd seen him in the post office, or wherever, perhaps because he seemed to be everything a man should be, and I might never be, in our small town. From what I knew, he'd led men into battle in Vietnam, been horri-bly wounded, and, as a marine major retired at thirty-three, turned his energies to teaching delinquent young men at an is-land school. He was one of those enlightened warriors, and when he offered his hand to me that day, large and work-hard-ened and attached to a forearm twice the size of my own, I was afraid to take it, afraid I might feel there a grip I could never equal.

The day was high, with the deep blue sky of late summer, and the fading scent of honeysuckle yet in the air, mingling with the salt. We were down on one of the Woods Hole Oceanographic Institution's docks, and the school's white fiberglass thirty-six-foot workboat, the *Harold Hill*, looked out of place among the ocean-sampling gadgetry lying about. George gunned the *Hill*'s Cat diesel as soon as I was aboard, and once she was ticking steadily, asked me to "Let her go amidships."

His tone implied that if I hadn't been there he would have gotten along fine. I let the line go, and we eased out into the morning chop of the harbor.

Our route took us through Woods Hole, a rock-strewn chan-nel whose current changes direction with the tide. So treacher-ous is the channel that fishing boats' insurance is eased if they promise not to use Woods Hole as passage toward the banks.

The mainland side of the channel is Penzance Point, which in the mid-eighteenth century was home to the Pacific Guano Company, importer of Chilean bird dung to be used in fertil-izer. Since then Penzance has become the neighborhood of the extremely wealthy, who have placed a guard at its neck, and have, over the course of a century, raised great houses as monuments to themselves. Built, of course, on guano.

The far bank of the channel is the islands Nonamesset and Uncatena, which begin the chain of the Elizabeths, at the end of which lies Penikese. They look as they did two hundred years ago. Meadows of salt hay and sandplain grasses reach away, dotted by sheep, crossed by gray fieldstone walls, broken up by thick groves of beech, locust, oak. A few houses are visible, but the car hasn't replaced the horse there. One coasts the rift between two worlds in the Hole, and once the passage is made, the old begins to replace the new.

As the *Hill* rumbled along at twelve and a half knots, feeling indomitable underfoot as she shouldered through the waves, George and I discussed the kids and the island.

"So, uh, what kind of persona do you think I should, uh, affect for the boys?" I asked him.

"Oh, I wouldn't do that," he said.

"Do what?"

"Just don't."

"Okay."

He looked out through the windscreen as spray peppered it and ran down the glass in streams. After what seemed a long silence, he said, "They'll see through any subterfuge. Be yourself, and don't say anything you can't follow up on."

Right, I thought. Be myself. But it was damned hard to rely on that in the presence of one as self-assured as George. I remembered the first time I encountered him.

When I was eight my mother and I had still lived in that house at the back of Eel Pond, the small inner harbor in Woods Hole, right across the pond from the drawbridge which separated the pond from the sea. I had ridden home from school one day in spring, and as I opened the front door, I could hear a deep voice from within the kitchen, someone discussing something with my mother. I wasn't used to the voices of men in the house, and I walked in slowly. I saw him then, a tall, strong-looking man who spoke with force, throwing around words like "mortgage" and "closing" and "realtor," words I knew had to do with selling the house. This man was to be the new owner.

They stood beyond the low lintel that separated the kitchen from the living room, he leaning against the counter that held the sink, my mother invisible, probably leaning by the big oak table. All I knew about him was that he'd been in the war that my mother and all her friends seemed to hate, and that along with him in that bag of disdain were guys like Nixon and Er-lichman and Dean. I was sorry we had to sell the house to him. Mostly, I was sorry to leave the house, because I knew the roads around there, the ballpark was around the corner, and I had a route to school right along the shore of the pond where I could walk in the morning and see what had washed up. I was going to miss the house, too. I was going to miss the warped foot-wide floorboards, and the faint line two feet up the living room walls that marked the tide of the hurricane of '38, and the old Franklin stove that sat in the living room like a primitive god, waiting to be fed. I didn't know where we'd wind up.

I went upstairs, heard the screen door slam, and watched from my window as he walked with a limp toward his pickup in the drive. We did sell the house to Cadwalader, and moved to the other side of the village, to a rented house on higher ground, and life went on. But Penikese remained a subtle presence.

"OKAY. So what about the college-boy factor here?" I said above the thrum of the diesel. "I mean, I'm not from the streets. What do I do about that?"

"Be real."

Okay, be real, I thought. Okay. I can handle that. Be real.

The *Hill* lurched as a rogue smacked her bow from the side, the remnant of a ferry's wake, and I felt my feet leave the sole as I held on to the grips overhead. George stood motionless at the wheel on his steel-filled legs. The *Hill*'s engine lost a couple of hundred rpm's and then regained her thrum as George peered out at the bay, watching for traffic.

"So, what shouldn't I do?" I ventured.

He shifted his weight. He is a thoughtful man, with a face capable of expressing moral outrage and compassion simultaneously.

"Well, what would it do to you if the ground shifted every five minutes?"

"Uh, it would make me nervous."

"That's what's going on with these guys."

"They're nervous?"

"Nervous as cats."

"Why?"

We were passing between Weepecket Island and Naushon now, and as George spoke he programmed the Loran, poking at its small keyboard with a big finger. After a moment it beeped reassuringly, and showed us in blue glowing numbers our latitude and longitude. Good to have that in a fog. George looked ahead again.

"One night Mother comes home and gives you a Hot Wheels car, okay?"

"Right. A Hot Wheels car."

"The goddamnedest Hot Wheels car you've ever seen, with fins and rocket motors and chrome wheels. Do you see that?"

"Yes. Rocket motors."

"And you are a happy little son of a bitch. Couldn't be happier, right?"

"Right. Chrome wheels. I'm happy."

"And then she cooks you franks and beans and reads you a bedtime story and tucks you in and the sugar plum fairies dance all around all night, right?"

"Right."

"So what are you thinking?"

"Uh . . ." I looked away, out the window at the brilliant yellow of scotch broom blooming on the green hillsides of

Naushon. "What am I thinking? I'm thinking I want to please Mom and I want another car, not in that order."

"Yes. So what do you do?"

"I behave."

"How do you behave?"

"Exactly as I did before."

"Right. But let me tell you what happens the second night."

The *Hill* coughed softly just then, and George swore under his breath.

"She's low on the starboard tank. I forgot to switch her. I meant to go to that port tank before we left."

He idled her down, and asked me to hold her head to wind while he kneeled stiffly and switched the fuel feeds under a panel in the deck. The *Hill* bounced easily in the swells, and I watched a couple of loons eyeing us just ahead. The switch completed, she raised her bow easily as he pushed the throttle down again, and the loons dove away.

"So what happens the second day?" I asked.

"You live the day the same way. You go to school, you eat your whole sandwich, you wipe your nose, you come home, and then the door opens and Mom is home. What do you expect?"

"A Hot Wheels car."

"That's right. But Mom comes over, and she's got a funny look in her eye. What does she say?"

"She says, 'How was school?'"

"No. You are a dismal failure, Mr. Robb."

"She says, 'I missed you.'"

"Abysmal."

"What, then?"

"She walks up close to you, looks at you, and then whacks you in the head, hard. Or her boyfriend does, or your uncle abuses you sexually in your bed when everyone else is asleep and tells you it's your fault."

George flicked the wheel to port to miss a lobster buoy.

"So, what does that do to you, day in and day out?" he asked.

"It makes me suspicious."

"It makes you a hell of a lot more than suspicious. It leads you to understand that the world may be going to give you a Hot Wheels car, or that it may be going to screw you, or both, at any time. It means that for these guys nothing is as it appears. There is no standard for behavior. Remember that. None. And it gives them X-ray vision, antennae sensitive to bullshit at a hundred miles. Sensitive to everyone's except their own."

But there was another thing going on, as George spoke: The islands which slipped by to port as we steered west-southwest—Naushon, Pasque, Nashawena—all were gently undulating ridges of glacial till, high points in a ridge carved ten thousand years before by Laurentian ice sheets flowing down from what is now Canada. The islands, although they had been farmed and logged off in historical times, had returned to what might resemble their pre-Columbian character.

Hardwoods grew in thick groves, supplanted by upland meadows, which in turn gave way to bogs and marshlands in the low places. And though there were a few houses on them, the islands were left largely to deer and coyote who swam the swift channels ("holes," in the local parlance) between them, to the wild. What moved past the eyes of a boy making the trip to Penikese was an hour and a half of wilderness, wild land on one side, the sea on the other. This was part of why I was back, to spend time with these lands, breathe their air.

"So you think you can handle these guys?" asked George, jerking me out of my reverie.

"Well, you saw my résumé," I said.

"Yeah. Publishing. Teaching. Construction. I don't doubt you can build a wall or teach a class, but how will you deal with a boy who tells you freely to go fuck yourself when you know your intentions are good? And this is a boy who has been defending himself against his father or guys a lot bigger than you for a long time. He's less afraid of a beating from you than of trying to trust you."

"Well . . ."

"What were your students like in Mississippi?"

"They were all African-American, it was a private school . . ."

"They were privileged."

"They were on scholarship, mostly sent from the inner city to get away from the violence, or they were from rural Mississippi."

"What were your problems?"

"The kids were tough, were used to guns and crack and short, hard lives. They were a long way from home, most of them."

"Why aren't you at that school anymore?"

"Lack of support from the administration. I had six classes of thirty-four, no money for books, and when I asked for it they docked my pay."

"Well, if we take you on here, I'll make sure you have the support. But you haven't answered my question."

"I don't know what I'd do, George. I'd have to know the kid."

He looked me straight in the eye as if I'd finally said something right.

"Good."

I wondered if this were my official interview. A first for me, if it were, conducted on a lobster boat above the roar of a diesel. I wasn't sure what the hell to do next. Cadwalader was a tough read, and I didn't want him to think me chatty. I risked another question.

"So, uh, what kind of treatment, or therapy, do you practice on Penikese with these guys?"

He looked at me as if I'd just questioned the use of breasts for nursing.

"The best therapy we provide, I think, is a lack of therapy."

"Oh."

The *Hill* churned on. I looked astern at the white wake unfurling behind us, and felt my stomach clamp down. Damn, I thought. I asked the wrong question. But then he went on.

"By that I mean we don't get them to lie down on a couch and rake through the shit of their childhood while they're on the island. See, most of them have never had the chance to be kids, and at their age I don't think they're really prepared to understand what they might come up with in therapy."

I was relieved. He hadn't been offended. The further we moved from the mainland, and the more I came to understand how little I knew about this place, the more I thought I wanted this job. Or at least a crack at it.

"How does that go over with the state?" I asked, looking for a neutral position.

"Well, there are different ideas about this. My feeling is that they're still children. The state . . . the state doesn't really know a lot about what happens on the island. They come out once a year and hand us a pile of papers about proper hygienic conditions and square footages for sleeping quarters, and we say thank you very much, and wait until next year. In the interim, they see a lot of relatively healthy kids coming off the island. What we try to do for the boys is give them six solid months of time to put between themselves and the lives that landed them here, time in which they can feel safe."

The plan, it seemed, was to give them a steady diet of wind, suns setting and rising, hard work, wholesome food, open space, some free time, routine, and the presence of reasonably well-adjusted adults. I could use a little of that, I thought.

By this time we had left behind Robinson's Hole, a narrow channel of swift water between Naushon and Pasque, and had drawn abreast of the mile-long Pasque, watched over by my friends Mal and Lynn, who are its caretakers. Mal would be out observing the coyote cubs, or sculpting, or getting the ancient Ford Farmall tractor running just to run it. Lynn would be painting or picking blackberries. Life out there, I knew, had a grace rarely equaled in more civilized domains. Pasque eased by.

"What do you think of Mal's old boat?" I asked George.

Mal's boat had a couple of asthmatic, smoky, seven-horse out-boards on the back. I always imagined them seizing in the middle of the Hole.

"He seems to get around in it, slowly." And then, as if pardoning a condemned man, he said, "He watches the tide well."

As the *Hill* labored, now hitting the short, square waves which had set up north of Quick's Hole where the wind met the tide, I clung again to the grips mounted on the ceiling, and looked for a way to pose my most pressing question. I knew some of the nuts and bolts of how Penikese worked. I knew it was a private school, founded in 1972 by George and his alter ego, a biologist named Dave Masch (known around town as a great fisherman, artist, chef, and raconteur). I knew it was a nonprofit, contracting with the Massachusetts Department of Youth Services (DYS) and the Rhode Island equivalent, and that it took eight boys (which sometimes became nine if a new one came before another left) on for a six-month term, during which the first two months were spent on-island without a break, and that after that they got every other weekend off. What I wanted to know was about Penikese's rate of success, but I didn't want it to seem to George that I saw this as a reason to stay or go. George's answer was provisional.

"Well," he said, "we don't know for sure how we're doing. How can you rate something like that? Going by the best figures we have, our rate of recidivism seems to be about seventy-five percent, and the state's seems to be about eighty-five percent, so by our best estimate we're saving perhaps one more kid in ten than the state."

"Are you happy with that?" I asked.

"Am I happy with it? No, it's goddamned depressing, but Pops (Dave Masch) is fond of saying that he thinks we turn a lot of potential murderers into car thieves."

"That's good."

"Good? I don't know if it's good. Do you think it's good? Maybe it's good. We may be playing a strong mitigating role with our kids. It's hard to say. What isn't hard to say is that the kids are hard to pin down when they're with us."

He paused here to squint out over the bay, look for trawlers crossing our bow as they headed out to the banks through Quicks.

I wanted to know what he meant by hard to pin down, but I didn't want to press him. At the same time, I realized that I was perhaps overreacting here, feeling too defensive. I didn't have much practice with guys like Cadwalader—these San Juan Hill types. And I realized, too, that I feared his judgment.

"Why are they hard to pin down?"

He began slowly, with the diesel thrumming in the background.

"Well, what I mean by that is that the kid who seems to be doing the best, to really be toeing the line on the island, may be the one who turns around as soon as he's off the island and fucks up."

Another pause here to look astern, see if anyone had crept up on us.

"The ones who are most screwed up are chameleons, see, in that they can adapt to any situation they're thrown into and do well. And they do this because they come from situations which are so arbitrary that the only way to survive is to be a chameleon."

"What do you mean by 'arbitrary'?"

"Hot Wheels one day, getting beaten and told you're a worthless shit the next. When you grow up in a situation like that, you tend to lack any concept of cause and effect. An arbitrary upbringing may be the worst thing you can do to a child."

Another pause here to squint out through the old marine's eyes at the bay stretching away. Having moved through the chop of the rip at Quick's, the *Hill* droned steadily now, and the spray from the bow covered the windscreen in rhythmic sheets.

At this point, George fixed his pale blue eyes on me, and spoke. I felt my distrust of him fall away in that moment, and at the same time understood clearly my doubt that I could ever speak with his assurance.

"What we try to teach on the island is that there is a direct relationship between what one does and the reality one experiences as a result. If we don't chop the wood, the house is cold, and meals can't be cooked. If we don't heat water on the stove, we can't take a shower. If we don't feed the animals, they go hungry. If we don't build community, we have none. We try to teach the basics on Penikese, and in the main, I think we do pretty well."

WE were thirty minutes away. Alongside to port slid Nashawena, a graceful three-mile-long island with one farm on it, serving a herd of Highland cattle and some sheep, making a bare living for the farmer. Ahead and to port lay Cuttyhunk, a bulky island rising a hundred and eighty feet to a high hill, home to a herd of deer and forty year-rounders who, legend has it, have divided into two camps and spend the winter feuding. I'm not sure we know how to feud properly in New England, so I imagine them just not speaking to each other, ignoring each other in the street, being violently silent, leaving the buckshot to the Hatfields and McCoys. And just ahead, to starboard, Penikese had begun to lift herself out of the sea.

On the chart, Penikese sits off to the side of the thrust of the Elizabeth Islands, which jut fifteen miles southwest from Woods Hole. It is something of a stunted sibling, out of alignment with its sisters, small, and resting almost at the end of the archipelago, just north and west of Cuttyhunk.

The island is not suggestive, not seductive. It is a runt, compassing just seventy-five acres, and lacking the marshes, heights, thickets, wetlands, and woodlands of the other islands. From any distance Penikese looks to be a desert island, seeming to lie impassive on the horizon, a low collection of bumps and swales not committed to anything other than being marginally above the sea.

The cove is easily approached in a southwest breeze, as long as you stay east of the reef called Gulls (an artful name, telling of its best indication of danger—the gulls who flock to fish in its shallow waters), from which rocky fingers extend several hundred yards. And it is a welcoming cove, looking snug and deep, until you run on the bar which crosses it about halfway in, or until the wind backs around south or east, bringing with it a rolling surf.

As we approached, the space was gradually whittled down. A few trees showed themselves in a hollow that I would learn was near the schoolhouse, and the blond salt hay looked less dry, with rosa rugosa and staghorn sumac clinging to some of the low places, out of the wind. As we came still closer, features began to stand out: the weathered gray house and outbuildings took on shape, the house's front door turned red, and the island took on bulk; I saw a few more trees tucked in sheltered spots, and a good hill at the island's center, rising maybe seventy feet above the water, marked by several sharp stones near its summit. And then we were pulling up to the dock, and Ned jumped onboard with a stern line, a taut, tall, half-wild metalhead . . .

2

SEPTEMBER 11. Saturday night. I am here for a trial week, as the schoolteacher, with three other teachers—Jack, the shift leader, a blond, stocky, bearded man of thirty-six; Gail, a pretty, brown-haired, capable woman of forty-five or so; and Jeb, a tall, brown-haired, thirty-one-year-old boatbuilder who teaches woodworking, among other things, out here—and seven troublesome boys.

After dinner, when things seemed under control and Jeb was washing the dishes in water heated on the woodstove, I asked if it would be all right if I went up the hill to watch the sunset. I didn't offer to take anyone with me, just said I might do some T'ai Chi up there for a little while. At this, Jack and Gail nodded assent.

So I headed out. I was desperate for a little quiet. I had been on-island for five or six hours, and in that time there had been none. Cyrus had wanted to play cribbage, Ned to show me where the "mices" came in the house, and Alan needed some help with a box he was making. James had wanted to play Ping-Pong, and so had Edward, and then they wanted me to go walking with them, and Sonny needed to know if I could go with him to check a lobster pot he was retrieving for a reward, and then Cyrus and Edward had gotten into a shoving match, and Ned had needed someone to help him look for his lost snakeskin, which had been draped on his shelf next to the death star he was making out of balsa wood, which was also missing, and then there was Alan who needed help deciphering the goddam miserable recipe book.

"Why don't this Beard dude just do everything in fuckin' teaspoons so I don't gotta know all this other shit?" he wanted to know. My answer, that three cups would be hundreds of teaspoons, was met with,

"So? So? I got six months, man."

And then there was wood to bring in with Edward, Mose wanted a spot (he was lifting down in the basement, and I think wanted me to see he could press 180 with ease, which he could, and I can, but not with ease), and then Ned needed to show someone how the pig pen needed rebuilding in the shelter, because

"Spahky's gonna drawp her piglets, man, and . . . 'cause that piece of wood on the bottom there, like that little low bench around the inside of the sheltuh, that's what keeps her from crushing the little bastahds when she's rolled against the side, that's all busted up, man. You think I could get some bonus points for rebuildin' it?"

was his question, one which I couldn't answer, so I referred it to Jack, who said from behind his magazine,

"Yeah, set him up with the tools and wood and let him go," which I did after consulting with Jeb.

All of this, and then an enormous dinner served up by Jack, roast beef and new potatoes and corn and biscuits and salad, all engulfed at the long table with seven boys grabbing at once for the dressing and the gravy and the Worcestershire sauce ("This stuff is the balls, yo") and being told to mind their manners and to ask please and to put their napkins on their laps and not to speak with their mouths full, all of this happening— I needed a break.

So I asked for it, and I took it. The air was sweet up on the

hill that evening, loaded with salt and honeysuckle and tran-
spiring leaf scent from Cuttyhunk a mile across the water, and
the sun was dropping into the bay. I did the first and second
sections of the Yang form up there, out of sight, and felt some
of my composure returning as I went through the old move-
ments—push, block, turn, throw, punch, breathe—while I
looked out over the dark green waters.

And then I returned to cacophony, as I opened the door and
walked into a gust of Cyrus and Edward playing Ping-Pong,
James dunning Jeb with questions about dovetails, a hip-hop
tune bumping out of the radio, which sat on a shelf in the
northwest corner of the house, and Jack mock-roaring at Alan
about the "goat-like odah" that rose from his area upstairs. Gail
played cards with Mose at the table, and Sonny and James discussed something quietly on the deck, smoking cigarettes and
laughing under their breaths. Jesus. I felt overwhelmed, full up
with the energy of it all. I waded in, played more Ping-Pong,
helped Mose write a letter, explained centrifugal force to Ned,
who then forgot it, went to the pier to check the tide with
Cyrus and Edward, played more cards with Edward and Cyrus
and Mose, talked about "cahs" and "bitches," and what they
did "wit their bitches in theah cahs" (come on, guys, they are
girls) on the deck as the guys smoked their last cigarettes of the
night, and looked at a book called *Russia—A Year* with Ned,
who enjoys books with pictures.

And then at ten on the nose Jack stalked across the floor of
the main room to the radio and killed the music. The Allman
Brothers had just finished "Southbound" ("I'm Southbound,
baby, lord I'm comin' home to you"), and were about to rip
into "Whipping Post." There were groans upstairs from Alan
and Sonny, and sighs of relief from Mose and Edward. Silence
came to the house like a gentle wind.

Just then Jeb appeared from upstairs and glided across the
floor to the table, settling his six-foot-four frame on the bench
adjacent to mine, and Jack sauntered heavily back to the table,
sat down, planted his large elbows in front of him, brushed his

hair back out of his eyes, and asked me how the day had gone. Gail sat at the far end of the table, reading. She looked up over her half glasses, an owl suddenly awake.

Jack, as I said, is a heavily made man of about six feet, with shoulder-length blond hair, arms that have seen a lot of the big crosscut saw that hums by the woodpile every morning, and a strong New England baritone that booms through the house. He has presence.

"It went fine," I said. "No threats, no intimidation, no real problems, at least from my end."

"Yeah, well, it was a good day, and you're on a little honeymoon with the boys right now, so enjoy it, 'cause it's gonna get roughah."

"Okay."

"But there's one thing," he said.

Gail looked at him, her brown eyes a little wide. Jeb watched calmly from the next bench, his big, capable hands looped over one knee, brown hair standing up in a sudden cowlick where it had been caught by his pillow. He'd been reading in his bunk upstairs.

"Yeah?" I said.

He took a moment, then turned his blue eyes back on me, and spoke quietly but forcefully. I could see, in this moment, why he was shift leader.

"That little stunt with the T'ai Chi, that can't happen."

I had had a feeling.

"Is that a bad thing out here?" I asked.

"Not the T'ai Chi. The taking off. You get off that boat, and you are heah, on duty, from the time those guys open their eyes until the time they close them, okay?"

"Yup."

"You need a break, you take at least one, better two boys with you, or they're on my hands or Gail's hands or Jeb's hands. Also, when the boys see you take off by yourself, they know you aren't there for them, and that's your job—to be there for them all the time. All of it. Okay?"

"Yup."

"They resent it when you're not there for them, even though they might not show it."

"Okay," I said.

"Now, how about you wait around down here till eleven or so, blow out the lamps then, and until then, keep your antennae up. Anything doesn't sound right, look into it."

"Okay," I said.

"Remembah, fire sounds just like the wind."

3

JACK sent me down to the schoolhouse with two boys this morning.

"Think you can handle it?" he said, grinning.

"Yeah, I think I can," I said.

"It's not as if I'm throwing you to the wolves, exactly," he said. "I'll be here, cookin' lunch, if you need anything."

We went, skinny Edward and big Mose and I, down to the schoolhouse. We walked the fifty yards past the fire pit and the little eight-tree orchard, down the brilliant green path winding to the schoolhouse with the red door. No one said a word. We went in and sat at the oak picnic table that serves as a big desk for all. And looked at each other.

"So, where do you guys keep your books?"

"Books? We don't got no books, man. She just been teachin' us out her mind," said Edward. Mose, a big, quiet black kid, tapped his head meaningfully with a long finger. They were referring to Patricia, the teacher on the other shift.

"C'mon, you guys have books," I said.

Mose looked wide-eyed at Edward.

"Mose is right, man. We ain't got no books," said Edward.

"C'mon, I know you guys have books," I said.

"Yo, that ain't even right, Dan. You callin' us a liar and you the newest, greenest staff on your first day of school, and you callin' us a liar. That ain't even right, yo," said Edward. At this, Mose folded his thick arms across his broad chest and turned away from me, stared out the window.

Neither one would budge, so I punted, walked back up the green path to Jack, five minutes after my first mission alone had begun. I knew they had books. I found him upstairs, calling in to shore on the radio.

"Said they didn't have books, huh? They're on the shelf there, above the red countah in the kitchen," said Jack.

Shit. I didn't know which were theirs. I walked again to the schoolhouse, feeling Jack's eyes on my back.

The school was empty. I headed for the pier, a minute away downhill, the easiest way to flee. They were in the fishing shack right on the way, sprawled on a pile of old moorings, sharing a cigarette in a mote of sun.

"Yo, what up, Dan?" said Edward, squinting up at me.

"School is up, and you guys are messing with me."

"Yo, that's cold, man. We just havin' a smoke, takin' a break, like," he said. I remembered he was the one in for arson, as I noted how tinder-dry the little building was.

"Did I tell you guys you could leave the schoolhouse?" I asked.

"You said you was going to go ask Jack. You didn't say nothing to us about nothing, did he Mose?"

"Nah, man, he sure didn't."

"Okay, here's the deal," I said, "You guys go get your books, bring them to the schoolhouse, and we'll get to work, or we can go talk to Jack, and figure out what your fines will be."

"Aw, shit, man, Dan's a tough guy," said Edward.

"No he ain't," said Mose.

And they went and got their books, trudging slowly up to the house in their ragged jackets, baggy pants falling off their hips, and then loped lackadaisically back down, books under their arms, papers trailing out of the corners.

So we got to work in the little school, as the chickadees worked over the steeplebush blossoms outside for their seed, with the corner of the bay and the channel beyond—Canapit-sit—just visible between the russet shores of Nashawena and Cuttyhunk; it went okay until we got into math. Mose, who is very smart, didn't feel like math today.

"Yo, I ain't doin' my algebra, man," he said, closing the book and staring out the window. I knew Mose was sharp, had been told he was capable of college-level work by George, and that he didn't show that to many people, so I said,

"Yeah you are, Mose. You're doing it. I'll do it with you."

His eyes narrowed. His voice was quiet. "Yo, man. I just said I *ain't* doin' it."

"All right, then make me a deal. Read for me for a half hour, and I'll let the math slide today."

But something had changed. In a moment I hadn't noticed, I had overstepped my bounds. Mose looked at me right between the eyes, maybe where he wanted to shoot me, gathered his books in one motion, and was out the door.

I AM employed now. George hired me. Why, I'm not sure. The next year of my life, barring homicide and act of God, is assured. The kids (Ned, Cyrus, Mose, Edward, Sonny, James, and Alan) are all trouble, to some extent. As Cadwalader says, everything they touch seems to turn to shit. Which is not to say that they have no potential.

And why I am working here, in the midst of this river of testosterone and anger, is not clear to me. I am scared. Yes I am a teacher, yes I want to teach tough kids, yes I want to make a difference, yes I want to live in a place where the ocean and sky whack me every day with their beauty . . . But what moves me deep down in these guys is not clear. I'm looking for something.

They are not big (except for Mose) or particularly intimidating (except for Mose), but there is always an implication of violence.

The cast:

Mose is big, well built, and quiet. Very quiet. He is a light brown kid from Springfield with small features and lean legs that taper into an upper body that saw the weights a lot when he was in lockup. He seems to be the silent ruler here. His story is that he shot a man who threatened him one night.

"He was comin' after my family, man, he was comin' in through the door, and he had a gun, so I just shot to scare him away, right through the door. 'Cause I'm the oldest in my family, man. He gets through me, and he's in. I was tryin' just to wing him, but he got one in the belly."

One of the other guys says that isn't how he heard it.

"Naw, he tol' me he plugged the dude when he was running the other way, got him in the back."

With a .357 Magnum. Mose is in for attempted murder.

Edward is a skinny, red-haired, raucous boy who reminds me most of a malnourished crow, always squawking about something. He is from a small town in Massachusetts, and came to us from a nearby juvenile facility—a minor-league jail, complete with razor wire and guard towers. Edward agreed to torch a fellow's boat for a grand, apparently. That got Edward a year in jail for arson. He never turned in his employer. Only Edward got burned.

Ned is yet another take on where our most disadvantaged wind up. He is the metalhead, mumbling and singing bits of satanic verse and wearing the black clothes and the bones-and-claws jewelry that go along with the image. With his scraggly, long brown hair, vacant stare, and Marlboro dangling from a sullen mouth, he is the embodiment of the headbanger. For a moment, and then he is off playing with a mouse or engaging a rooster in conversation, or theorizing on the whereabouts of the ospreys, the big fishhawks that hunt often around the island.

"I sawr 'em fishin' right off of Tubbs. That's where they always go, man. They know wheah the fishes are. That's where the blues are man, right out theah."

I've found that Ned can't read very well, and that his math skills are sketchy—we're tiptoeing around fractions right now—and that for all his bluster, he is the most peace-loving character on the island. His sense of right and wrong seems cemented in place, which is remarkable to me, considering that his childhood was spent with a father who seems resolutely to have abused his family, whose last wife is rumored to have disappeared. Ned is "slow," but I can't say whether he is retarded, or simply so browbeaten by growing up in a household predicated on abuse that he is "behind."

What is different about him is that he hasn't committed any crime. He is with us because he had run out of possibilities in the Department of Social Services (DSS), running from residential treatment centers, getting beaten up in foster homes. Penikese was Ned's last option.

Blond-haired Cyrus is another anomaly. The child of a college-educated, divorced, professional couple, Cyrus has been in therapy since he was three, and has the jangly blue eyes one would expect in a fellow who ate his victims. He says things like, "You staff are so pretentious," doesn't think twice about telling us to fuck off, and wears the baggy, falling-off-the-hips pants of a hood. I've heard that he broke into a few cars, took a few radios, and maliciously vandalized a few sites. He walks around with the attitude of a drug lord.

Alan is our king of substance abuse. His main problem seems to be that he can't stay away from what will get him high, whether that is acid, "fawties" (forty-ounce bottles of beer), dope, or glue. A big, strong, quiet kid with curly blond hair, gazing out at the world through big gray eyes that look continuously dazed, he is quick with algebra, and is with us for charges that stem from his substance abuse problems.

James is a lanky, blue-eyed, raw-boned kid from Lawrence, with a stoop that gives him the aspect of a much older person, and with what seems a genuine wish to do well on the island. He is an excellent woodworker, turning out boxes faultlessly joined with dovetails. On his arms are tattoos of the names of rock bands, and his best friends are wrapped up with a small-time gang back home. He came to us after beating his mother's boyfriend senseless with a chair.

And Sonny gave me that first tour. That is the student body at the moment—we are one short of our capacity—and it is apparent that whatever specific crime brought each of the guys here, most of them probably have varied résumés.

4

THE island makes me damned uneasy, in some ways. I have made the journey here twice now as an employee, once for that trial week, and now again as a full-time staff member. I'm elated to be here, on the front lines, as it were ("as it were"— no wonder they look at me like I'm from another planet), fifteen miles from where I grew up. Maybe I can pry one of these guys up, help him see light, breathe the thin air of . . . whatever the hell it is we have to offer. But I am a scared man much of the time out here, walking with a gait that says my legs are strong and I am strong, and doing twenty chin-ups like they're nothing, and looking back at Sonny with a clear, unflinching gaze when he jumps quickly at me as he walks by, he making all the motions of sucker-punching me except letting the blow land, his fist six inches from my face as he looks into my eyes to see if there is fear there, and I seeing it all coming as he approaches, from his posture and glances stolen at me to see how I hold myself, if I am vulnerable, and knowing that when it happens I will move not at all, nor flinch, but will stay loose and look calmly back with my eyes nailed to his as if to purr, "You naive little shit, do you really think you're going to catch me out like that? You're lucky I didn't take that poorly led right by the wrist and break it in half, twist you onto the ground."

I don't like it, that part of it. But there is such a culture here of riding the edge between being hard men and nudging the boys toward a more conciliatory place. Cadwalader, of course, walks with the muscular gait of the wounded (yet still deadly) warrior. The other shift is anchored by Tom Q., who I like tremendously, six-foot-two of quiet Vietnam vet and ex–Secret Service man, a big-hearted man. He has no limp, has a way of looking through a kid when the boy is contrary, a look which is just an inventory of where his first blow might land. A very honest look, never a finger lifted, a hand laid on. Just implied violence: Do it our way, succumb to our rules, or else (maybe). Why am I here, one of the oppressors?

WEDNESDAY, after mid-morning coffee break, James and I walked to the schoolhouse along the narrow green path that meanders past the little orchard. I raised my eyes to the bay reaching away to Nashawena in the distance. It was a rare, high day, and the sun was hot even as the air was cool and clear.

"Jesus, it doesn't get a lot nicer than today, huh? Clear as a bell. I feel damned lucky," I offered. James knew what I meant—he felt it too, the electricity that comes with breathing on such a day—but he couldn't let it in.

"You feel lucky, huh? Well, I ain't. Fuck that, man. I mean, yeah it's pretty, but I wouldn't be here if they hadn't fuckin' sent me."

He threw his books on the table there and slouched down in his Carhartt jacket.

"All right, then, what are we doing today, man?" I asked, giving him some control of the morning.

"Nothing."

"After that."

"I'll start with history."

"Yeah, and then what?"

"Math, and then I'll work on the essay the bitch give me."

"Patricia? Patricia is not a bitch."

"She's a fuckin' bitch, man. She gave me a essay on top of my readin'."

"That's because she wants you to do well."

"No it ain't. It's so she can say to George, 'Look, I got one a'them assholes on the island to write a essay for me. How about that?'"

"All right, as long as you do it, you can feel about it how you want. But let's start with journals. Fifteen minutes."

"Fuck that, man. I hate writing in my journal."

"Look, I'm writing in mine."

"What you writing about?"

"Someone."

"Who?"

"You write, and maybe I'll tell you."

"Dan's got a ho . . . sorry—girlfriend, hah hah hah. What you writing about, what you did with her last week?"

"Write and maybe I'll tell you."

"What you did with her? Was it in the shower?"

"Hey, man, write, and I'll write, and then if we feel like it we can share."

"I'm writin' a letter to my bitch, yo, that's what I'm doing."

SEPTEMBER 20. A strong north wind blowing, and the waves break themselves on the isthmus, lifting spray high in the air. Autumn is here a day early, hard, undeniable, and we are in its thrall, as a vast sky of the clear deep blue that comes with the north wind looms overhead. Talking of great winds at the long table at breakfast, as the big cook stove threw off a wall of heat, Alan recollected a snowstorm of last spring.

"Oh yeah. I remembah that storm. It blew so hahd that the rain was going sideways and bouncing off trees. I was walkin' to my friend's house in that, freezin' my frickin' balls off." Another bite of French toast. Then, a faint grin. "I spent that day drinkin'." Another bite. "Whiskey. We got shattahd."

I sit at the big oak table in the schoolhouse with Cyrus. We both write in journals, and the wind buffets the solid little building. Alan's comment comes back to me, as I consider the weather. Such a loss of a good wind on Alan. In a few minutes, after finishing up some geometry, Cyrus and I will take a look at Thoreau and Emerson. Perhaps this kid will see a little of himself in "Why I Went to the Woods" . . . not likely, though. I know it sounds trite to read the seminal version of the Spartan life to a juvi in a program in the outback, but what better source than *Walden?*

We went outside, and sat on the wellcap among the milk-weed and steeplebush, and read carefully the first few paragraphs of Thoreau's "Why I Went to the Woods."

" ' I   W E N T   to the woods because I wished to live deliber-ately,'" he read in a quavering voice, "'to front only the ess . . . ess . . . essential facts of life, and see if I could not learn what it had to teach, and not, when I came to die, discover that I had not lived.'"

"Whoa," he said, and then, "Man, this dude is heavy, man," and then he went on.

"'I did not wish to live what was not life, living is so dear; nor did I wish to practice resignation, unless it was quite nec-essary. I wanted to live deep, and suck out all the marrow of life, to live so sturdily and Spartan-like as to put to rout all that was not life . . .'"

C Y R U S was suitably confused by all of this, and the ten or twelve lines that follow it, and I was hard-pressed to extricate it for him. We sat on the south side of the schoolhouse, out of the wind, I sitting on a plank, he smoking a generic menthol and squinting at the bayberry and pokeweed; he was trying to puz-zle out how his time on the island had anything to do with Thoreau.

"What does he mean by 'deliberate'? Ain't that what a jury does?"

"Well, it is, and that's what he means—taking one's time, going carefully."

"Oh. Hah. I have a hard time with that." He paused here to whip a stone into the thicket.

"So, what do you think about this 'sucking the marrow out of life' business?"

"I don't know. Sounds vaguely perverse."

"Well, what's marrow?"

"The stuff inside of bones."

"Yeah. So if you want to get every bit of nourishment out of an animal you eat, what do you do?"

"Cook it. Eat it. Fuckin' puree it. I don't know," and at this he waved his cigarette in the air.

"You eat everything, and then you even crack the bones and suck the marrow out of them, like wolves do. That's how Thoreau is saying we should approach life—suck everything out of it."

"Oh. A real vampiuh, huh?"

"Yeah. So how about Spartans? Do you know about them?"

"They were them gladiator guys, right?"

"Yes. And they lived simply. No luxuries. No cookies, no Cadillacs, no movies."

"Fuck that. Why's Thoreau want that?"

"Because that's how he wanted to live."

"Wait. Don't tell me. Thoreau wanted to, to simplify, get to the bottom of things by getting away from the distractions of life, right?"

"Yup. Good. And that's what we try to do here."

"Well it ain't workin'. These guys are just as screwed up as they were when they got here."

So, we moved to Emerson. I set Emerson up by asking Cyrus if he thought Thoreau should be accepted as right.

"Each person should have to decide this him- or herself, obviously. I mean, everybody's got a brain," was his answer, so we lit into non-conformism, looking at Emerson's line "Whoso-ever would be a man must be a non-conformist."

"What do you mean, everyone should be a non-conform-ist?" he asked, squinting at me in the sun.

"I didn't say that. Emerson said that."

"Yeah, but you're teaching it."

"So you can decide whether it's right for you."

"Well, what the hell, how could everyone be a non-con-formist? Nothing'd ever get done."

"That's good, Cyrus. You know, this is tough stuff, they study this as freshmen in college."

"No shit?"

"None. Where were we?"

"On everybody being a freaker, we'd never get anything done," he said, walking away from me on the edge of an up-turned board like a tightrope walker.

"I think he meant something different than that, man. I think he meant that every person should think for him- or her-self, and then decide if he wants to go along with the crowd."

"So?"

"So, do you agree?"

"I don't know. I got to think about it."

He fixed his jangly blue eyes on me, and then whipped an-other stone into the grass.

"There you go."

"What?"

"You're right there."

"Shut up and let me think!"

I REMEMBER a ball game. It was played on a raw spring day on the Cape in 1978, the day I began to die. Carl Yas-trzemski and Freddy Lynn and Jim Rice and Luis Tiant and Carleton Fisk and the rest of the Red Sox were just beginning their run for the pennant in the American League, but I didn't know that, yet, didn't know that their year would end at the hands of a stumpy Yankee shortstop named Bucky Dent, who lofted a murderous fly ball over our left-field wall in the seventh game.

The sky was gray that spring day, and low—not a day on which the ball would carry well, and I was trying out for a Little League team. It was my second team, because the coach of the team that played on my home field—a tall, gangly, potbellied man with graying hair—had to cut me, he said, because all of the positions were taken by kids who had been on the team the year before (or by the friends of his son, I knew was the hidden phrase).

So he cut me. The year before I'd broken my arm, it was my last year of eligibility, and he was saying it was all over for me. But he sent me to another team, where I had, he said, one game to win a place.

The field was in Falmouth, and when I was dropped off there were some boys I knew from the big middle school there, boys who seemed harder than any of us from Woods Hole. Four or five of them milled around by the backstop, warriors in purple nylon jackets that said "Falmouth" on the back, chewing bubble gum and spitting on the ground.

I was there early, and didn't speak to them, but went and sat on the bench and sucked in my breath and waited and held my Rawlings Bobby Grich autograph glove in my lap. The rest of the team trickled in from station wagons that stopped on the road to let them out.

When the coach got there I went to him and told him who I was. He was a blunt, stocky man of forty who wore his ball cap far back on his head, and he looked at me blankly for a moment, scratched his short hair under his cap, looked at his clipboard, and said,

"Yeah, Coach Weld told me about you. Whyn't you go out to right field for the first couple of innings?"

I hated right field. Left was my field. But right was better than nothing.

First time up I hit a home run to deep center that bounced off a pitch pine beyond the field. Second time I doubled to center off my friend Phil, doubled off his sidearm scroogie he

had told me was unhittable. In the next inning I threw a man
out at the plate from deep right field. In the fourth inning the
coach pulled me, saying he had to let others play.

We won, I had knocked in half the runs for us, and at the
end of the game he came up to me as I sat on the green bench,
and said,

"Well, you had a good day. I don't have a place for you.
There's a team that meets here on Saturday mornings you can
play for."

"But I hit a homer and a double," I said.

He shook his head and turned away, started putting his bats
back in their long green bag. He had cut me. Saturday morning, I knew, was the day their farm team met. I knew they were
the rejects from the system—I'd played on a team like that
three years before. I turned and walked away from him, my
good, dusty glove tucked under my arm, cursing the whole cor-
rupt system. Fuck them all, I thought, all men, all of them. It
was clear to me, in that moment, that there was no trusting the
men in charge.

My mother was there to pick me up in the old red Ford
wagon, and as I got in the car she knew something was wrong,
but I couldn't tell her. She was my mother, who would never
understand. She would tell me it didn't matter, it was just a
game. My dad might have understood—he knew baseball—
but he was gone. And I felt different because of that, I the kid
who wasn't part of the team, the kid without the father. I had
been cut; my blood ran onto the car seats in my mind. I was
cut. I was fucked.

Which all sounds maudlin and sappy until you remember
the leverage of those days, remember the ferocity of your little
peers, their cruelties and name-callings, the seriousness of their
rehearsals for the hardnesses of life, the dangers of trust, the be-
trayals, the sweetness of being accepted and the tangles of re-
jection.

These boys out here on the island—they were given no acceptance in a deeply psychological sense. They were cut.
They're here because they were cut.

5

T H E day dawned blustery, gray. I awoke to a strong southwest
wind off Nashawena, banging the window in the south wall of
the staff room, with flocks (should be called jubilations, or ex-
altations, like butterflies) of barn swallows roiling through the
skies over the island, headed south to Florida, Costa Rica. A
long way.

Yesterday, as we worked on the stone wall around the potato
patch, Ned found a mouse trapped in a hole with a puddle at
the bottom. He did CPR, breathed on the creature, trying to
revive it—the little fellow lying faceup, buck-toothed, in his
dirty hands, with Ned's skull and crossbones amulet swaying
just above.

"Ned," I said, "put the mouse down. You know we don't
pick up the wildlife out here."

"No. He ain't dead. I sawr him breathe. Look." The mouse
lay in his hands, motionless, whiskers moved only by the
breeze. From the cove came the sound of wavelets curving in
from the bay and coming softly onto the beach.

"Ned, I think it's dead. Why don't you put it under that
bush, let nature decide."

"No, man. I'm gonna save it. Look. He moved. Hey,
mousy."

It had gasped; amazing, after lying in the puddle at the bottom of the hole, probably all night.

"I'm givin' him mousy CPR," which he began again, the long-haired metalhead, veins popping on arms I'd seen do twenty chin-ups with ease, standing in the drizzle with a mouse cupped in his hands, breathing life into it, a samaritan.

"Ned, Jesus, you can't give the mouse CPR. Mice can have diseases . . ."

"Leave me alone, man. I'm gonna save him, and put him in a box and keep him in my room."

"Ned . . ."

He looked me in the eye. "Yo, man, what if you was this mouse, Dan, where would you want to be?"

"Inside by the stove, but we're not going to put him there, Ned."

"Why not?"

"Because we're not going to bring a mouse into the house."

"There's a gazillion of 'em in there already."

An impasse. Finally, we decided the mouse would do best if left to dwell under the hay pile by the barn, with a cache of food, deep in a hole burrowed with our arms. But even then we kept discussing, under the tarp that covers the piled hay. The sweet hay, the southwest wind crackling above the tarp, our voices simmering with the debate of what was best for the soggy rodent.

"We gotta bring him inside, man, it's his right."

"Over my dead body."

"You ain't got no mercy, man."

"Yeah, I'm a hard-ass, Ned."

And I wondered if Hanta virus, mouse-borne, could have made it to Penikese. What a way to go, I thought. Killed by a mouse.

Though I was tempted just to let the mouse check out, I particularly wanted to encourage the streak of compassion in Ned, as he seems to have been the focus of so much systematic abuse as a child. His feeling toward the mouse offers good proof of his general outlook, it seems to me, and the simple attention paid to the issue, to gnashing teeth in friendly argument with the boy, tells him that his thoughts matter. This feels like a kind of fathering.

Later, we scouted for good wall stones and firewood on the north beach, as a gentle surf wrapped around the island and broke alongside us, and the light fell. Oblivious to my mission, Ned instead found old fishing lures in niches between the rocks. Then, just beyond the leper graveyard, we climbed the little bluff face, and walked back overland toward dinner, Ned clutching half a dozen rusty lures wrapped in an old glove. The wind had built enough so we had to lean into it, guinea-hen chicks scampered around in the half-light, and as we topped the rise near the great rock, we could see kerosene lanterns beginning to glow in the house windows in the distance. Cyrus was in the kitchen. He'd be the one lighting the lamps.

ONCE, when I was ten or so, coasting sandy back roads on my fat-tired Schwinn, I surprised a kid, a guy I knew was a "student" from the island, kissing a local girl under a little railroad bridge. I stopped, and just watched them for a moment. She had long, dark hair that shone. They seemed as if they were drinking each other in. It was quiet under there, and dark, and cool. It smelled of the tar on the massive timbers that spanned the one lane, and of the damp stone retaining walls on either side. I liked it under there, too.

Then the kid, who had blond hair and a wispy beard, looked at his girl, looked at me for a moment, and said, "Scram, kid," quietly, like he was Clint Eastwood. I tried to look him in the eye and skid the bike around in one motion. Instead, I laid it down, and looked up as I did to see the girl smiling up at him. He hadn't taken his hands off her waist. I pedaled away.

Another time, when I was sixteen, I was out in an old wooden sailboat, one I had patched together that spring in the driveway, the old family Herreshoff twelve-and-a-half. The wind was up, stiff out of the southwest, and I was sailing alone, driving her hard to windward up the bay, bound for a little cove called Hadley's Harbor, talking to her, hoping that none of her old fastenings would let go. A white lobster boat bore down on me by Can 13 at the mouth of the Hole—they were in a hurry—and I eased off the wind, let them pass. I was looking up at the gaff, wondering if the old piece of spruce might break, if I should throw a reef in the sail, when I heard a voice.

"Hey, asshole, whyn't you watch where you're goin'?" A squat kid in a Dolphins cap was standing at the stern of the *Harold Hill*, the Penikese boat, lifting a sentinel finger to me, mingling his voice with the diesel fumes in the *Hill's* wake. He was headed out for some months on the island.

And there were other encounters. One time, as I stood in the bank to deposit a check I'd earned teaching sailing, George stood with a couple of kids in dirty jeans and sweatshirts at the back of the line. They started talking.

"What you mean they ain't gonna give it all to me now?" said one kid.

"You get the rest when you're done with the program," said the other.

"Nah nah nah, man, they gonna give me what's mines now, or Ima fuck some motherfucker up!"

There was complete quiet in the bank. An elderly woman in a pumpkin-colored overcoat, standing in front of me, turned around fast to look at the speaker. Her lower lip trembled. George already had them outside, a hand on each boy's collar, lifting them so they stood on their toes. We watched him mouth words at them through the window, the veins in his neck standing out, each boy's eyes wide and upturned.

There was something about those kids that spoke to me, not those two in particular, necessarily, although I admired their fierce grammar, but those kids who were so much on the periphery of life in that village. I felt that way, too, marginalized somehow, even though I did well in school, held a job, had a friend or two.

A couple of years later I read a book by a family friend named John Hough called *A Peck of Salt*, about two years he spent teaching for VISTA in the ghettoes of Detroit and Chicago in the late sixties. It was one of the finest books I'd come across, sparely written, with lines about his students like,

> "My uncle say he gonna kill my mama," Taylor said. It was the first time he'd spoken. His voice was husky and tired. He was fifteen and last night he'd seen the blood of his father on the hands of his mother. Taylor had gone down and watched him die.

Jesus, I thought then, to teach kids like that, who were going through so much, to try to help them on their way . . . —that appealed to me. And seeing these guys around Woods Hole occasionally, guys serving time, guys who had been in that kind of world, made Penikese appealing. I hadn't even started college yet. The teaching would have to come later. But that was the teaching I wanted to do.

WE have a new guy: Wyatt. He is a new one to me, but not to the island. This morning we all watched the *Harold Hill* appear, a speck on the horizon, then watched it grow into a boat, and then I was left in the house while the others went to meet her as she charged into the cove and then lost speed, settled down in the bow, coasted in; I sat on the deck with a cup of coffee, listened to the wind hunting around the corners of the house, and watched the knot of people at the end of the pier next to the white boat. They stood there for quite a while. Then I saw the boat detach itself from the pier and turn again out to sea, saw the green tractor start slowly along the pier pulling a load of pig feed and groceries in the gray wooden wagon behind, watched the humans break into smaller knots, begin to drift up the hill toward the house, and then everyone disappeared behind the thickets of sumac that line the rutted road. First to reappear were Jack and Wyatt.

I saw a wiry five-foot-eleven young man, bristling with energy as he told some tale to Jack. His hair, dark brown and bleached blond toward the ends by the sun, was in dreadlocks pulled back into a ponytail; his eyes were blue, and as he walked up the path he seemed caught in a film that couldn't move fast enough to capture his motion. That was the end of my ease, as I had to be up to greet the guys when they came in. I shook Wyatt's hand.

"Pleased to meet you, Wyatt," I said.

He said, "What up, bro?"

From what I've heard, he spent six months out here, graduated a few months ago, and wandered around at home in a small town, finally getting charged again with malicious destruction of property: He and his pals smashed several hundred pumpkins in a local field. His caseworker decided to send him a wake-up call, and shipped him to lockup in Brockton, where they check on you all the time, you don't go outside at all, and each evening they watch you change into your mandatory pajamas. It is jail. After a few days of that, Wyatt wrote George a long letter, pleading to be allowed to return to Penikese. Jack, Jeb, and Gail all seem happy to have him back, volatile as he is. And one of the signal differences between Wyatt and the others, to me, is that his town, unlike that of any of the other boys here, is *my* town. He is not of my village, did not grow up on the same streets as I, but he is of my town.

ALSO, we now have Jerome, a short, polite, brown-skinned guy from Cambridge, whose reputation does not precede him. Mose is soon to go into the onshore program, a kind of halfway house, and Jerome takes his slot out here. He has adopted Jeb, and the two of them make a funny couple. Jerome has never met anyone like Jeb, and it is a riot to hear him quiz Jeb as if he were from Mars.

"What you gonna do this weekend, Jeb? You gonna see your woman, or are you gonna build a boat out of a tree?" said

Jerome as they sat at the table after dinner, the lanterns lighting their faces softly as they played cards.

"Yeah, I'm gonna see my woman, Jerome. What's it to you?"

"Jeb ain't gonna see his woman. Look how funny that boy look. Ain't no woman gonna put up with him. He too tall and skinny. He eat too much. All he be eatin' is vegetables. All he be doin' is snoopin' around the tomato patch, lookin' for leftover tomatoes he could eat. No woman gonna put up with that. He ain't got no woman." (Gales of laughter here.)

"Jerome, I may be funny lookin', but at least I'm gonna be somewhere else this weekend," said Jeb, smiling.

That quieted Jerome down, until he found the next point to needle Jeb with.

"Man, you got four T-shirts on. How come you got all them T-shirts on, Jeb, you afraid someone gonna come and take those nasty old shirts?"

"No. That's how I stay warm, Jerome, I layer."

"Jeb a crazy dude, man. He afraid someone gonna take his old T-shirts off his back, man. You crazy, Jeb. You worser than homeless."

And they go on. Jerome, who is with us on a gun charge, is obviously very fond of Jeb, who is such a solid guy, and may be the first man Jerome ever felt confident enough around to needle.

DURING off weeks I live in a cottage in town. It is a rectangle, one room, with a partial wall toward its south end and a curtain that makes the one room two. The ceiling is high—a cathedral ceiling, so called. Indoors the place has glossy pictures of Greece and Rome in frames on the walls and prints of works by Miró and Picasso. They are good, and lend the place a feeling of the cosmopolitan that I do not. The outside is shingled. In fact, I reshingled it two years ago for the owner. Inside there is a large arts and crafts chair with a green cushion, and a thin dark wood table with two leaves, a heavy dark wood set of bookshelves, a small green couch, and my stereo. There is also an oak desk which sits in front of a window facing the sea, and one other dark wood chair. A small kitchen butts off the east side, as does a small bathroom in which there is a massive clawfoot bathtub which is always very cold. Nothing in the cottage is mine but the stereo, the bedclothes, the motley books on the bookshelf, and the scattering of papers and journals that lie on the desk, in fading sun, as I see it now. The chair with the green cushion is what I dream of when I am on the island; not the only thing, but close. It is quiet in the cottage, and the sea is not far.

When a shift ends it is Friday. The boat comes to us in the morning at eight-thirty or so, a tiny white block behind a mustache of spray thrown either side by the bow on the horizon. If you look away for a few minutes and then back it has grown. It is a phoenix, and because it is the end of a two-week cycle when it comes, it means that those boys who have earned a weekend home can take it, the promise of it in their eyes as they sit in the early sun at breakfast, and then as they do their chores with care and energy because they know they are the chosen ones for the weekend. They are coming out of the wilderness, after an hour and a half on a lobster boat and two more on a bus, back into the world.

I long for that boat, I have found. Yearn, even; to think my own thoughts. We clean the place up, and then at eight-thirty the boat is at the dock, and we are shaking the hand of George or the weekend crew as if we were going home from the war, and the boys are showing off for the nonfamily members by talking loudly and swearing and lifting the heaviest bag they can with one arm. Then we are pulling away, and the diesel picks up, and I feel the fatigue of the week overtaking me, the sweetness of dropping my guard, the ease of slouching and watching the wake flattening and spreading behind us. I have a few words with Jeb, Jack, Gail, perhaps take a spell at the wheel as the islands walk slowly by, and finally we are backing into the slip in Woods Hole, and I am waving to the crew, shouldering my bag, walking down the main street, Water Street, in my Carhartt pants and battered clothes. I walk the half mile home, along the shore of the inner harbor, to the cottage, open the door, close the door, sit in that chair on the green cushion. Just a wall to look at, a wall that does not backtalk.

Get me out of this warren of thieves and pissing-out-the-mouth carpetbagger youths, I think pretty often, although rarely do I word it so. More often, these past weeks, it has been, What the hell am I here for, taking this beating? I have high ideals, want to teach them to write, to inspire, and am deflected at every damned turn, it seems, or almost, ricochet off their hardened shells of "Fuck that" and "Fuck you." What can I write but that if it's the truth? The words leave me cold, but there they are. So I am disappointed in them for their lack of rising to my occasion, and I am disappointed in myself because I am putting conditions on my experience, i.e., I don't want to be here if I'm not changing the world visibly and now. I want results. What a whiner.

S O N N Y and I found a dead barn swallow in the grass next to the wagon road yesterday. Or nearly dead. We couldn't tell. A beautiful little guy, with iridescent green breast, nestled in the tall, dewy grass alongside the wagon track, missing his eyes. Perhaps he lost one to a branch, another to a beak, and so settled to earth, gathered his legs beneath himself, to grow cold gradually. Darkness.

"Little cocksucker's dead?" said Sonny, as he knelt next to the perfect little bird.

"I don't know, man. Think so?"

"I think he bought it," he said, quietly.

"Kinda looks that way. But you know, you really can't say for sure that it did that other thing."

"Did what?"

"What your name implied."

"What name?"

"What you called him."

"What, 'cocksucker'? That's a damn term of endearment, Dan, man. I didn't mean he DID that. Fuckin' A." He rolled his eyes. "Lighten UP!"

I never know what they'll say.

To watch the swallows from the deck as they bank after flies, or as they hurl themselves into a dive and then flip out, careening back up into the blue above the garden, above the overgrown potatoes, is to witness play without the word "play" between myself and it. It's a jazz; I don't think most of the guys hear it yet.

No more of that for this one. Sonny buried it, very solemnly, on the hill above the house, cupping its soft body between his hard brown hands, and laying it in the earth among the many small graves of departed animals there. He marked this one's place with a small cross of sumac twigs tied with dental floss. Ululations of his kind flutter south to Costa Rica these days. They'll be back in May.

WEDNESDAY afternoon. I began work with Alan, the big blond kid with dazed gray eyes and a taste for acid, on the stone wall along the south side of the garden. The day was a high come down from Canada, the wind out of the north, the sky limitless, deep blue, the air crisp—carrying the scent of salt, of dying leaves—and rare, entering into one with the ease that cool water is taken in in slaking a thirst. I can think on such a day, can conjure a little. As I looked out, the bay sparkled, with a darker band of water south in Canapitsit where the wind roiled the north-flowing tide.

We could have been farm workers in Steinbeck's Salinas Valley—anywhere, in torn denim pants and old sweaters. We got the balky John Deere out of the barn, hitched up the gray wooden wagon, and headed to the isthmus which joins the island to its peninsula, Tubbs. Alan drove in low third, at the three miles per hour allowed the students, and I walked alongside; the slowly turning balloon rear tires reached about the middle of my chest.

We had already looked at the wall and its prior construction, standing in the waist-high yarrow and goldenrod. Inspecting the improbable collection of fieldstones, Alan was unimpressed. At fifteen he is a slouching five-eleven, and nearly as big as I am, with big shoulders and blond, curly hair pulled back in a ponytail.

"How many rocks we gotta get?" he asked.

"As many as we can. The bigger the better."

"Why don't we just put up a goddam fence?"

"Well, this is how they used to do it. The frost'd push the rocks up out of the ground, and the farmers would make their fences out of them. And they'd last for years. Centuries."

"They never fall down?"

"Well, yeah, but you put them back up."

"Which is why we should build a fence."

"Well . . . ," I said.

"Well?" he said.

"Well, we're building a stone wall," I said. "Let's go."

The kid harbors an intellect, I thought, behind that big, sleepy face. So why does he want to kill it so bad?

We lurched along the meandering track, shouting occasionally above the motor and wind.

"What would you rather be driving?" I asked.

"A Mustang five-point-oh, doin' a buck twenty, sitting beside Janet Jackson," he said. He leaned back in the rusty seat and imagined it, smiling to himself, while Sparky and Melissa the pigs snorted at us as we rolled past their pen.

The track wound through the old north pasture on the way to the isthmus, and we moved there through a landscape reminiscent of the island of 150 years ago, when it was farmed by Silas Mayhew, with the old fieldstone walls meandering along the borders of the fields.

We rolled past an old bog, moved through a strip of salt hay between it and the cove, and finally gained the beach and turned south along it, where it is paved at its spine with smaller stones. Within fifty yards we began to see larger stones close by.

We put a layer of these in the wagon, and then another layer, each stone weighing thirty-five pounds or so, each one blond or brown or russet granite, rounded by the surf, each one requiring a walk down the rocky beach toward the breaking three-foot waves, a low stooping to curl the fingers to its rounded contours, a heave to the shoulder, and then a stumbling walk back up the stony beach to the weathered wagon. This forty times, and all the while the wind was at twenty knots, the surf coming on the beach, gravel clacking as the waves receded, this in our ears, the wind bending the grass, gulls wheeling.

And then, hardly speaking, we loaded three large buckets of chinks—smaller stones—into the wagon, started the tractor, and proceeded to spin the wheels into the rubble of the isthmus. Alan screwed up his face, looked at me as if I were the dumbest of the dumb men in the world. We would be ridiculed for stranding the tractor on the beach. The rosa rugosa and goldenrod stared at us, listening. So, we discussed it.

"Too many goddam rocks," rumbled Alan. "We *gotta* take some out."

"All right, let's take half out, get it on solid ground, reload it, and go."

"Shit."

"We have to work until five o'clock, anyhow."

"All right, but I better be getting some pretty damn good scores."

We unloaded half of the stones. The sun sank, casting a golden horizontal light as we unhitched the trailer, dug the wheels down to level, and eased the tractor out. Alan sighed with relief as she pulled free, and stood as he steered her in a broad half circle to harder beach. We hauled the trailer over to level ground, manhandling it over the cobbled pavement of the upper beach, and reloaded our stones, bringing them slowly home through the fields with the wind and sun at our backs.

* * *

T H E N we unloaded them again, prized up a few stones left by the old masons, and began our new section of wall.

"See, we want to build a wide base, and then come in toward the top."

"You mean like a V upside down?"

"Right."

"Why didn't you just say a V upside down, then?"

"I didn't think of it. You did. That's good."

"I gotta think of everything. So we need the flat ones on the bottom, so it's sturdy."

"Right," I said.

"I fuckin' hate this," he said, as if he were putting salt on his food, and then he found a big flat one, and placed it, and went on, taking his time, playing blocks, looking for the right combination of flat and round in the failing light.

"You know how these stones got here?"

"Who gives a shit?" he said.

"I do," I said. "They came in a glacier. You know what that is?"

"A river of ice. Shut up, man, I'm tryin' to work here."

"Ten thousand years ago, the glaciers came down from New Hampshire and Vermont and ended here, and they brought boulders and stones—"

"I know. All right, man, you did your teaching," he said, making a place in the air for that with his hands. Then he made another place in the air with them. "Lemme do this now."

So I looked for stones myself, and reflected on the route that these stones had taken to get here: glacial till, left here as the litter of the ice tongues that withdrew ten thousand years ago, brought in the guts of a river of ice, rounded by the sea, now brought up from the sea to divide the land into parts, to separate pigs from potatoes. Another division.

* * *

I REMEMBER clearly the morning my parents told me they were separating. I was three, and they leaned over my bed, which was narrow, and told me this, something like, "Don't think this changes anything, but Dad's moving out," and what I remember is telling them that was not okay.

Then, a little while later, I remember watching my father's back as he walked down the stairs outside the house. They were cement, and had a black wrought-iron banister running up both sides, and he was walking down the steps away from me. He had a brown tweed jacket on, and brown leather shoes, and he was carrying two brown suitcases. He put them in his car, which was a Jeep back when they still said "Willys" on the side, and he drove away.

A little while before he left that day, he knelt down in front of me and tightened my belt for me. I have a picture of that. His hands are big, bigger than mine will ever be—farmer's hands, or a ballplayer's hands—and he is cinching the belt gently tighter and saying something to me. I can't make out the words in the picture, which is black and white, and shows me standing there in front of the big window that let the mono-chrome Pittsburgh light into the living room. The light is stark, as if all of the coal burned to smelt the steel in that city had burned the color out of the air, and it reflects off his hair, which is smooth with Vitalis, and shows his strong jaw and the depth of his dark eyes.

There was no abuse in that household. No harsh words that I could hear. Just nothing, no father anymore, and my mother sobbing over the dishes in the sink.

6

THIS is how things happen out here on a typical day.

We all sleep on the second floor of the house, reached by a narrow staircase/ladder that drops down into the middle of the living area. Up here, the students have adjoining areas separated by partitions, each with a bed and the inevitable warren of shelves and homemade cabinets holding myriad shells and old lures and girlfriend pictures and cologne bottles and shards of the past life of Penikese.

TWO of their areas are in a slightly higher loft reached by a short bridge. The most senior kids live there, and it is seen as a privilege to do so. We (the staff) sleep at the end of the floor in a room divided from the loft by a porous wall, in which there is an open doorway flanked by two loosely curtained window frames. In our room are four bunks, one in each corner, with a central bench above which is mounted the marine radio, our only contact with the mainland. A locked chest of medical supplies sits under the window, which looks south.

Gail, the woman on our shift of four, rises at six and goes downstairs, where she starts the fire in the cook stove, heats water, makes coffee, sits by herself at the long, heavy table, reading perhaps, or just looking out at the dark cove, the flashing green—two, then one—of the Lone Rock buoy, the long white flash of the mid-channel marker, or the steady beam of the light at the farm on Nashawena, three miles across the water.

This is her choice; it gives her an hour of solitude before the rest of us get up and begin complicating the day. At seven she climbs heavily up the stairs, and wakes Jack, the shift leader. He is up first, as soon as she is gone, bounding out of bed and jumping into his pants, which he has carefully left ready, stepping into the legs and pulling them on two at a time. It can be done. Then Jeb and I stagger up at intervals, and the three of us rumble down the stairs and bumble to "the pole" (one of the two gate pillars, a little way up the wagon path from the house, left from John Anderson's 1860s manse, which exists now only in photographs), to piss in the long and relieving way one does when one has refused to leave bed to go out into the cold night.

Which we do, and then return to drink inevitably strong, dark coffee, sweetened always with condensed milk, and to grade the students' performance from the day before. We do this in eight categories (up on time, cooperation, maturity, honesty, effort, initiative, skill, care). At twenty-five points per category, and two cents per point, they can earn four dollars a day, which is not great money, to be sure. But it is theirs, and we can take it away. It is a good lever.

At seven-thirty we wake the boys, the innocence of sleep is banished, and they have half an hour to smoke, curse, and drink coffee before exercises begin. At eight we go out on the deck and exercise, with Jeb leading us in stretches for twenty minutes, at the end of which we do a couple of sets of push-ups and sit-ups, run the quarter-mile loop down to the pier and back, and finish with a set of pull-ups and dips, and a game of volleyball. By nine we are in the house for breakfast, which is eggs or pancakes or French toast, oatmeal, bacon or sausage, orange juice. Like all of our meals, breakfast is had at the long, heavy table, dark and smooth with years of use, which defines one end of the house, and which, I am beginning to realize, defines the social life of the island. The "board" is where it all happens.

And then, after a ten-minute cleanup of areas, we go to work. One boy is "in kitchen," doing chores, two boys are out with Jeb, building a boat or making something in the forge, two boys are with me, struggling through school in the school-house, and two boys are with Gail or Jack—whoever isn't in kitchen—chopping wood or cleaning a sty. There is endless possibility.

Break is at eleven-fifteen, lunch is at twelve-thirty, with much good food served up, some always landing in the pig bucket. Even the pigs eat well out here.

WE have free time from one to two-thirty. We work again from two-thirty to five, and in the afternoon my work is something manual, as school is only in the mornings. We have more free time from five to six-thirty. Then we eat dinner at six-thirty, then free time again from dinner until ten, when all is quiet upstairs. The radio plays from seven until ten: an hour and a half of rock, an hour and a half of rap, and then blessed quiet. No Walkmen out here, and everyone is in bed at ten-thirty, with lights out at eleven. This rhythm seems to work, and it disturbs the boys if the schedule is thrown off. I have been able to write this schedule down, sure that ninety-five out of a hundred weekdays on the island would almost precisely fit it. Oh, and we have no phone, nor any power but for the photo-voltaics that charge the heavy batteries from which we run the refrigerator and radio. We light with kerosene lamps.

Jack is a career educator, and has been at Penikese, off and on, for eight years. In another life he would be a chef or fisherman, and somehow manages to look both parts. Jeb has a degree in engineering from Berkeley, and has worked as a boatbuilder for the last four or five years on the Vineyard. He can narrate the workings of the solar system or discuss, far into the night, ways of building plank-on-frame boats, and wins the long-distance kayak races around the Vineyard. His clothes are usually decorated with red lead or epoxy, or whatever potion du jour is being used to hold a boat together.

Gail, the woman to whom we are indebted simply for her presence, not to mention her genius with the kids, is a pretty, rock-solid, no-nonsense type who manages a hardware store when she's off the island. She can convince a seventeen-year-old car thief that the best thing he can do with his afternoon is to make strawberry shortcake for the rest of us. Try that sometime. They are remarkable people.

There is another shift of four that works the first week to our second of each two-week cycle. Heading it is Tom Q., who is yin to Jack's yang, with a similar cast to back him.

YESTERDAY we walked the island's perimeter for exercises before breakfast, a mile and a half over rough ground. All morning Cyrus had been pushing us. "Fuck that, fuck you, fuck what we do here, I don't want to, I'm not going." A quarter mile from home, as Cyrus and Sonny and I swung through some tall grass near the cellar holes of the leper houses, Cyrus tripped me from behind. I stumbled down into a hole obscured by the tall grass, and felt one knee twist under me as I went down. I was up fast and then moving toward him, seeing red.

"You want to fuck with me, little punk? Huh? C'mon, pussy. Do that again and I'll break your face."

I stopped. Cyrus had taken two steps back. His mouth hung open, and he was getting ready to run.

"I . . . I . . . I," he said.

"Just don't trip me," I said. "Don't mess with my legs, stay away from my legs, my knees, my body. Don't fuck with me — you know I don't mess with you — and I won't be in your face."

"All right man, chill out, it was just a j-joke, Dan man."

He was shaken. We finished the walk.

Later, after lunch, Sonny loped up to me on the deck where no one else could hear.

"Yo, Dan. Don't lose it that way."

"Huh?"

"Like you did at exercises."

"What do you mean?"

"Don't show us we could get to you, man. It shows us you got weakness, that we could play on your mind, when you lose it like that."

"It was nothing, Sonny. I just didn't get much sleep last night."

"Okay. Whatever. Just wanted to give you the word."

"Thanks, Sonny."

"Take it easy, man," he said, and loped away.

But he is right. I am angry, and it worries me.

SEPTEMBER 23. The time here is both wonderful and hard for me, in that I am afraid of so many things out here, and not afraid at the same time. Take a morning. We staff all sit at the table after the standard ablutions and evacuations. The sun is well up. On the stove there is a battered pot—tin, blackened, fragrant, dented—full of black coffee. I fill a chipped green mug with it, splash in condensed milk from the eight-ounce can that sits on a dark plank embedded in a timber that holds up the kitchen ceiling, and consider the reign of internal terror that awaits me in the passing of the day. I sit with Gail and Jeb and Jack at the long table. Outwardly I am calm. Jeb scribbles in a blue book, says,

"Yeah, he was all right, Jack, he was okay, and he tried to put the screws in straight, although I think it's impossible for him to do it, but he really tried."

"Give him a twenty-three, then," said Jack.

"Twenty-four."

"Jeb! A twenty-four for Jerome? Feelin' generous, huh?"

"No. He earned it."

"You got to leave them somethin' to aspiah to, Jeb."

"Twenty-four."

"Okay. Your call. Gail, how was Mr. James in kitchen?"

"Straight fifteens."

"That good?"

"Yup."

"Anythin' specific?"

"He spit in the dishwater when he thought I wasn't looking."

"Such angels we have in our care, Gail."

I CONTRIBUTE my fourth of the grades to the blue books. Within, I wonder how school will go, will they work with me today, will I be caught being less than athletic during exercises, fail to complete ten chin-ups or twenty dips, or whatever, or trip as we walk to the schoolhouse, land in a pile of poetry books and newspaper clippings, have them kick me in the shins? Or will they jump me, behind the school, my two students, Mose and Edward, just because they can see that I am not cool, not down with their thing? Yet I am cool, outwardly, I know I am, seemingly. So cool.

And then there is the part of me that wants to do this job so well, which of course is arrayed against the part that sees its futility, that I'm never going to sway a single kid, might as well be in New York City playing jazz, screw all of this big-heartedness and damned good citizenry.

Then one of them rumbles down the stairs, Cyrus perhaps, in a T-shirt and ripped jeans, pours himself a cup of coffee, looks up blear-eyed. Standing near the stove now, I say cheerily,

"Hey, man, how'd you sleep?"

And he says,

"Fuck off a minute, woodja?"

And that I am a fool for trying runs through my head, along with the thought that here before me stands an asshole who I am paid to love.

7

OCTOBER 1. Mose has gone in to the onshore house, the school's halfway house in Woods Hole. They all have high hopes for him there. George plans to enroll him in the local community college. I'm happy for him, and for me. He was an intimidating presence—too quiet, too strong. They can have him.

It's not that I don't like Mose. It's that he has an edge which I take to mean he could snap, and that's unsettling. Perhaps it's that I'm new to this, and perhaps it's that he might snap. It's a hard call. We all, the men out here, rely on a mystique to keep the pups at bay. We don't mix it up with them, wrestling or playing hard, for the most part, as it is good to preserve our unknown strength. And the strange part is that they want us to have that, some mysterious physical and even mystical fighting power they can then aspire to.

"You picked that up like it was nothing," Wyatt said to me the other day when I picked up a fifty-pound dumbbell with one hand. It wasn't "nothing" to me, but he wanted to see it that way, wanted me to be strong so he could look up to it. I didn't let on that it felt plenty heavy, and I suppose there's a fine line there; I don't want to encourage the threat of violence out here, especially in myself—there's little difference between the implication and the practice. But I must admit that I let slip the other day that I had studied T'ai Chi for a number of years. I wanted that lever, that unknown, on my side.

TODAY began with a question for me from Sonny, the tough eighteen-year-old from Charlestown (Challstown) who gave me a tour when I first came to the island. We were in the wood shop, a drafty, high-ceilinged and wood-framed building, doing exercises before breakfast among the many half-finished birdhouses and cabinets that lay scattered on rough table tops, as it rained outside. We were in a circle, in our ripped island clothes, following Jeb through his normal routine of stretches and strength exercises, when Edward spoke up:

"Jeb, why we gotta do the same goddam stretches every day? I'm sick of doin' this fuckin' quad stretch."

"These are good stretches, Edward," said Jeb. "Just do 'em. You get through them every other day, and it's good to keep a little routine, so if other things don't go right it doesn't throw us off." Edward seemed cool with this—he'd just had to release a little pressure—but I *had* to jump in.

"And Edward, don't swear, man. You don't have to swear all the time."

This wasn't a particularly bad thing to say, but it fit a pattern that wasn't making the guys happy. Sonny jumped all over it. Loudly.

"Hey, Dan. Why the fuck don't you mind your own fuckin' business with Edward here? He wasn't beefin' with you, he had an exception to what Jeb was doing. Why you go pokin' your nose in that, huh?"

"'Cause I didn't like to hear Edward swear. That's my business," I said.

"Yeah, but you don't gotta fuckin' jump on Jeb's toes, there, or on Edward's toes. It ain't none of your fuckin' business until Edward gets in your face, and I'm sure all of us would like to know why you think you gotta be 'third man in.'"

Silence. Sonny had a point, everybody looked at me, and I was at a loss. I grasped for some way to get beyond the silence of the room without losing their respect.

"Sonny. How about . . . How about you and I talk about this later on. I'll think about it, and we can talk about it later, all right?"

Silence.

"All right?"

Finally, after a protracted look that said, "I could hit you in three places that would take you down, any one of 'em," Sonny gave me a sullen nod, and returned to the posture of the arm stretch we were in the middle of.

Thinking about it later, I saw Sonny was right. He needed a bandage for a cut finger before lunch, and as I got it for him, I told him so.

"You were right at exercises, Sonny. I thought about it, and I shouldn't have jumped in there. That was Edward and Jeb's business, and none of mine."

"You got to keep your nose out of where it don't belong, Dan," he said. "I mean, I seen fools get filled full of holes back where I'm from for a lot less, you know what I mean?"

"Yeah, I know. I'm learning out here, Sonny."

"Learn faster. Thanks for the bandage."

"Sure."

WE spent the afternoon lobstering. Alan, James, Ned, and I launched *Smoke*, our pulling boat, and checked the ten pots which lie on the far side of the cove, scattered among the rocks in the shallows there. *Smoke* is long and narrow, blackened and fragrant with pine tar and turps, and heavy, carrying her way many yards after the order "all stop" is given. Thole pins are mounted in her gunwales rather than oarlocks, and when one mans the sweeps, pulling hard for fifteen minutes as a greasy baritone sings out, "Pull, pull, pull, you bastahds, pull . . . ," it's easy to imagine the long row out to a whaleship coming up the bay, a trip often made by the pilots who lived on Penikese in the early 1800s. Which of course I told the guys about. James took it up with me.

"There aren't any damn whales around here."

"I know. That's why they sailed for them, up north off Canada, and south to Antarctica, and up in the North Pacific, around Cape Horn."

"What the hell'd they want whales for?"

"They boiled them down for their oil, which they used in lamps and for lubrication."

"They didn't eat the bastahds?"

"Not so much. The Japanese still really like whale meat, though."

"Big hairy dirty cocksuckuhs—I wouldn't put no fish oil on nothin'."

"They aren't fish, man. They're mammals, like us."

"How you gonna tell me a whale ain't a fish. It lives in the water, don't it?"

"Yeah, but they give birth to live young, just like we do, and they breathe air with lungs like ours. They have to come to the surface and breathe."

"What, lady whales got tits and all?"

"Well . . ."

"No shit. So how come the milk don't just leak out in the water, like when they're way down deep and the pressure's up and they're bein' squoze like in a vise?"

"That's a very good question, man. There's a book on whales in the house on the shelf right next to the radio . . ."

James hauled and baited while the rest of us rowed, trying to keep the boat from being swept down and away from the island by the strong north-flowing current and fifteen-knot breeze. Alan and Ned rowed strongly all afternoon, saying all they wanted was to stay away from the bait, which was old cod and had been sitting in a cooler on the pier for three or four days. It was rotten, blue and green in places, and in the midst of lique-fying. James's hand dripped with liquid fish when it came out of the cooler. I didn't want to touch it any more than they did, but the lobsters, discerning in their tastes, like that carefully aged fish. We got four keepers, and the boat came out of the water easily, everyone heaving in unison as we hauled her up the beach on cedar rollers.

COMING back from lobstering yesterday, around four-thirty, with the sun low in the sky, we walked up the wagon path and came upon Edward sowing winter rye in the garden from a red bucket slung over his shoulder. Barefoot, naked but for shorts, he walked the 150-foot length of the garden, broad-casting with his big right hand, a nineteen-year-old adolescent arsonist for a moment a farmer in seventeenth-century England, absorbed in the rhythm of his task. And then the four of us pitched in to rake the seed under. And that's what I love about this place—its ability to create an entirely new time for these boys, a place wholly separate from the planet upon which they became, an atmosphere of fresh, untried airs.

"You guys don't know how to fuckin' rake," he said with a grin, as if he had been doing this all of his life. With luck his seed will take, and we won't lose topsoil to the winter gales.

NOVEMBER, 1989. A memory. Woods Hole, Massachusetts.

The granite steps we were sweating into place weighed five hundred pounds apiece, and had to be nudged into their cradles with pry bars, looked at, and then prized up again so we could fill under one corner or another, level them up. I worked with Jimmy Fahey.

"C'mon, Jim," I said, "lean into it."

"Hey, I'm gettin' old," he said. "Twenty-seven on Friday. I deserve to slack a little."

He was strong, had thinning sandy hair, had been three years ahead of me in local schools; in spite of the fact that we worked alongside each other, had come up in the same town, I felt he had something I didn't, an assurance I lacked. It was forty degrees out, the sky was gray; steam rose from the shoulders of our battered sweatshirts.

"So what do you think about the death penalty?" I asked.

"What, you mean whether there should be one?"

"Whether it's right."

We leaned on our bars for a moment.

"That's a tough one," he said. "But I don't think it works. I don't think it's evenhanded. Minorities are sentenced much more harshly than whites for the same crime. So, right now it isn't just."

"Yeah, it's not," I said, disappointed. Agreement meant we had to find something else to debate as the steps slid into place.

Eel Pond stretched out to my right; the few hulls still in the water were mirrored on that windless November morning; the *Sarah Jane*, a graceful fifty-foot sloop, lay motionless upon her upside-down self, her white hull slightly hogged at the chainplates, yet still seductive, low, slender. The old wooden schoolhouse watched over the scene from a small hill; a cormorant surfaced near the muddy shore, droplets of water falling from her narrow bill; Jim would grunt, throw his weight against the pry bar, and I would do the same on my side; gradually we worked the gray granite slabs into place.

"What are you going to do next?" I asked him.

"What, today?"

"No, when you're through with this job."

"I don't know." He looked out over the pond. "I've been with Bill three years now. I sit in the kitchen after work, you know, watch the sun go down, sit there as it gets dark, drink a cup of tea. I try to figure out what's next, but I don't have the slightest, man."

We worked the second stone into place, the bars ringing on it.

"That's good to hear you say," I said, finally.

"Why?"

"That's what I do, too. All the time. Try to figure out what's next."

"You think you're near?"

"I don't know. I feel like there's something I can't see holding me back."

He looked at me a moment, then said, "I know one thing. You'll know hard work when you leave this job." As he said this he held out his right hand, palm up. It was callused along the base of the fingers, the skin hard and dark. I held out mine. It looked the same.

We leaned on the bars. Jim put his toe on the stone, and I heard the scrape of sand on his boot sole, and then the distant hum of a car's tires on steel grid as it crossed the drawbridge. We looked out over the pond, then put the bar muzzles back under the stone, began to nudge it home.

And then a voice stopped us.

"What in hell are you guys doing, tearing up my neighbor's lawn?"

It was George Cadwalader, walking stiffly toward us, dressed in weathered work clothes.

"What's going on here?" he said. "Who in Christ's name told you to make it easier to walk up that hill?"

"Hey, George," Jim said. "You got any pots out, getting any?"

"I'm still fishing about seventy."

"How many're you getting?"

"I'm gettin' a few," said George cagily. "Price's in the crapper, though. Nobody eats lobster in winter. What's going on with these steps? They look crooked. I don't want my neighbors showing up on my doorstep with their ankles askew."

"Well, we'll, uh, we'll try to get 'em in there right, George. We were thinking that threshold by your front door would look nice at the bottom here," said Jim.

"Over my dead body," said George, grinning, then allowing that "They look good."

The discussion ran out, with George saying something as he

walked away about "good luck" and "squashed toes" and us turning back to the work.

"He's a character, huh?" I said to Jim.

"Yeah. But from everything I hear, a better guy would be hard to find."

"You ever think of working for him?" I asked.

"On the island?"

"Yeah."

"I think those kids would eat me alive."

N E D ' S voice: "I used to just spend time out in the garage, you know. I'd just go out there and take stuff apaht, like, you know take a car apaht and take the stuff I wanted and put it together some way, like in another shape or somethin'. And they used to not be able to find me, which made them mad, so when they did they'd tie me to the table or somethin', or to my bed in my room, 'cause that was heavy, and I couldn't drag it through the door.

"The bad paht was when my father used to get mad. Then he'd beat us, or he'd chase me around the yard with a wrench or somethin'. Somethin' big. And then he'd lock everythin' up, locks on all the cabinets, like. It wasn't hard to run away, though, 'cause he's pretty slow.

"But then they took me away, and put me in a fostuh home. And I got beat up there so they put me in another fostuh home, and I got beat up there, so they put me up at Atkins Group, and I got booted from there so they put me in another fostuh home, but the lady there wouldn't feed us and she stold our clothing checks, so I said fuck this and I ran, and they caught me and brought me back, so she beat me up, so . . . they put me in the Reynolds School, and I was there for a while, but then there was this sandal [sic] there, and the shit all hit the fan, and this guy got fired for no reason, so then they put me in another fostuh home, and finally I ran from that 'cause the lady there wanted me to kiss her but she was rasty and old, so I wound up here, and I been here for a while now.

"It's all right, but I wish there was other stuff to do, 'cause after a while you run out, and there's nowheres to go, like just
walkin' around the mall or somethin', anythin' like that, or like
a place where you could get somethin' to eat that wasn't just
like island food, like a burger or somethin' like Chee•tos. But it
ain't bad. I been here longer than I been anywheres except for
Reynolds. It ain't bad here, really."

FIREWOOD. We carried wood for seven hours today.
Dan Clark's barge arrived just after breakfast, a rusty platform
with a small crane astern, stacked with fifteen cords of five-foot
logs, all pushed from one side by the *Elsa Jane*, a stalwart little
tug out of Vineyard Haven. Johnny Pimental and Marty
Amundson of Woods Hole were the longshoremen, two guys I
had seen walking the streets of Woods Hole as I grew up, working men in Carhartt jackets, not afraid to walk around unshaven or filthy from hard work—the strength of the work
filled them with an honest energy that came through a door
ahead of any appearance. They were putting chain around
twenty logs or so at a time and swinging them onto the pier
with the derrick. Then we carried them, two or three at a time,
up a small hill to be stacked along the wagon road. A long
chain of men and boys and one woman moving with wood,
under the sun, trudging up with logs of beech, white oak,
cherry, black locust, coasting back down. The boys were good
for an hour or so, and then the unfamiliarity of working hard
and long began to tell, and their backs began to hurt, and they
were short of breath, needing to sit down.

"C'mon, James," I said, "let's go. I'm getting ahead of you."

"So, get ahead. Knock yourself out."

"I'm sitting next to the stove all winter, then. You get to sit
by the door."

"Yo, I been working for a half hour straight, yo," he said,
then, "I ain't sittin' by the door," flung his cigarette butt away,
hauled himself up off the stone pier wall.

I stared at the butt smoking on the gravel.

"Oh, my bad, Dan. I got it." He picked it up, and began to follow me back down the pier toward the stack at the end.

"You guys are fuckin' slavedrivers, yo," he reported next. "I can't wait to get out of here."

When I walked past again with a load of wood, the butt was back on the rocks, smoking. But he was carrying wood. I let it slide, conscious of the possibility that I was a nag.

And they kept on, although they were still pulled toward sitting, smoking. It seemed to go in waves. Only Wyatt kept on without letup. I asked him what he thought of it. "Sucks," was his reply.

Later in the afternoon I looked up from my load and saw again the long line of men, boys, and woman, still snaking up the hill, still moving wood for each other, and then I turned and looked out over the cove beyond, with Tubbs tawny brown in the high sun, the sun glistening on the ten-knot waves between us and Cuttyhunk.

A YOUNG woman filmmaker came recently to the island to shoot footage for her thesis, a pretty brunette with a warm smile and finely sculpted features. She dressed in a collegiate, preppy way, wearing a tartan jacket over a white, long-sleeved sweater that fit closely and showed off her breasts and curves. Which the boys were quick to note.

They surrounded her fast, swarming, boasting of getting high ("Yo, we got so blunted, yo, that night"), or stealing a car or losing the Five-O's (cops) in a chase. They felt this would impress her. Of course, it did, in all the wrong ways. She seemed a lovely girl.

Which made it all the more difficult when at lunch James gave me a knowing, lecherous look as she bent over her equipment in the house. Later, he expanded on his thoughts as we stood in line for dinner:

"Yo, Dan, what did you think of Jenny, man?"

"She's attractive, James."

"Yo, I'll take her up to da outhouse and fuck her there, man," he whispered. "I'll give her a yellow shower and then fuck her in the ass." All of this said with much hilarity, much smiling.

"Jesus, James, that's disgusting. Get your head out of the gutter," I replied, and then we were called.

"Line *up!*" Jack bellowed. We lined up.

"Have you washed your hands, Mr. Washington?"

"Yeah, Jack," said Alan.

"I didn't see you anywhere near the sink, Mr. Washington. Go to the sink, sir, and wash 'em. . . ."

Man, I thought. Where do I begin? I thought she was attractive, too, but . . . this is way out of line. How do I express that it's okay to note a woman's beauty, or to fantasize about her, but not to speak of violating her? Maybe just like that . . . James is not a violent type, and gets along here as well as anyone, yet there is this dark energy even in him, this possibility for wronging another that asserts itself so easily.

We talked about it later, as we lifted weights in the dim basement that evening.

"James, uh, I know you were just messin' around, but it's not okay to talk about a woman that way."

"Yo, Dan, what is she, your sister or somethin'? She wanted me, I could tell, man."

"James, whether she wanted you or not, it's just not okay to talk about a woman that way, you know? We're about respect out here."

"Yeah, respect. All right. I don't think I'd see you respecting her if you were in the backseat with her, now."

"Hey, even if I were in the backseat with her, it would be up to her to say what was okay. If she wanted to do something . . . unusual, then she and I could talk about it . . . but that's a big part of it, her being part of saying what's okay, and humiliation is not okay."

"Yo, man, I was just kidding around, man."

8

NOVEMBER 5. 9:30 P.M. Walk outside, and it's like your eyes fell out of your head. It is dark. Aeolus rants, throwing squalls at us, peppering windows with hard drops of rain and shrieking around the chimney, sucking air out through doors and windows on the east side of the house in a chorus of faint moans. Everyone has sought a warm corner. As I'm lying in my bunk, the conversation of the boys on the other side of the porous wall sifts through. I look up at the soot streak left on the plywood ceiling by two decades of kerosene-lamp smoke, rising through evenings like this from the lamp on the shelf next to my head. The room is dim, warm, roughly finished. There are faint smells of old socks, adhesive tape, old wool, Gold Bond foot powder, sunbaked wood, cologne leaking from a kid's dresser, dust. Supplies overflow the shelf space and hang from rafters—a surplus stretcher, crutches, boat models, extra blankets, fishing rods. I am up here "relaxing," with antennae up for a scuffle, a word thrown too hard. What I hear from Sonny, who doesn't know I can hear him telling his story to James and Edward:

"Yo, like, so we messed these two guys up one afternoon, kicked the shit out of them in a alleyway, and they, they was *messed* up, yo, but like, it turned they just so happened to be the son of the so-and-so of Somerville, they was connected, so we're screwed. So my boy's like, yo, you can use my lawyer if you want, but so, we went to 'im an' he said eight-fifty up front an' eleven hundred dollars a day after that, so we were like, 'Yo, chill, man,' but he said, 'Yeah.' So I went down, you know what I mean?

"I, yo, I . . . like *yo*, I got caught rippin' this fuckin' Camry and shit, and they nabbed me, and I was like, all right I'll go, but then when I got to court I got hit up with all this other stuff, *mad* stuff, and they was talking seven years, so I got it talked down to eighteen months in lockup, and, like, yo; if I could get out of here for, like, a month, if they would let me outta here for a *bare* month, I could pay this dude his bills and he'd go to court and he'd talk some *mad* shit, and I'd be outta here, Jim.

"But, like, my friend, yo, he was going to Mexico, and he said what do you want? I said a couple of cases. He left me his apartment, and a case of *Remy*, and it was mad, man. I dropped him at the train, man, loaded. Yo, he sells these watches, man, a little clock, for, like, they're nothing, like, twelve hundred for these little motherfuckers, little, like that. Yo, it's mad."

It's mad.

NOVEMBER 12. "Stonewall Lesson."

This is teaching: As he bitches, as he watches,
place another stone
broad and flat
upon its hard brothers and sisters,
rock it until it rests on three points.
Slap it for good measure.
Straighten up. Look at it a moment.
Look the kid square in the eye.

Realize you don't know what the hell you're doing.
Don't let on.
Then look out over the island,
the cove with cats' paws of wind sweeping it,
the grassland of Tubbs, a little bit of Kansas.
Look at the isthmus which holds off the sea
to the north.
You still don't know what the hell you're doing,
but he watches you look,
wonders what is he seeing.
You watch the land,
lead his eyes to it,
ground him that way.

NOVEMBER 14. 9:30 A.M. We are in school. The air has a bite to it, and is still, so you can hear water licking at the rocks, distant surf across a mile of water, over at Canapitsit—the residue of a storm out to sea—and the mournful call of a loon who swims languidly across the cove. He lifts his bill toward the sky when he trills, and his wake spreads behind, a widening V. He is the summer species of loon, soon to be supplanted by the winter, and perhaps his call is good-bye. Nothing else is heard, except Wyatt calling me a "punk motherfucker" under his breath, and the scrape of Cyrus's pencil on his journal as he details, he tells me, the depths of his sexual frustration.

There should be more wind at this time of year; perhaps the calm is the shift to the next season. All of the harbingers of winter have come or gone. The ospreys, the graceful fish hawks who nest on poles at either end of the island, have gone, headed south to Central America, as have the terns and the summer variety of cormorant, along with the swallows, who moved overhead this month in flittering hordes, chaff on the wind.

"So Wyatt," I said. "What will it be like to go back home when you get out of here?" He sat at the table, his journal open in front of him.

"Bitchin', yo. It's gonna be great. Be with my girl all the time, get back in school, yo."

"You think that's going to be easy?"

"After this? You bet."

"So what happens when you're sitting in a class you hate, like business math, with a teacher who is dull as a post."

"I'll just smile."

"C'mon, on the tenth day of dull-as-mud math, you'll smile?"

"I don't know, man. Why you sweatin' me?" he said.

"'Cause you're going to have to face it."

"I'll deal with it when it comes along."

"How?" I asked. "What about the cops? They're going to be looking for you to screw up. What are you going to do about them?"

"Man, they are so dumb. I like to screw with them because they are so dumb."

"Right. And that's why you are locked up, right? Because they're the dumbos? You're not going to be able to screw with them anymore. You're gonna have to toe the line."

"I'll just taunt them a little."

"No. You have to be perfect, or else, man. Or else you're screwed, you're right back here."

"Man, the problem is that there's nothing going on up at home. It's just dead. We get so bored. You got to do something, just to break it up."

"You can't do that anymore."

"I know. What am I gonna do?"

I ASKED Wyatt the other night, as we lifted weights in the basement, why he had done what he had. The lanterns cast a warm dim glow on the damp stones of the foundation, and we could hear footfalls as people moved around upstairs. He thought for a moment.

"We were just running around outside at night, having a

good time, and then we came on this field and there were all these damn pumpkins, lying there real peaceful like big eggs, and we just started throwing them at each other, and smashing them over our heads, and pretty soon it was just mayhem, man, and it was like war. We couldn't stop it. And then after a while we looked around and they was all in pieces, just lyin' around in pieces, like on a battlefield. It was kinda eerie."

Then he was up from the bench, pounding the heavy bag that hung from a joist, moving faster than my eye could follow in the dim light. After a couple of minutes, he sat back down.

"Why'd you do that?" I asked.

"I dunno," he said, breathing heavily. "Felt like it."

"Do you ever get violent at home?"

"Nah. Unless somebody messes with my girl, yo. Then I'd fuck 'em up, like this (he shadow boxed), and like that. I'd fuckin' wreck 'em."

"Anybody ever do that to you?"

"Nah."

We did another set of bench presses, Wyatt working with 125 pounds, me with about 150. I am not much stronger than he, and not for much longer, either. He is sixteen.

"So what do you want to do next?"

"Go back to school, be with my girl, yo. That's all I want to do, go back to school, and be with my girl."

"So, do it."

"They don't want me back in school. They'll do anything to keep me out of there."

"Why? What'd you do?"

"I just didn't do anything I was supposed to, and I told the principal he was a fuckin' faggot."

"Oops."

"Yeah."

He is a compelling kid, and one who I can't suss yet. I get the impression he is carrying some cultural energy that he displays only in his hair, but perhaps this is just his way of being as different from the other boys as possible. Which is strength, on some level. I've never seen him before, which in this town (of which Woods Hole is only a part), with its broad acreage, open borders, many hollows and coves, and twenty-five thousand souls, is not unusual.

E DWA R D is gone. Two days ago I gave him a ride down to a fancy coast town where he had a court date to review his status at the end of his sentence. He hadn't been an angel on the island, but he had grown a lot, and we were all fond of him

"This is a nice car," he said as we drove away from Penikese. "It's got all the dashboard on it, and stuff. Can I smoke? Wheah's the ashtray?"

"No you can't smoke, man. That makes me a passive smoker, man . . ."

"C'mon, man. I'm busted out today, I'm free. This is celebration day, man."

"All right, all right, you can smoke, seeing as it's a big day."

"Cool. You got a match?"

And there I was, handing a match to a convicted arsonist.

We didn't talk much about the upcoming meeting with the judge. "The Judge" seems to have great stature among these guys, and even their respect, and it doesn't seem to be good form to speak of the court or the judge much. So we talked about food and the island, and finally lapsed into silence. Edward, I could see, was stressed-out.

We met his mother, an extremely tall, narrow, frazzle-haired woman of forty with her brown hair in a long braid down her back, at the courthouse, and waited with Edward's lawyer for his case to be called. Edward fidgeted and made excuses to go to the bathroom. Other minor felons milled around, stubbing their hundred-dollar sneakers on the floor, leaning back with their arms crossed in front of themselves and their ball caps far back on their heads, posing for the other minor felons, saying things like, "That's fucked up, yo," and "I been locked up there. It ain't so bad, yo, but there's this one dude who will

have you for lunch, yo, he will swing on you . . ." Like golfers,
they compare notes on the various courses they've been down.
Finally, we were called, and the judge, in the stately old court-
room, hurried through the review, saw that Edward had been
doing okay, and staring sternly down at him over his half-
glasses, gave him his release from Penikese.

"I hereby remand you to the custody of your parents."

Edward, standing straight at the defendant's table in his
white shirt and jeans, was happy, and also wore a rather lost
look as we pounded him on the back.

I took him over to the family diner, where they fed me a
tuna salad sandwich. His stepfather, a stolid Polish man, stood
mutely behind the counter, and seemed less than overjoyed to
have Edward back, but the mother was full of smiles and stories of how well Edward would do in the future. "He's a good
boy. He really is. He hopes to be a lawyer."

WYATT'S voice: "My first memory is when I was eight and
we were fuckin' peltin' down the highway in this old beater
Ford, it was a Galaxy, and I said, "How fast does it go, Dad?"
and he said, "I dunno," so he floored it and it got up to ninety-
five, and the whole thing was shakin' and then we started going
down a hill and we're both just screamin' like it's the best thing
ever, and the speedo broke a hundred by the bottom of the
hill, and then one of the rears blew, and I looked back and
there's smoke and rubber all over the place and the car starts
whalin' around the road, and then finally my dad can't hold it
and we go up on the shoulder and he throws me under the
dash and then she rolled like three times, and then it was all
fuckin' quiet, so quiet, like you could hear crickets and shit,
and then I hear my dad moanin', and I look at him and he's
holding one arm, and he looks at me and says, 'You all right?'
and I was, so I say 'Yeah,' and he says, 'Wait here for Mom. I
got to go 'cause if the cops find me in this car, I'm fucked.' And
then he just like got out of the car and vanished in the woods.
Like a ghost. He could vanish anywhere, my dad.

"So I did what he said, and that was the first time the cops took me down to the station. They know me pretty well now. The next time I saw him was like two months later, and he moved back in with us for like a month, and that went okay for a while, but then they started again, you know, like, fighting, and he was drinkin' real hard, and one day when he was passed out Mom dragged him out and put him in his car somehow and drove him like a couple miles away and just left him there and walked home, and she was crying when she came back . . . and I guess that was the last time he lived with us.

"I learned a lot from him, but he's too unstable, you know, to have in the house, really, but he's good at what he does, you know.

"But all I think about now is my girlfriend, yo, that's like, it. All I want to do is go home and go up to my room in the attic and go to sleep with her in my arms, that's all I want, and the sooner I get the fuck out of here and back in school and back with her, yo.

"But I keep worrying that I'll get back in trouble, 'cause there's nothing to do back there but hang out, and me and my boys we get tired of all the shit and the pace, and the cops are sooo dumb, man, so dumb, and it's just so slow, and after a while you want to do something to juice it. Like, that's why I stole the tractor-trailer. We were like, yo let's get *out* of here, kid, some-how, and we found the key, and I saw a news show on a kid who stole one once, so I remembered how to run through the gears, and we got to fuckin' Framingham before anybody stopped us. But they didn't like that much, tryin' to put all kinds of vehicular assault shit in there on us and shit. And I'm just worried that it's going to happen again, you know, like I lose perspective, and then we're just tearing something up or going down the highway a million miles an hour, tripping our asses off.

"That's one thing I'm not stoppin'. It's too good, trippin'. It's like, you don't understand, it's another world, and you, like, learn shit out there, and nobody's judging you, and it's so good to drive on that stuff, or to just do anything, anywhere. So much better than what you get otherwise.

"But that's all I want, is to go home and be with my girl, that's all I want. But I'm worried." Yeah.

DECEMBER 1. Wednesday. I had a few rare moments of liberty yesterday. Wyatt and Cyrus (our transcendentalist) and I were repairing a dory whose main frames, amidships, had ripped away from its hull on both sides. We were working in the boat shed, up near the outhouse, and things had gone along well, with a fire in the woodstove to warm us (after we got the chickens roosting there to vacate) and the dory sitting on blocks in the middle of the big, open room. We had cut a sister for each frame—port and starboard—and had the hull of the boat drawn together with a Spanish windlass. We had a brace and bit, a caulk gun with a canister of 5200 Marine adhesive, screwdrivers, and coffee steaming in battered plastic mugs. Chickens clucked outside the big double doors, and sleet angled down into the grass outside. The floor was a Pollock of paint from previous jobs. Everyone was calm, and for the moment, everything seemed possible. Cyrus said,

"We got the damn warmest assignment, yo, fixin' the boat, yo, by the fire. This is the balls—all them other cocksuckers are takin' it on the grill compared to us, yo."

(Cyrus's mother, I was reminded, was a lawyer, his father a teacher. He wanted, apparently, to be downwardly mobile.)

"Cyrus, clean up the language," I said.

Then, after going over our equipment again in his mind—this was a day I'd prefaced as a day for practicing "preparation"—Wyatt said, "Hey, we don't have screws. We need some of them brass screws, Dan, the longer ones to go all the way through the hull into the sistahs."

"Yeah, we're gonna screw into your sistahs, Dan," chimed Cyrus.

"You are right, Wyatt. Completely right. We need some bronze screws."

"I said brass."

"Did you? I thought you said bronze."

"No, I said brass."

"Well, I guess you were thinking bronze, because that's what I heard, and you were right about us needing bronze. Good job, Wyatt."

"What's the diff?"

"Well, look at these two shorties, here. The lighter one is brass. It looks more golden."

"So?"

"So the brass will corrode, the bronze won't."

"What's 'corrode'?"

"Rust. So where are we going to find some long-ass screws?"

"Dan said 'ass,'" said Cyrus.

Then everyone had a theory, and we agreed to split up, each covering a different depot of bent and salvaged screws. Wyatt would go to the box in the forge, Cyrus to the fishing shed. I would go to the carpentry shop. We agreed to meet in the kitchen for a refill of coffee in ten minutes, and then return to work.

We ambled down the hill together, slitting our eyes against the sleet, and then split. Inside the carpentry shop I climbed the short flight of stairs to the main level. From the basement Jack rumbled,

"Who's theah?"

"Dan here, looking for screws."

"Your boys being excellent this mawnin'?"

"Yup."

"All right," he said, and resumed his conversation with Jerome (Jeb's sidekick) and Reggie, a new student from Dorchester, Edward's replacement. He is a bantam who becomes a panther on the basketball court, and he and Jerome, who are from similar neighborhoods, seem to have much in common. They were down at the big worktable, standing on the old cement floor, mending lobster pots.

"See, the lobstah comes in here through this funnel, then he goes in here with the rotten fish bait, and this funnel keeps him from going back out."

"Why he can't just go right back out?" asked Jerome.

"Sometimes they do, but they're not really logical thinkaz, Jerome. They have a lot of good instincts, but not so many problem-solving skills."

"So what do we got to do?"

"We gotta fix the netting, like on this one, fix the hinges on top if they're broken, fix the runners on the bottom if they're broken, fix the latch on the door, make sure each one has a bait bag . . ."

Jack's voice went on as I rummaged in the screw box that sat on the battered workbench. I imagined him flipping the trap around as he spoke, the boys on either side of him a little awed by his strength.

"And when you're done, I give you a buck for an easy trap, and two bucks for a hard one, all deals to be negotiated before work begins."

"What's 'negoliated'?" asked Jerome.

"Negotiated. Do the deal first, then do the work. It means getting with him to make a deal," said Reggie.

"Oh, you gonna chisel me on that shit, ain't you, Jack?" said Jerome, smiling (I could hear the smile in his voice).

"Oh yeah. I am a chiselah, bawn and bred," said Jack.

"So how good do lobstermen do?" asked Reggie.

"You mean in a year?" said Jack.

"Yeah. How much they make?"

"An average guy, working hard, maybe forty-five grand in a good year."

"That's mad loot, yo," said Jerome.

"That's his gross, is what it is. Well, let's figure it out. Say his costs are this—ten thousand on his house, and ten thousand on his boat."

"That's twenty thousand. He still got twenty-five," said Jerome.

"Four thousand on insurance, eight thousand on vehicles and gas, three thousand on traps and equipment. How much is that?"

"Twelve grand," said Jerome.

"Fifteen," said Reggie, correcting him.

"Ten grand. He still got ten grand left," said Jerome, clearly hopeful that the lobsterman would be a kingmaker.

"He's got a family. Five grand on food, and five grand on expenses, like clothes, presents at Christmas, snow shovels . . ."

"So he's breakin' even," said Jerome, losing hope.

"He's still got to put something away for college for his kids."

"Dude is screwed. He oughta get into real estate," said Jerome.

"And then"—Jack paused here for effect—"some kid boosts his cah out of the A&P lawt."

"Now that's a low blow, Jack," said Jerome.

"Does two thousand dollars' damage."

"C'mon," said Jerome, feeling the heat. He'd stolen a couple of cars, and Jack knew it.

"It happens. So, you have to be real good, or you have to work a second job."

"You hear that, Jerome?" said Reggie. "You're oppressin' the lobstermen, man."

"Shut up," said Jerome, laughing.

I listened as I set my selections aside. Two good long bronze screws, one with a buggered head, and a hot-dipped galvanized one that would do. It would rust, but not any faster than the boat would rot.

Jack had a way of being with the boys that I admired. He never seemed to say overtly, "I care about you, kid," never admitted that. But he was always moving smartly through the day with a couple of boys in tow, showing them how to be, teaching as he went.

"What's the matter with this piece of wood for a runner?" Jerome was asking.

"That's pine," Jack said. "It'll rot. We need oak."

"What's the difference?"

"White oak won't rot. It's harder. Feel how soft that pine is. Push your nail into it. Now feel this oak."

"It don't matter."

"It mattahs."

"You're just makin' it difficult, Jack," said Reggie. He was going to fit right in.

"Yup," said Jack.

But you could tell they liked knowing about white oak. I knew I'd hear Jerome explaining to a new arrival in a few weeks, "See that? That's pine. That's some shit wood for traps. What you want is white oak, 'cause that shit don't rot."

The new boy would say, "How you know?" and Jerome would look him in the eye and say,

"'Cause I know these things."

I HAD my screws. I headed for the house, not wanting to give Wyatt and Cyrus more than a couple of minutes without me. Both were there, standing by the cook stove, sipping steaming coffee.

"How'd it go?" I asked.

Wyatt, suddenly dancing to an inner tune, his dreads wrapping across his face as he shook his head, opened his hand, showing me two good long bronze boat screws. Cyrus had found four.

"Excellent. Have these guys been excellent, Gail?" I asked.

"Gentlemen," she said from her seat at the table. "They just came in."

"You didn't give us no time to screw around," said Cyrus.

"Any time. Let's go," I said, and we headed back out into the sleet.

"You think we can get that frame done by lunch?" asked Wyatt.

"Now that we've got screws, no problem," I said. "As long as you guys work."

"Yo, how much do a boat cahpenter make?" asked Cyrus.

"Cyrus, you know that isn't how you were brought up to speak," I said.

"So fuckin' what?"

"So you're an impostor, and you sound like a kid trying too hard to be cool," I said.

"I asked you how much," he said. I let it go.

"A good one, maybe thirty grand a year."

"Whoa. Thirty grand, that's mad loot, yo," he said.

"Well," I began, "let's look at his expenses."

"Yo, how you know it's a 'his,' Dan? You're a sexer, Dan man," said Wyatt.

"That's 'sexist,' Wyatt."

We had it done by lunch. Two weeks later Cyrus and Jerome hauled a trap mended by Jerome in a boat fixed by Cyrus. I rowed. It sleeted that day, too.

9

DECEMBER 2. Thursday. It sleets outside, and morsels of ice tattoo the windows in the gray evening light. The house is quiet, strangely. Gail is making dinner, and the smell of baking bread is rising through the floor of the staff room, where I lie on my bed, which is covered with a thick blue wool blanket.

We got the first news on Monday morning, after breakfast. All of the guys had headed out. Jerome and Cyrus were working with Jeb on the transom of the skiff they're building up in the wood shop, and they were probably getting the hens out of the woodstove there so they could light a fire. Gail, Wyatt, Ned, and Reggie were cutting wood in the lee of the house, sheltered from the wind, using a big two-man saw to cut the logs down before splitting them. Alan and Sonny were with me in the school, bitching about writing in their journals, and Jack had left James to start on the breakfast dishes while he called in on the radio upstairs, just to check in. It was a clear day with a north wind that brought the waves down the bay to land hard on the isthmus, so there wasn't much static. I came in looking for a biology text just as Jack raised Pops.

"How are you, Jack?"

"Finest kind, Pops. Come back."

"I've got some hard news, Jack. Clear the kids out of there."

The sun slanted in the window, and Jack caught my eye, nodded to the open door. I checked the loft.

"They're out," I said.

"Okay, Pops, go ahead," said Jack into the mike.

"Wyatt's father's been missing since last night. They think he may have died along with another guy in a quarry in Amesbury. Looks like they missed a turn in the road and jumped the car out into the middle of it. They're not sure . . . It doesn't look good."

"I see," said Jack.

"Don't tell Wyatt what's up—George wants to do that. Just tell him there's trouble at home and George will tell him the rest. We're sending the boat out soon's we can."

The man, from what I know, was a mechanic, sometime carpenter, and longtime drugger. I think, from the look on Wyatt's face as he walked out the door, headed for the boat, that he knew.

T W O nights ago Jeb and I went down to the forge, after the boys were in bed, to work on Christmas presents. On the way, walking through the little orchard, I could see the dark bulk of the house to the north, and the light in the staff-room window, up under the gable, warm yellow light of a kerosene lantern. Jack was up there in his rack, reading Steinbeck or Hemingway, I'd be willing to bet. Gail was in the kitchen below him, reading Patrick O'Brien at the big dark table. Her lanterns threw the same warmth out the old twelve-lighted windows there. Above us, the stars hung, cool, limpid, and I could hear the bell in Can 13 over at Cuttyhunk *donk* in the light swell. That meant a slight southeast breeze—a breath—and that our hammer strikes would perhaps be faint in the house, along with the creak of the big bellows.

Jeb was in front of me, and as we moved toward the little stone building he disappeared into the darkness of the hill into which it nestled like a mine entrance, leaving me with just the sound of his feet in the dry winter grass, and then the sound of a clothesline turning a rusty sheave in an old block as he pulled the door open, raising the counterweight inside.

He struck a match, it scraped and flared, throwing his shadow immense against the rough stone wall, and he lit the lantern he'd brought, turned and lit mine, and we trimmed them, both began rounding up paper, kindling, and coal.

"The forge," once a storage building, had been roofless for a long time, and Jeb and four boys in three afternoons of frenzy had roofed it with wood and tin. He'd then built the actual forge from an old car-wheel rim, bits of a barbecue and odds and ends, and rounded up old anvils, hammers, mallets, made bellows and tongs from scratch, and generally provided a wonderful teaching place—a first course in engineering and metallurgy, with the bonuses of fire, heavy hammers with which to pound, and the lessons of Icarus—for perhaps three hundred dollars. Three hundred dollars, I'd say, and thousands of dollars of his skill and time, which he very nearly gave away.

"What are you going to make, Jebber?" I asked.

"I've got to finish a set of tongs for a fireplace, and a floor lamp, and a bunch of coat hooks."

"All tonight?"

"Most of it's done. You?"

"I'm thinking four or five hooks and a candleholder. That's mostly done, too."

"Cool. You want to pump or kindle?"

"I'll pump," I said, and grabbed the handle tied to the end of the bellows rope, which ran up to a pulley and then back down to the end of the bellows. He already had paper and scraps of wood assembled at the center of the fire bed. He lit this, and as I began to pump the two-by-three-foot bellows, he threw a few small chunks of coal on the little blaze.

Soon we had a fire, and were each working a piece of iron—cherry-red at its end and throwing sparks into the dark room with each blow of the hammer. We were lit in the face by the red glow of the coal, our forearms holding iron and hammer, sinews plain—all resembling a Soviet propaganda poster of the 1930s. Our blows rang out—*tin, tin, tin,*—from the little building, and I wondered if the boys could hear us, if they would dream of track-laying in a chain gang.

"How long you been here?" I asked Jeb as I finished my first coat hook.

"It'll be two years in a month," he said, his tall frame bent over his anvil. He hit his piece once more and dug it back into the fire. I leaned on the bellows rope, and the fire hissed and brightened as the long breath flowed through it.

"You knew that," he said.

"I guess I did," I said.

"How come you ask, then?"

"I guess I'm just wondering how long I can take it."

"It's hard to know," he said, "but people have put up with a lot more."

"Oh yeah. It's not the Gulag, that's for sure." I leaned on the rope. "I guess that's relative, though. In your mind, it depends on what's keeping you here, and what your alternatives are."

"You mean what you could do otherwise?"

"Yeah. I can think of a couple of otherwises I'm kinda missing out on."

"Yeah, I've got an otherwise, too," he said.

His piece was almost hot enough again. I had time for one more question.

"So do you like the on-again, off-again thing, the dual life?" I asked.

"I guess I don't mind it. I guess it gives me a chance to have a break from both lives."

"That's a point."

"I wouldn't want to do it forever."

"I bet Jerome wouldn't mind it if you adopted him."

"I think you're right. But he'd get sick of my life pretty quick. Shoot, I live more simply at home than I do here. He heard me when I said I had a hot tub, but he didn't hear me when I said it was wood-fired, with an old oar for the water jet—hand-driven."

The end of his iron bar, soon-to-be tongs, was white with heat now, seconds from burning. He pulled it out, let it cool for a moment, then went back to work on it, pounding it out, his eyes dark, lambent in the firelight, focused on his work. We kept on for a couple of hours, finally walking back to the house at about 1 A.M.

A one-quarter and waning moon had risen, over the cove and the bay beyond, and shone silver on the grass, silhouetted the apple trees and sumac limbs, and Jeb's large form, walking dark against the bright sea.

Strange. I had just worked hours alongside this guy, and had broken bread with him for a week on top of months of weeks with him. We had watched each other's backs, had faced danger and boredom together (as I had with Jack and Gail). Yet I didn't know him, or them, really, beyond the isle. Here we met, agreed to guide the boys together. But cross the water, and we scattered. Fine. But I regret it. We are a family here, a professional family. There, ashore, we lose that focus, go back to our separate lives.

DECEMBER 21. A forty-knot gale blows, southeast, which would make landing at the dock impossible. If the weather holds, we will be here an extra day or two. The waves tear into the cove, light green on top, dark green at their core, wrapping themselves onto the beach as if trying to fuse with it. They are determined, it seems.

We fed the pigs earlier, Wyatt and I, and until they heard us coming with the slops they lay alongside each other in their shack, sheltered from wind, listing to one side, big piles of pig flesh, warm, floppy ears relaxed onto the flanks of their fellows. Melissa, the smallest, lay on top and between the grande dames Bacon and Samantha, with her trotters tucked down between them. Everyone is subdued in the midst of the blow, and seeks warmth in others.

The other day at lunch Alan asked for the salt:

"Pass the fuckin' salt."

"C'mon, Alan, you know how to ask."

"Oh. Sorry." (Genuinely) *"Please* pass the fuckin' salt."

10

January 1. Yesterday, an old friend and I drove to Chatham in my cranky Volvo to hike Grand Island, a four-mile lozenge that points south along the inner forearm of the Cape. We picked up Wyatt and a pal of his on the way out of Falmouth.

There were four inches of wet snow on the beach, but below the wrackline the sand was hard and smooth, and we walked the length of the island in an hour and a half, trading stories of misadventures, and staring down together at oddities in the sand—sand dollars, pieces of a book, costume jewelry. We made small talk, but after a while I sensed that Wyatt had something to say, so I asked how things were at home since his father had passed away.

"They're all right. Kind of quiet. I think about him a lot, that he's probably happier where he is. That's what's kind of crazy about it all—life just wasn't kind to him, wasn't kind to him at all, and I bet he's just a whole lot happier where he is."

"How come?" I asked, hoping to draw him out, and knowing that I was doing so largely because I was curious, not because I was doing Wyatt any favors.

"Nothin' ever seemed to go right for him. You know, he came from two worlds, know what I mean?"

"Two worlds?"

"His mom was white, right? But his dad was a quarter Cape Verdean, and his dad grew up there for a long while. You know where that is?"

"Yup. So you're Cape Verdean a little, too."

"I'm a sixteenth. And Irish and Dutch and German and a whole heap of shit thrown in on that. And my father, he wound up kinda in two places, and he couldn't pass for one or the other, know what I'm saying? And on top of that he was just too intense for the world, and it didn't understand him, didn't know how to take him, you know? But it was fuckin' weird at Christmas with him not there and all the family sitting around sort of totally conscious he wasn't there and still having a good time, in spite of it. I mean, he would of wanted us to have a good time, but it was weird. He's happier where he is, I know that. I fuckin' know that."

And then he was picking up rocks and throwing them as far as he could out into the water, their landings marked by small geysers.

JANUARY 8. We expect a new student, Ken, from the toughest juvenile facility in the state, any day. He is a terror, from what we've heard, although Dave Masch, co-head of the school with George, assures us that he's okay. Dave is large, a jovial, beefy man of fifty with a big mustache who stole cars in Detroit before he went to Harvard, and who sees guys differently than those of us of lesser stature. "Okay" to Dave might mean "terror" to me.

YESTERDAY it sleeted hard, after several days of intermittent snow. In the afternoon we played hockey on the north pond in old skates and boots. No one had a pair of skates that fit, and the game was one of eluding in slow motion. It was Reggie's first time, and he was unaccustomed to the lack of grace he found on blades.

"Yo, man, these things is worser than I thought they was going to be. I ain't got nothing for ankles," he said as he struggled around on the old skates like a bird with a broken wing, his ankles bending almost to touch the ice.

We canceled work for the afternoon in order to play, and we played until the light failed around four-thirty, as the hundred shades of brown in the high grass of the hills became gradually gray and less gray and finally black.

In the final light, standing in the reeds at the edge of the pond, left by the others, Ned and I gazed up at the oval bulk of a snowy owl perched on the osprey pole. The great bird was a dark place against the barely lighter sky; above us, self-sufficient, imperturbable, his head (this would be a male too young yet to win a mate in the breeding grounds further north) turned with the precision and assurance of a god, scanning for the rustling that spoke small mammal feet in the thicket. He was aware. I told Ned to pay attention. He didn't hear me, as he gazed up at the owl.

And now, today, in school, the stove roars; though it is mild out, we have it stoked. It gives the place a center. I mentioned this earlier.

"Don't you guys think the stove kind of gives the room a focus?"

"What you mean 'focus'?" said Ken, the new guy, who seems to have settled right in.

"I mean, like a bit of a center, like a spiritual center."

"What the fuck you talkin' 'bout 'spiritual center'? You crazy, man. The stove be warm, that's all," said Ken.

"He's geekin' out, man. He's a fuckin' geek. What you want?" said Sonny.

"Hey. Watch the language," I said. And then I began walking knowingly into the minefield. "The Romans used to worship Lares and Penates, the household gods, and one of them was the god of the hearth, and the hearth is the fireplace."

"I don't know about you, Dan," said Ken, thoughtfully, interrupting, shaking his head. "You a little wack upstairs. Know what I'm sayin', Sonny? The stove be warm, warm, that's all it is. All right? Now shut up an' let me do my math."

"You got it, Ken. The stove is warm. Do your math."

Sonny did his geometry. I tried to help Ken, but he refused, insisting he could do it himself.

He is a big kid, two hundred pounds on a thick five-ten frame. But what I notice are his hands, which are big and pink and densely scarred around the knuckles, and his brows, which too are scarred, have borne many blows. I notice too his voice, which is strangely musical, rising and falling easily in pitch, and whose words in their shapes seem to be taken from Black English, e.g., "I ain' gon' do that."

I remember Edward saying, as we anticipated Ken's arrival from jail, "Ken's got a pair of hands on 'im, that's what I know."

The day Ken came to us, it was blowing twenty-five knots, and he was fairly green as he climbed up from the boat, his knuckles white as he held the sides of the ladder. He didn't say much that day to anyone, but since then I've had some conversation with him, often down in the cellar, where we lift weights and where I am careful not to lift anything unless I know I can move it. I want to seem strong. In one of those talks, Ken said:

"You know, it's weird, Dan, but I ain't been restrained here yet. I don't know why, but I ain't gone off on no one yet."

"Why is that weird?"

"'Cause I used to get restrained every day at the juvenile school. Every day, I'd be in a fight or I'd go for somebody and they'd have to hold me down."

"We don't do that much here," I said.

"I know, but it's weird, like I don't feel like I gotta straighten nobody out like that here."

And then he lay down on the bench, slid under the bar, and pumped out ten reps with 180 pounds as if he were lifting a broomstick.

From what I know, he grew up in reform schools, having been put in that environment when he was seven or eight, among much older boys. He has been in training to defend himself since he was very small, and seems to see the world as a place where one can attack, intimidate, or defend. Peaceful coexistence doesn't exist.

I told Ken to sleep well as he headed up the stairs the other night, and he shot back "You too," before he knew it. His eyes widened with surprise as he went up the stairs. I think he was shocked to hear the kindness in his voice. It is there, buried.

A F E W nights ago we played our regular game of spades at the dining table. It is a jailhouse game, and this was a quiet game, as the tension of the risk each team had taken hung in the air. The only sounds were of cards sliding out of hands, the soft hiss of kerosene lamps, breaths being taken in and held, and an occasional palm slapping the table to take a book. In that quiet something began to gnaw on a bag of flour in the shelves behind Ken.

"What's that?" he asked, his eyes big as plates.

"It's a frickin' mouse," replied Cy, his eyes half closed, and with that Ken's cards were fluttering in the air as he screamed and ran out the kitchen door. A moment later we heard him scream again, and he ran back in, just about taking the door off its hinges. Scared of the dark. He is scared of snakes, of going to the piss pole at night, of riding the boat to the island. But he sure isn't too scared to tell me to fuck off and die, the way he did the other night when I asked him to carry his lamp more carefully, with one finger on the base of the glass chimney so it wouldn't fall off.

Can I be the guy these boys need?

11

I RECALL the fright I felt those first days on the island, largely because I still feel it. I was scared of what they might do, what I might do in reaction. Then, there was only one, Mose, who looked damned strong, who was too quiet, who I'd heard had shot somebody, but the others were unknowns, sulking young men who had seen everything. I wasn't sure what they had been exposed to, but I had a pretty good idea, a composite formed from comments dropped, a glance at a few files. I could imagine.

I pictured them witnessing, in the corner of a dim room in a seedy apartment, their drunken mother beaten by their drunken father, or raped by a new boyfriend who never came around again, or I saw the drunken mother or father coming for the small boy, and felt the blows, what those must have been like, the flat of a hand against a cheek, or a fist connecting with an eye socket, the flash of light that came with the blow and the feeling as the face began to swell, and then more blows raining down, a boot toe in the ribs, the rolling into a ball, and the only one to cry out for the one behind the blows.

And I imagined any of them might crack, see his last vestige of self-regard slip away, do something rash. What? I could see

Cyrus lighting a fire in the basement and then going to bed, the ensuing inferno as the kerosene in the house went up. Or James, while splitting wood, going back into the time when his mother's boyfriend beat her, forgetting where he was, taking a swing with the axe at whoever, next to the tomato patch, with the bay in the distance, sparkling in the afternoon sun. That would have been a mess.

Or I'd envision one of the guys coming after me for something I'd done, some way I'd shamed or offended him, coming at me from behind a parked Pontiac, with a gun or a shiv, having nothing to lose. They weren't all small, they all knew how to fight, and even the small ones could carry a gun. I am still scared, I am still unsure of myself, I am still wondering how I'm doing.

Not long after he left the island I ran into Mose on the street in Woods Hole. I was walking north on School Street, headed downhill, just beyond the old school. Leaves were still thick on the trees, and I was looking forward to the view I would have of the pond to the west, the boats lying at anchor there. And I saw a man, tall, well built, walking down the hill opposite me. At 150 yards I saw by his gait that he was in good shape, fleet, moving fast with an easy stride, no limp, no weakness there, the gait of a thoughtful man, too, somehow present, the feet touching heel-toe, neatly, in line.

At a hundred yards I saw that he was black—a rarity in Woods Hole. Visiting scientist, no doubt. At fifty yards I saw that he was Mose, walking back to the onshore house from George Cadwalader's. He saw that it was I, and his gait changed. He ditty-bopped a little, sunk into one hip, syncopated his stride, and then we were face-to-face, and I was shaking his hand.

"How you doin', Mose?"

"All right, all right. You?"

"I'm all right, resting up a bit. Hey, I hear you might be heading to college, man. That true?"

He smiled faintly, looked at the stone wall across the street. "Well, maybe. That's what they all seem to want."

"What matters is do *you* want it? Right?"

"Yeah," he said, his eyes finding a piece of road nearby to look at, flickering across to mine for a moment, then back down to the road.

"I won't sweat you on it anymore, man. Hey, good luck with it, anyhow."

"Thanks, man," he said.

"Let me know if I can help out."

"All right, then."

"Okay, take it easy."

And we parted.

I walked on, thinking how strange it had been to run into him there, where so much of my growing up had been done. And how much stranger still for him, a young man from the projects of Springfield, strolling a quiet street in the heart of a well-to-do village.

He must feel at odds with this middle-class, scientific place, I thought. Must feel out of sorts, far from home, alien.

Three weeks later I went by the on-shore house on Friday during my off week, to meet with the teacher there, pick up some old textbooks to take back to the island. On my way in I ambled into the kitchen to scare up a cup of coffee. Mose sat at the little table there with a skinny boy named Rudy across from him. Each had a bowl of cereal, and as I entered, Mose said,

"Nah, do it like I said or Imona fuck you *up!*" I walked through the door on *up*. From Mose's inflection, and the way he was staring at Rudy, I could see he meant it.

There had been rumors wandering around that Mose was having other boys sell crystal meth. on the ferry docks, that he was intimidating them, that he had a gun locked in a drawer upstairs.

I said, "How you doin', Mose?" trying to sound as cool as I could.

He looked hard at Rudy, turned the same gaze on me, did not speak.

"How you doin', Rudy? You all right?" I asked.

"Yeah, I'm all right," he drawled, and concentrated on his cereal. "This milk sucks, though." He looked scared.

"Mose, you want to tell me what that was all about?"

Silence.

"Mose, man, you know we aren't about that here. Rudy, would you mind giving us a little space?"

"Yeah, man," he said as he eased out of his chair, clumped out of the room.

"Mose, man," I said as soon as he was gone, with my arms folded over my fast-beating heart, "I don't like to hear you talking to Rude like . . . like he's your boy. You know that isn't right."

"Look, man, I don't want to talk to you. And I ain't your man."

He sat with his elbows on the table, looking at Rudy's chair. I felt like I was driving too fast along a road I didn't know.

"Mose . . ." I began.

"Your word ain't shit in here, Dan," he purred, looking up at me through slitted eyes. "Why don't you just chill, 'cause you don't know shit about what's goin' on in the real world in here."

"I can't just chill," I said, sitting in Rudy's chair. "Tell me what that was all about."

"Yo I ain't tellin' you shit," he said, looking now through my eyes at the trademark on the back of my skull. And then he was up and gone, the screen door slapping the frame behind him.

He went home to Springfield that weekend, was picked up by the police on a drug possession charge, and went back to jail. All of the plans for him to attend classes at the community college went down the tubes. It may have been just too much, trying to fit him into a world he didn't feel was his. I never did get out of Rudy what it had been about. "Snitches get stitches" was all he'd say, but the whole thing scared me, raises my blood pressure even now. How could I be a father to that boy/man, who may have shot to kill, has broken the will of tougher beings than I in a fight, who knows the inside of prison, who (I later found out) has children of his own. This plays on me, is underneath the surface of every interaction I have with these boys. Can I father them? And Ken awaits, and Wyatt, and the rest.

BUT I am learning. About reactions. About why I am here. When I was small, before we moved to Woods Hole, things were often dark. Or I *thought* they were.

The first house I remember was a duplex in Pittsburgh, two mirror images stuck together, with front doors next to each other. Ben and Bette Zweig lived next door, and it was there that they raised their boys Jim and Benny, there they had the promised American Life. I remember going, when I was about four, to "help" Ben plane a door. He had the thing on its side in the upstairs hall. Ben, who had white hair except on top, who was big, it seemed to me then, big enough to manhandle a door, and Bette, who was petite, wore her blonde hair in a bouffant and who fussed pleasantly around us, bringing lemonade, laughing musically. Their floors downstairs were bright hardwood, and in the little family room they had a small black piano with pictures of family and a vase of fresh flowers on top.

On our side, I remember green carpets, a dark, inorganic green that wasn't quite military, but that seemed to lean farther toward a military shade than anything else, and a black couch, and the furniture was dark wood, and the light was less bright, it seemed, than over at the Zweigs'. But what I may have been feeling was something different in the mood.

My father was gone almost from the time I was born. What I remember most is his absence, the silence of this, and odd things, like how his shoes sat in the back bedroom upstairs, these symbols of how he moved through the world, lined up along the wall. They sat there all day, quietly, shined, the dim light glinting off them, the smell of Kiwi polish in the air. Sometimes a pair of brown socks would be thrown lightly over a pair, or a pair of brogues would have appeared, and a pair of wingtips vanished, the brogues slightly scuffed. I followed these developments closely, so little else did I know of him. The next morning there would be the brogues again, polished, and the smell of the fresh polish in the air, as if by magic. I remember wondering why I couldn't see him ever.

I recall my mother being down about this, crying over the dishes a lot, and reacting fearfully to the universe, sitting on the couch with her head in her hands, or grousing about the socks thrown carelessly over the shoes, the lack of neatness there.

I recall her standing in the doorway of the kitchen one afternoon, in a brown wool skirt and a white shirt, her hair bobbed and brown, an attractive woman wringing her hands and talking to herself, and then looking over to see me standing under the table in the dining room, watching her; she stopped and smiled wanly, and then turned back into the kitchen, and began to cry, leaning over the sink with a hand on either side of it and her arms straight.

And of course, when I was three the shit had hit the fan— my father, the good-looking, eloquent, likable journalist split. He hit the road in a secondhand Triumph sedan, driving cross-country on a soul-searching junket, telling my mother he would probably move out when he returned in two weeks, which he did. To my mother, it seemed to me, the world was a patently unfriendly and disappointing place, and that was the message I got at four: Life is hard, joyless; you can expect things to go wrong.

Evidence from the larger world bore this out. On TV Walter Cronkite, who I trusted, talked of the Vietnam War every night, of soldiers killed, helicopters downed, and showed pictures of men with rifles, stooping as they left the open door of a Huey and fanned out across a paddy, looking for someone to kill. My mother would come and turn off the TV, try to keep me from seeing, but I saw—it was the age of assassination. I knew the names, even then. Kennedy had been shot, Medgar,

Malcolm, and then they got Martin. All of the hope for that time, it seemed, had been killed.

I remember vividly my mother and her friends, attractive women in their thirties, speaking in subdued voices around the picnic table in the yard of who "they" would shoot next. That's the kind of thing that makes an impression on a four-year-old—who is going to get shot next. They talked about him like he was a friend, addressing him by his first name. She and her friends smoked Chesterfields and never laughed for long. And then they got Bobby, too.

And it made me angry, angers me still, to feel alone there, in that memory, to feel that I was going through it alone, without support. That is what angers these guys of whom I write.

I AWOKE at five today, and looked up at the smoke-stained plywood ceiling bathed in fading moonlight, heard the jabbering of the starlings in the privet on the far side of the woodshop, and the breaths of eight boys and my three colleagues as they slept.

I pulled on tan work pants over long underwear, pulled on a pair of gray wool socks and my Redwing boots, another white T-shirt and a blue turtleneck, threw on a thick gray wool sweater and a beaten-up green sweatshirt over that, breathing evenly all the while, trying to watch my hands at work, and walked as quietly as I could over the worn plywood floor, my soles scraping on the sand there, through the boys' loft and down the ladder stairs to the all-nighter. The door moaned as I opened it; I threw a couple of chunks of oak in on the embers, and spun the draft screw open a quarter of an inch so she'd heat up. It clanged softly as I turned it.

Then I walked out to the pole through the dusting of snow that had come in the night, and watched the horizon beginning to glow to the east as I pissed, steam rising in front of me, the stream paddling on the frozen ground and then breaking through the frost and soaking in. Naushon Island was the horizon—across three miles of millpond-flat water (glowing white with cloudlight reflected) it was seven square miles of dark thicket and meadow and deer down in the tall grass for the night. That was a part of where my voice came from.

And then I meandered to the schoolhouse with an armload of wrist-thick splits for the little stove there. I loaded it, first with twigs and then larger wood, put a ball of crumpled paper just inside the door, lit it, watched flames lick at the paper. The rough spruce walls of the little school were lit up, and I sat there, on the floor, my back to the wall, watched the flames move through the wood.

I had made it to this island, I thought, made it back from the publishing job in London, back from the teaching job in Mississippi, back home from days alone in the Mojave, come home to this coastline, to know . . . my origin, perhaps, from where my voice arose; how the hell I was supposed to find that in the flames in the little green stove, in the shadows on the walls of that schoolhouse, or in the voices of the boys who studied there . . . I didn't know.

There is a way of seeing, I'm told, that suggests that we choose the circumstances, choose the parents, even, that we will have in the next life, the next incarnation. I don't know if I believe that, but it casts a different light on it all, when I entertain it. If it is so, then what am I here to learn? How can the perceptions of abandonment and simple absence of emotional support that I felt as a child be reconstrued as lessons there for me, lessons even to be grateful for if I can bring myself to a level of awareness high enough to see them as such? And what about these guys, how much can their upbringings be seen as their own postdoctoral study in the psychology of dysfunction in the American home, and they as the experts in this, if they can only take none of it personally, or as of their own making, see it as if from a high vantage on which they perched prior to this life and said, "Yes, I'll take one alcoholic mother with patterns of sexual and verbal abuse, and one murderous father with limited self-awareness and a pathology for self-destruction.

Those two ought to serve me well in learning compassion and unconditional love."

Did they bargain on having their memories so foreshortened and their awareness so cloistered as to forget the choices they made then and what they are here to learn now?

AT quarter to seven I damped the stove down, and ambled up the path, past the eight little apple trees, to the house. The sun was just up, reflected in a long, straight line over the bay, and Gail had the big cook stove breathing hard, with its damper along the back set to "kindle," heating water for coffee. She sat at the long table with a book.

"Where you been?" she asked, shaking her brown hair out of her eyes.

"Down starting the stove, watching the sun come up."

"Up early today."

"Yeah, well."

"They don't appreciate it, you know," she said.

"What?"

"You starting the stove early so it's warm."

"Maybe they'll remember it down the line."

"Maybe." She smiled as she said this, and turned back to her book.

I thought of the Robert Hayden poem, "Love's Austere and Lonely Offices," in which he wrote of his father starting the coal stove in the dark, early in the morning, which deed—which *love*—lay unappreciated by the poet until he was grown and moved away.

12

JANUARY 9. One afternoon last week Jack said to me,

"I'd like to go out with three and check the traps. How about pumpin' some water up to the cistern with one, then grab some driftwood for a sauna?"

"Okay," I said.

"How about you and Reggie?"

"Fine. What's Jeb doing?" I asked because Jack liked us to know where everyone was, for safety's sake.

"He's got two going on the boat in the shed, and Gail's replacing the stovepipe in the school with Jerome."

"All right," I said.

"Hike," said Jack.

So I found Reggie in his area, and we rambled down to the well, which was right next to the schoolhouse, and began connecting the pump to the six hundred feet of piping which ran up the hill to the cistern. The day was unseasonably balmy, so we were in old sweaters, and Reggie was, as usual, excellent company.

"We don't need no water, Dan. We'll just drink milk and soup. We don' have to do this," he said as we moved from connection to connection, he working steadily and carefully.

"Oh, we gotta do it."

"Oh, I see. Forcin' me. I want a hearin', I'm filin' a griev-ance. This is inhumane. I'm callin' the ALCU."

"That's ACLU."

"Whatever," he said. I admired his playful ferocity, and was struck by how easily he bantered with me, when most boys, new to the island, were shy or intimidated by conversation. Perhaps he'd grown up with a lawyer or teacher before the streets had got him. They all had good minds, but here was one less cowed, less buried than most of the others. Then he asked, pointing down the well,

"Hey, how come all that water out there is salt, and this is fresh?"

"Let me show you," I said, grabbed a piece of paper and a green crayon out of the school, and drew him a picture of the freshwater table rising up into the earth of the island with the saltwater all around. He saw, as I said words to him like "strata," "density," and "cline," and then we were attaching the pump, and he wanted to know how that worked, so I explained the im-peller to him, and the pistons and cylinders—internal combus-tion—and drew that for him, too, and he saw, and we started the pump, and watched it for a moment, and then he said,

"Hey, how we know it's comin' out at the top?"

"Well, we better find out. Why don't you truck up there, and watch the ruler on the side of the cistern. The water rises slowly, so you'll have to watch for a minute or two to see . . ."

And he was gone, a slight kid jogging uphill through tall grass. A criminal. I watched him climb away from me, and af-ter several minutes he stood at the top of our world, pulled open the hatch to the cistern, and gazed down into what I knew would be a dark pool of cold water, or himself, silhouet-ted against blue sky, clouds. He gazed a long time down, and then (how I loved seeing this, a young man from hard streets alone on an island hill) he looked a long time out to sea.

As I watched him up there, Gail and Jerome were coming down the path, Gail carrying her tools, Jerome three lengths of stovepipe and several elbows. As they passed with nods and entered the schoolhouse, Jerome was asking,

"You sure you know what you're doing with all of this?"

Her reply was lost in the buzz of the pump.

Several minutes later, after Reggie had returned with a report of rising water, he and I stuck our heads in the door. They already had the stove repositioned on a small hearth, and Gail was explaining how they would attach the new pipe.

"See, we have to decide where it'll sit in there, and then we drill holes through both pieces, and put one of these screws in each hole."

"How we gonna drill? That's metal."

"We just drill with a metal bit, same as you would with wood."

"Really?" said Jerome.

"Yup," she said, and in one motion slid a bit into the chuck of her banged-up cordless drill, grabbed the chuck tight in her left hand, and pulled the trigger. With a whine the chuck closed hard on the bit, and Jerome's eyes widened as he saw how fast she did this. Reggie and I were just leaving as Jerome said,

"So how do the smoke know to go out the pipe?" and I heard Gail start in:

"Well, the smoke is a gas, like the air going into the stove, but the molecules in the smoke have been excited—warmed— by the fire, so the smoke is less dense . . ."

Later, at dinner, after Reggie and I had gathered a barrelful of driftwood for the sauna, Jerome was full of questions about the staff, as he tried to recalibrate his sense of us.

"So, Jack, you know how to fix a woodstove?"

"Yup."

"And Dan, you know how to cook dinner?"

"Badly."

"Gail, you could, you know how to check the lobster pots?"

"Yup."

"Jeb-man, you could cook dinner?"

"Oh yeah. You gotta try my tofu-turkey, Jerome."

"That's nasty, man. You could drive the tractor, Gail?"

"Yup."

"Dan, you could garden?"

"Yup."

"Gail, you could garden?"

"Yup."

After a while he quieted down, and ate, thank God. Clearly, however, his understanding of our limitations had been changed. Along with his impression of his own limitations, we can only hope.

JANUARY 11. After breakfast today, I sent Reggie and Wyatt down to the school ahead of me.

"Take your books, and don't open the stove door. Just leave it alone, okay?"

"Yup."

When I got there Wyatt was sitting in front of the stove with the door wide open, and Reggie was slumped over the big table in his down jacket, holes patched with duct tape.

"What did I ask you not to do, Wyatt?" I said.

"Huh? Oh, my bad," he said, and slapped the stove door shut.

"It's too cold to do school, man," said Reggie, groaning.

"It is, huh? Well, maybe it'll warm up in here some," I said, wondering where the morning would take us, but then Reggie reached for his journal, and opened it slowly, and just as slowly began to write the date at the top of the page, and I thought, We might have a good day in here after all.

Reg is withdrawn today—maybe the weather's working on him. He is lean, steely, a mongoose on the basketball court, with laughing almond-shaped eyes and a brilliant grin that he flashes at will. I know that smile sometimes hides anger.

When he was first here he was eager to do the right thing. He asked if he could help, often neatened the cream and sugar tray that sits on the dark plank sticking out from the massive central post in the kitchen. I appreciated his efforts. They were refreshing; but I thought they might end, that we might see a different side of Reggie. Recently he's been slipping. I think I know why.

He is so bright, with enough awareness and verbal acuity to slide back and forth between a Dorchester street dialect and the college dialect spoken by the staff. He's able to move between worlds, and that's hard. It's a question of loyalty, at some level, in the end. "Whose version of English do I speak, which one is more a part of me?" he might ask himself. In language is a tacit statement of origin and identity, and every time Reggie shifts, he addresses this, if only unconsciously. He reminds me of students I taught down south.

Several years before coming to Penikese, I'd taken a job at the Piney Woods Country Life School, an historically all-black boarding school in rural Mississippi. Every student at Piney Woods was of some African descent. Most were from inner cities around the U.S., sent by relatives who hoped to save them from the killing there. A few were from Mississippi, and a handful were from Ethiopia. I taught English to seventh-, tenth-, and eleventh-graders, two sections of each in classes of either all boys or all girls, and coached baseball.

As I taught, it became clear that before I could get my students to commit to learning "English," I had to break through the hard question of just what good English was, as opposed to bad or incorrect English, because every day seemed to offer me (the interloper, the possible bigot, the highfalutin', stuck-up boy from the North) the chance of offending most of the students in the room with pronouncements like "That's not how you say it," or "That's wrong."

This problem, and its answer, were made clear to me by an English class on gerunds, one day in September.

I had given my eleventh-grade class a practice quiz, in which I gave them the infinitives of five verbs, and then asked them to put them in the present-progressive form. Given the example "He (to run)," the student was supposed to write "is running."

I explained this, with eloquent commentary and diagrams on the board, passed out the mimeographs, and sat at my desk for five minutes while they wrote. Then I wrote the answers on the board, asked them to correct their own, and then to start reading the first five pages of *The Bear*.

Almost immediately Marken Rutherford stood by the corner of my desk.

"Mr. Raaa, I got to ax you about this, please," he said.

"Sure, Marken, what's up?"

"Well, you say, put these verb in the 'ing' form, in the present-time tense, so it be happening now, and I did that, but it don't match what you wrote on the board."

Marken was just about my favorite kid in the school. He was quiet and big, not yet full-grown, but six foot one and hard. He carried himself with an easy dignity that became effortless grace on the basketball court, where he was a large point guard, in the school of Magic Johnson. His intelligence was clear in how he worked the court, assessing the instincts and talents of the players around him, seeming to move through them as a man would when playing with boys. And he respected others. This was clear by how he moved among his peers, by how he addressed them, and me. He was attentive. He smiled easily and genuinely. He was curious.

His face was a network of scars, suffered in a car accident when he was small, I speculated, or perhaps in a dog attack. And he spoke with a thick Mississippi country accent—at times beautiful, slowly musical and somehow dramatic ("I sho' don't see where you goin' with *that*, gurl."), and at times completely incomprehensible to me, which is an asset in a language spoken by an oppressed people among their oppressors. I didn't see his speech as lacking sophistication.

"I mean, Mr. Raaa," Marken went on, "I don't see how this work."

And then he looked at me with eyes every teacher wants to

see: open, clear, trusting, intelligent, fiercely wanting the truth. I could read the answer I had prepared in my head.

Marken, it went, he "be running" is wrong. We never use "be running" in the English language. "Is running" is right. And as I reviewed that in my head, I could see my pat answer was wrong, misguided, potentially damaging.

It became clear that to tell Marken his way was wrong would communicate to him my belief that not only was his way of speaking wrong, but that his parents and the entire linguistic tradition on which he had been brought up were wrong. Now, "wrong" is a word I use to connote factual incorrectness, or moral denunciation. Neither of these fit Marken's situation, for within his linguistic tradition "be running" *did* connote the present-progressive form in a systematic and regular way. It was correct within the absolutely standard grammar of the dialect he spoke, fully recognizable to anyone conversant in it. Further, he was not doing anything ethically negative by using the "be running" construction. He wasn't wrong, I realized, privately smote; further, anyone who thought he was wrong was ignorant! (Which was me! Yipes!)

I looked out over my class. Thirty-two heads bent over their books, wading through the first paragraphs of *The Bear*. Doubtless there were more "be runnings" out there. The Ethiopians, Coptic Christians from the north of their country, speakers of Amharic, wouldn't mind being told they were wrong. They had no tradition in English. But every other kid in the room might. I looked up at Marken. He was still looking down at me expectantly.

It was, after all, not many days since he and the rest of my students had called me Professor Robb. I had asked them why they called me this, and they said because they had been told to. Then I asked a colleague, Professor Carpenter, who taught history, and was black, why this was.

"Well, you see this is a holdover from days, not thirty years ago, when a black man in the South ran the risk of being lynched if whites overheard him referred to as 'Mr.' That was considered uppity. So, all male teachers at Piney Woods were called Professor or Reverend by their students, and by their fellow teachers, too, as a matter of safety," he said. Then, cocking his head, he said, "But you're in kind of an odd place with that, aren't you? See, if they get lazy about what they call you, it could still get them in trouble somewhere else. They have to be aware of what they say and how they say it. *All* the time."

I was teaching in a community where, thirty years before and *less*, the wrong salutation could cost a man his life. I had to mind *my* way with words.

"Marken," I said, "I think this is going to come up with a bunch of the guys, so I think I'll just explain it to the whole class right now, all right? But thanks for bringing this up, man. You asked an excellent question."

He took this in, and with an easy "Cool, Mr. Raaa," headed for his desk. I wondered as I rose if I could say what I needed to without insulting everyone.

"Hey guys," I began, walking toward the blackboard. "Marken just asked a great question, and I want to discuss it with you for a few minutes, all right?"

Thirty-two pairs of eyes locked onto my head, interested, if only for moments.

"Marken wondered why I gave 'is running' as the answer to number one, rather than 'be running,' if they mean the same thing. Did anyone else wonder that?" Half of the class nodded.

"Anyone have any ideas?" No one spoke, but many sets of eyes wandered around the room, wondering if anyone would.

"Okay, I guess I'll just explain, then. See, I had an English teacher when I was a kid, Mrs. Doyle, who would have told you that 'be running' is wrong all day long, that it's 'bad English.' I'm here to tell you it's not wrong. It's one way of expressing what we call the present-progressive tense."

I wrote "present progressive" on the board, and then a definition—"happening *now*, verb ending in ing."

"The difference between 'he be running' and 'he is running'

is that 'he is running' is how you express the present progressive in Standard English, and 'he be running' is how you express the same thing in what I would call another dialect. James Baldwin called it Black English. They are two different dialects, you need to know both, and neither one is right or wrong—they are just different."

"Which one we need to know more?" asked O.G., a tall, skinny kid who sat in the front row, and listened hard every day. I paused. Here we go, I thought.

"You need to master both," I said. "Standard English is what's used in college, and on job applications, and in job interviews, and in business communications, and in government and law. Standard English opens doors to you. And you need to understand, if you grew up speaking another version of English, that that version isn't wrong or opposed to Standard English. In fact, if you want to write a great play or a story or a poem that sounds right when people speak, you have to know every dialect they speak." I was struggling, and their eyes were rolling in their heads, and then I knew I had to tell them about my friend John, who I had known in England.

"Let me tell you about a friend of mine in England. His name is John, and he is from a part of London where they speak a particular dialect. He is very smart, but a lot of the other guys we were at college with looked down on him because he spoke a particular way."

"What he sound like?" asked Countee, a muscular, squat boy from a small town in Mississippi.

"'Roi," I said, "'e sowndead loik dhis: Whoy dhon' yoo stop chryin' t' be sow hoy an' moy'ie, Den? Cum bek dahn to urph, man, an' 'av a poin' wiv us."

They shook their heads. "What he say?" said O.G., laughing and shaking his head, and Hamikeo, a tall, quiet kid from L.A. said, "That boy have some problems," from the back row.

I said, "He said, 'Right, why don't you stop trying to be so high and mighty, Dan? Come back down to earth, man, and have a pint with us.'"

"What 'a pint' mean?" asked Jamal, a small, bright-eyed kid who sat near my desk.

"In English bars they sell beer in big, pint-size glasses, so that means 'a beer.'"

"Oh. So you broke down and had a beer?" asked Jamal.

"I probably did, but the point is, John was and is very smart, and he didn't speak in Standard English most of the time." (I didn't even mention here that English Standard English differs from American Standard English.) "He spoke the way he did growing up in his neighborhood. Why do you think he did that?"

"'Cause that was comfortable to him," shot back O.G.

"Right. Why was it comfortable to him?"

"'Cause that was how his moms and his pops and all his people spoke," said O.G. again.

"Right! All right, O.G.'s on a roll, guys. Who else has an answer for me? How did he feel when his teachers said 'You sound like a ruffian, John.'"

"What's a 'ruffian'?" asked DeRoy, a hard, lean kid from Flint. He grimaced as he asked, as always.

"A crackhead is a ruffian," said Neville, a tall, quiet boy from New Orleans, a sphinx speaking from the middle of the room.

"Good, Neville. A crackhead is an example of a ruffian. Somebody who is rough, who might beat you up."

"Lousy," said Ketla, a gangly, serious kid from Ethiopia. He was several shades darker than anyone in the room, which lowered his status among the other students, and he was an "Ethi," which further lowered his status. His eyes fairly crackled with intelligence, which hurt him even more in their ranks. He'd just learned "lousy" the day before, and was eager to use it.

"Veddy lousy in this reprehenzible way so to act," he said.

"Yes. Very lousy," I said. "Good, Ketla. Why?"

"Because the teacher wasn't just rankin' on his speech, she was rankin' on how his whole family spoke, how all his people spoke," said DeLisle, an angry-looking, sullen kid from Detroit who rarely spoke. "I been through that shit. Oh, my bad. But that teacher was dissin' his whole crew, so he probably told her to step off."

"You're right. He did. And, he also went on to get an M.D. He's a doctor now. He can write in Standard English, he can speak in Standard English if he needs to. He can operate easily in that mode. On the other hand, he's proud of his heritage, and he likes how he grew up, and where he grew up. And he saw he had to learn the standard grammar if he wanted certain things in life. So, 'be running,' 'is running.' Which one is right?"

"They both right," said DeLisle, his dark eyes fierce. "More than one thing can be right."

"Yes," I said.

Marken had listened quietly to the whole exchange with his arms crossed on his chest. He looked at me after DeLisle finished.

"What do you think, Marken?"

"I got it, Mr. Robb," he said softly, coming down hard on the final *b*. "That answers my question."

"Cool."

B A C K on Penikese, after Reggie and Wyatt had written in their journals, they each did some math, and then it was time to do some writing. As a lead-in, we talked about nonviolence versus violence, after reading over some of Dr. Martin Luther King Jr.'s writings.

"What was the dude doing in jail in Birmingham if he's such a smart guy?" asked Wyatt.

"What was he doing there? What do you think he was doing there?" I asked.

"Fuckin' time, man," he replied. "He was pickin' his nose waiting for his old man to bail him out."

"Watch your language, Wyatt."

"Oh, my bad."

"Thank you. He was in there on principle, right?" I said.

"He was in there 'cause of what he believed," said Reggie.

"Right. But what do you mean by that, Reg?"

"He was in there 'cause what the white sheriff was doing down there with the hoses and dogs wasn't right, and he was protesting," said Reggie.

"That's lame. Dude gets thrown in jail on purpose. I woulda fuckin' wrecked 'em all, man. Man, the blacks were deep, man. Mad deep, there was so many of them out there protestin' they coulda taken the cops easy," said Wyatt.

"Watch your language, Wyatt."

"Which part?"

"The 'fuckin'' part."

"What's amatter, are your ears burning, Dan?"

"Yo mama," I said to Wyatt.

"He said 'yo mama' to you man, hahahaha," said Reggie, and we all grinned for a while. Then Wyatt said,

"But the dude's still questionable for taking it sitting down, man."

"So what are the benefits to him of finding a nonviolent way of achieving his goals?" I asked.

"Goals? Dude got thrown in jail, man. That ain't my goal," said Wyatt.

"Yeah, but they got the buses and the seats in the diners and the rights to be who they wanted to be," said Reggie.

"Without what?" I said.

"Without violence, man. That's what you want me to say, right? Without V-I-O-L-E-N-C-E," Reggie said, spelling it out. "But it isn't always that simple, because he wasn't on the street with crackheads who bus' your head looking for their next score. I mean, sometimes you got to take the law in your own hands," he said, shifting in his coat, and then taking it off as the little school warmed in the rising sun, which came through the latticed east window, along whose inner sill lay a feather of snow.

"'Cause if you don't," he went on, "you ain't waking up the

next day to take care of your baby sister, man. And that is not right."

"So, what do you think of Dr. King's methods here?" I asked.

"They were right, 'cause he could afford to work that way, because he had the respect of the people on his side," said Reggie.

"Nah," said Wyatt, shaking his head. "He had the respect of the people, maybe, but as soon as he lay down and let them throw him in jail, then they got him, them spigots, and there's nothing he can do."

"That's a good point, Wyatt. It's 'bigots,' but that's a good point. So where does the law come in?" I asked.

"What law? He broke it," said Wyatt.

"That's right, but how did he view it?"

"He thought that if he broke the law, even if it was an unjust law, then he had to suffer the consequences if he was gonna be able to say that he respected the nation whose law it was, and due process, even if he didn't respect the law," said Reggie, leaning back, as if he were reading the ingredients off the back of a pack of cupcakes.

"Yes!" I said, thrilled. "That's right, I mean, that's right, Reggie—do you see that, Wyatt?"

"What?"

"Do you see that King is trying to change things, even by breaking laws he thinks are unjust, but with respect for the system and the nation's legal structure? So, if he does the crime, he pays the time."

"Yeah, I see it, but I think that it's uh, it's too, it's too like you man, too many ideas getting in the way of actually doing anything, like, it all sounds good but the guy's in jail, that's the bottom line, and I don't, I don't really see how that's . . . winning."

"Well, King wanted to gain equal rights for his people, right?" I asked.

"Yeah," said Wyatt.

"And he also didn't want to stoop to the level of the people who were oppressing his people, right?"

"Yeah, the fuckin' spigots, man. He wasn't gonna use the

hoses back on them, like I woulda, fuckin' mop 'em off the streets, and biff the doggies in the nose," he said, making a swooshing sound with his mouth and jumping up with an imaginary high-pressure hose and dousing Reggie and me.

"Bigots, Wyatt. Watch your mouth," I said.

"Hey, yo, man, I'm tryin'," he said.

"Yes you are, man," I said, "and I appreciate it. So, he didn't stoop to their level, he showed his respect for the American system of law, he protested what he felt was an unjust law, and he got what he wanted peacefully, right?"

"Right," said Reggie, "but the man wasn't dealing with no crackheads on a regular basis, is all I'm saying."

"Well you want to know what I think?" said Wyatt.

"What?" I said.

"Man was a fuckin' lunatic."

"Wyatt—"

"I'm just kiddin'! Calm down, yo. He's got a point. I'll think it over. I just never met any sherriff you could peace-out like that, yo, by letting them throw you in jail."

"So what do we do about a guy like Hitler?" I asked, moving us into the work we'd done on world War Two.

"That's the kind of man you ain't gonna talk any sense to, that's what I'm sayin'," said Reggie, relaxing in his seat and looking over at Wyatt with his eyebrows raised.

"You remember what he did, Wyatt?"

"Yeah. He incinerated the Jews and he attacked the whole world, along with the Japs—"

"Wyatt . . . ," I said.

"The 'Japanese,' I mean, and the I-talians, and then we cleaned all their clocks in the long run."

"Yes. So, was that the right thing to do?"

"Yeah, it was the right thing to do. The man was a, uh . . . that word . . ."

"Bigot."

"Yeah, bigot, and he was loony tunes if he thought he could rule the whole world."

"Reggie?" I said.

"Yeah, it was the right thing to do, to stop him. But only after all the other options was used up, and they were."

"So you think that violence is okay if you've tried everything else?" I asked.

"Yeah, man, and sometimes the options get used up quick," said Reggie.

"That's what I'm sayin'," agreed Wyatt.

"So what about Switzerland?"

"Their cheese sucks and they all go around in leather shorts . . ."

"Wyatt . . ."

"It just slipped out, man. Sorry."

"All right, so what's their angle on the whole thing?"

"They are mad deep, and everybody's got an assault rifle, and knows how to use it, so nobody messes with them," said Wyatt.

"Well, that's some of the story. You remember the word they use to describe their political position?" I asked.

"'Neutral,' man, like in a car. Neither forward nor reverse," said Wyatt.

"Yes! Good, Wyatt. So, what do you guys think of that approach?"

"It be working for some dudes around my neighborhood, 'cause nobody be messin' with them when they know they're strapped," said Reggie.

"Yeah, but is that a good way to go through life?"

"Instead of not going through life? Yeah, it's a good way," said Reggie.

"No, I mean, always being on guard. Wyatt, stand up and stand like you're ready to wreck me," I said.

"What, like this?" he said, standing up tall, chest out, cocking one fist by his ear, holding the other one out to block, and gritting his teeth.

"Yeah. Now how does it feel?"

"Like I'm gonna wreck you."

"No, how does it feel to stand like that?"

"It's tiresome, man. Yo, I gotta lie down." And he did, right there on the floor.

"You know what I mean, Reg?" I asked.

"Yeah, everybody be on edge, and the fun ain't there when you always on your guard."

"So, would you want to live in Switzerland?" I asked.

"See, it would be safe there, like, I mean even Hitler stayed away from them, man, 'cause they was packin' some heat, and I gotta say I got respect for that, but I see what you're saying, Dan, I see that," said Reggie.

"So how would you do it, if you had to change something? Would you go by King's standard of peaceful nonviolence, or would you pack heat and mind your business like Switzerland, or something else?" I asked.

"I'd start out with King, and then work my way toward the violent end if I was still being messed with by the other guys out there," said Reggie.

"Yo, I'd be like Switzerland, man, just bad ass and don't mess. That's the way to go, just kill the fuckers if they try to take me over," said Wyatt.

"Wyatt, man, watch the language," I said.

"Yo, Reg, man, I'm being oppressed, I'm gonna have to waste Dan now, 'cause all other options have been exhausted," he said, spraying me with imaginary machine-gun fire, and then he was out the door, which Jack had just opened to tell us it was time for break.

"Yo, man, it's too hot up in here, man," said Reg as he went out. The snow on the sill had melted.

Later, he wrote, "You should only use violence when you have to, like when your family or your friends are threatened with violence and you have to defend them, that's the only time you should use violence. Any other time is not all right with me, because then you aren't utilizing the other possibilities you have, such as discussion, or walking away."

But what if the violence is within, and to withhold it is a sort of violence as well? Where to put it? Wyatt, it is clear to me, hasn't discussed any of his background with Reg. Nor should he, I guess. But I wondered how this might have changed the conversation if he had.

13

JAMES may be gone soon, heading out after his six months. When he came here, he seemed vulnerable, and looking for friendship. We played cribbage, lifted weights in the basement in the evenings, and a dim picture emerged of his home life. His mother dreams of going to Montana, buying some land, of settling there. That's what keeps coming up—"When we go to Montana, I'm gonna get me a dirtbike, and we'll have a house, maybe a double-wide, and things will be different."

I asked him a pointed question on a recent evening. He was sitting on a rough-hewn bench, with his head drooping and a twenty-pound barbell hanging from his right hand. Mice scuttled on the beams in the dim basement, and the barrel stove in the sauna creaked as it heated up. For some reason, the question caught him when he was open. "What was it like for you growing up, James?"

"What do you mean?"

"What was your mom like?"

"She was always drinkin', man. She'd come home from work, and she'd pull out the bottle, and by the time I knew it she'd had three or four, and she'd got evil."

"Like what?"

"Swearin' at me for what I was watching on the TV, or telling me I was a good for nothing kid and get the hell out of the house and go play wit' the assholes next door."

"What about your dad?"

"He wasn't never around."

"Never?"

"Hardly fuckin' ever. He'd come around when he had a lit- tle loot and spread it around a little, take me and my sister to Mickey D's, but then he'd blow it all in a poker game and get beat up after, and we wouldn't see him for a while. Now my mother lives with another dude, and I hate him. All he does is drink and beat up on her. I went for him with a frickin' chair; that's why I'm here, man."

"Why?"

"Why'd I go for him?"

"Yeah."

"'Cause he drank a lot, and he'd beat up my moms, and I didn't like how he was lookin' at my little sister."

"Where did you live?"

"In the projects, man. Right where they be sellin' crack out the house next door."

"What did your mom do for a living?"

"She worked in stores until she got too tired of ringing up stuff, then she'd quit and go back on the dole. Every six months."

And what doesn't change, from week to week, is James's an- imosity towards his mother's boyfriend, his love of the old boat he and his buddy are fixing up, and his raunchy sense of hu- mor.

But he and I have run the course that a parent and child of- ten run. First, we were good buddies, had an easy rapport. Then, when I had to ask him not to do some things, like smoke in the house, I became the damned authority figure. Now, on the eve of his departure, gone is the banter we shared pushing weights in the cellar in the dim light of kerosene lamps. He is silent, morose, or sarcastic most of the time, which I can't take personally. He's scared of what waits for him out there.

It's clear that I have to detach further from the lives of these guys—not change my behavior, but change my understanding, sink less ego in the outcome of life out here. Although James has been less personable in his last days here—which I attribute to the uncertainty he faces back home—I also see I'm not just myself here—I am a figure of adulthood, and will be liked and rejected often, according to whatever stage of the psychological journey a kid is in. But I'll miss lifting weights with James, and the moments of connection I felt sitting on the deck with a hot cup of coffee, after an afternoon of wood-splitting, when we discussed a fine point of morality, or the looks of a car.

The other day, as we sat on the deck, looking out over the cove, watching the colors change and fade as the sun went down, he said to me,

"Yo, Dan, how could you drive a Volvo, man?"

There was no wind where we were, stretched out in Adirondack chairs on the leeward side of the house, bundled up, each with a cup of coffee. We had been gathering stones for the wall around the garden all afternoon. James pulled on a generic menthol cigarette occasionally, and gestured with it as he spoke.

"I get in the driver's seat and I turn the key."

"Yo, you know what I mean, man, like it's a Swedish box, man, with no curves and no details that . . . like on a '84 Camaro like my boy Eduardo has, yo, that thing has curves, man, like where the hood goes forward from the fender, yo, it's sexy."

"Well, you have to get to know my car—it's got a lot of room, and it's a tough old mother, and it's a diesel, so it's easy to work on, and it's—"

"Yeah, but the guys who drive those are the guys who all work in them shiny computer buildings on 128 and who commute, man. It's the boring guys."

"Are you saying I'm boring?"

"No, man, I'm saying your car is boring, so boring. You ain't gonna rake in no chicks with a ride like that, man."

"Well, I hear you there, James, but maybe this is a good time for me to let you in on a concept."

"What?"

The light was lowering, and objects around the garden—fence posts, the stones of the wall, the two leafless pear trees at the north end of the garden, the slats of the compost bin, the carpentry shop with its rough gray shingles, even the tall grass of Tubbs in the distance across the cove—had begun to take on a glow, an integrity in the low light, as if there were a life within them that could only assert itself in the dying light of the evening.

"Well, hmmmm. No, I'm not sure you're ready for it," I said.

"Oh come on, don't pull this maturity-trip bullshit with me."

"All right. See that leaning fence post next to the compost bin?"

"Yeah."

"And you see the big stone there in the middle of that span of wall?"

"The big triangle one?"

"Yeah," I said. "Now, what do you think that fence post thinks of the stone?"

"It don't think nothing."

"Right. It just accepts that stone, right?"

"Fence posts don't think, Dan."

"Assume this one does. That is called 'tolerance,' James. When you accept the way something else is, and don't judge it."

"What do you mean, 'tolerance'?"

"I mean acceptance, no judgment."

"You mean I shouldn't go off on you about your boring car."

"I mean, what do you think that fence post, or this island, thinks of you?"

"It don't think nothing of me, it's a island."

"It accepts you as you are, doesn't it? No judgments, doesn't care how you dress—how does that feel?"

"You're a crackhead, man."

"I thought maybe you weren't ready for it."

The light was even lower now, and the real quiet of a windless evening had set in. The cove was millpond flat, and we could hear Jack and Reggie and Jerome talking at the pier, two hundred yards away, where they had been repairing lobster pots. James took another pull on his cigarette, and watched the smoke come off the tip of it for a moment, then said,

"Well maybe you didn't explain it good the first time, this tolerance shit . . ."

That was one of those good conversations.

14

SCHOOL. Just Ned and me. The wind is steady at forty knots out of the northwest, and ice growls down the bay, setting up fast against the island. Even now it looks impassable, the thick white plates of the soft salt ice pressing together, an impatient crowd; in an hour or two the pack around the island will be impregnable. Even the *Hill*, with its bronze-sheathed prow, can't punch through the frozen sea. We are isolate.

And the snow drifts, is driven nearly horizontal, gathers in the tall grass with a chirr, as gravity narrowly exerts greater influence than the wind. The waves in the bay would be huge, but for the slick of ice that calms them. And instead of writing the times of sunrise and set, high tide and low on the little blackboard which hangs by the front door of the house, as was his duty this morning, Sonny, the tough Italian, the truth teller, wrote "Fuck Penikese" with a big smiley face next to it. The weather has us all in a corner; we are quick to strike out.

So to school. When Ned and I came in today, once we had stopped up the cracks in the door with newspaper, and fed the little green stove some wood, Ned sat down to write in his journal (a boy who writes hardly at all) and has now scribbled out three-quarters of a page. I asked him what he was writing so hard about, but he said, "Leave me alone, man. Can't you see I'm busy?" So I did.

The other day, after Alan called him "a frickin' retahd," he threw himself off the ten-foot-high deck, landed easily in the garden, did two handsprings and three forward flips, tore off his shirts, climbed the fifteen-foot obstacle-course wall, flung his long frame off that, landing and rolling like a good para-trooper, and tore off up the hill, clad only in pants, snow flying up from his boots as he ran; and then he was gone, his foot-prints leading over the hill, disappearing from view. He came back, calm, clothed, a half hour later. Never did he threaten Alan. I suspect that's what he writes about. Ned, although he has a different style, may be the most enlightened kid out here.

And it may be because he doesn't judge so much, doesn't lapse into qualification when there's a question about why something happened. He seems to let his anger out, but not to attach it to himself or anyone else, as I do. I would have thought, after all he's been through, he'd have come to the conclusion that something was wrong with himself, but maybe he hasn't.

WHEN I came to the island, I had grand notions of trans-forming the lives of the students by giving them an apprecia-tion for the world of ideas via the reading and writing of literature. We were going to read, goddamnit, we were going to write, and in spite of their balkiness the project of creating real literacy in my students *would* proceed.

To which they said, "Fuck that." What I have found so far is this: Some of the guys are capable of extended periods of con-centration on a subject, and some just aren't. Some are sad-dled with disabilities such as dyslexia and attention deficit disorder and the insecurities that can accompany them, and some are just plain paranoid about being shamed. It has be-come clear that while one guy might read *For Whom the Bell Tolls* with ease, and then write a reasonable response on the theme of ethics in time of war, another guy can struggle with a Hardy boys mystery, and then completely tune out when it comes time to think about what he has read. Still another student is so phobic about school that he has difficulty just being in the schoolhouse, or anywhere, for an hour at a time, never mind actually working on something.

What I see is that cultivating a positive attitude toward learning in these guys—getting them to see school as a nonthreatening part of their routine—is far more important than squeezing out the mastery of any specific skill. Attitude, in many cases, is everything, and it is clear that I am engaged in damage control with 70 percent of the boys who come through the school door. They have been convinced, either maliciously or otherwise, that they are not capable of doing work in a normal classroom. Beneath it all, they want to be able to function as normal kids, to have that world open, but the fear is in charge.

Because of this, a lot of my creative solutions to the endless classroom dilemma of "what the hell to do to interest rebellious students" fall flat. The poems of Etheridge Knight, full of rhythm and vibrance, slipped easily beyond them when we read them in class the other day. I couldn't believe it, that even the poem I thought was guaranteed to generate a few minutes of interest in the toughest of them—"Feeling Fucked Up"— was a wash. I tried to teach it to Jerome and Sonny. Jerome asked all of the questions.

"What he mean 'fucked up,' and why he say 'fuck marx and mao fuck fidel and nkrumah and Jesus and the disciples and alligators'?" asked Jerome.

"Well, remember the last line?" I said.

"Yeah."

"What's it say?"

"It say (reading), 'So my soul can sing.'"

"And what's it say in the line before that?"

"It say, "'All I want now is my woman back . . .'"

"Right," I said.

"Write what?" asked Jerome,

"No. Right. That's why he says forget all that other stuff."

"What stuff?"

"Marx and Mao and Fidel and Nkrumah and Jesus and the disciples."

"What's Marx?" he asked. I wanted to hug him for that.

"Well, he was a German guy who said we should redistribute the wealth in the world, give some of the land to the poor, and some of the money, even things out, and his thoughts influenced the revolution in Russia when they kicked the czar out of office."

"What's a zar?"

"'Czar' is the Russian word for 'king.'"

"Write it on the board."

"Write it on the board what?"

"Write it on the board please Mr. Wise-Ass Teacher."

I did. "Czar."

"That's Russian?"

"Yup."

"Why they going and making another word for king, man? We already got one. When they kick him out? They did that recently, it's in the paper?" he asked.

"No, no. They did that in 1917," I said.

"Oh. And Marx said they should take the rich people's money and give it to the poor folks?"

"Yeah, distribute it evenly."

"Yo, I like that Marx dude. What's Mao?" he said, stabbing his stubby finger at the word on the page.

"He was the head of mainland China when they won their revolution in 1949, and he knew all about Marx."

"They was buddies?"

"No, but he had read Marx's ideas."

"Yo, he be payin' that Marx dude off for his ideas, that's how all y'all collegy guys do it, right?" said Jerome, leaning back and laughing.

"Well, sort of . . . uh . . ." But he was stabbing at the page again.

"What's Nkrumah?"

"Kwame Nkrumah was the first president of Ghana, a country in Africa, from 1960 to 1966. He helped end European colonialism on that continent."

"Where's Ghana?"

I pointed to it on the map of the world that hung on the south wall.

"He kicked the white mans out of there?"

"He worked to liberate Ghana, yes."

"Why this dude saying screw him?"

"'Cause he doesn't want to worry about any of that political stuff, he just wants his woman back. He's in love."

"This dude need to go find his woman and tell her what's up. And he need to stop takin' the Lord's name in vain, 'cause he gonna get a lightnin' bolt up his ass right quick, and he need to stop usin' the f-word all-a the time because it's just being lazy, like you told us, and he could find a more interesting word, like, like, like 'bamboozle.' Yeah, 'Feelin' Bamboozled.' That got a ring to it," he said, with firmness in his voice, looking me straight in the eye.

"Well, that's maybe good advice. What do you think of the poem, Sonny?"

"I think it fuckin' sucks."

"Why?"

"'Cause it's a piece of shit."

"Well, tell me a little more."

"A little more? All right. I can't fuckin' stand this poem. I hate poetry. Fuck poetry." View of Sonny's back going out the door.

"Sonny, get back here, man. Don't ruin your day."

"I fuckin' hate poetry."

Always let them have the last word.

THE schoolhouse. The wind is at three knots—barely a breath—and the mercury stands at minus four degrees in the

sun. The ice has set in, and with it a quiet that pervades the island. We are locked in. The fire roars in the little green Jotul,
and Ken sprawls on two mattresses in the loft, leafing through
his journal. Jerome has begun on his geometry, and seems
content for now, but I know that the tension of not knowing
how we will get off the island tomorrow will bubble up in him
soon. I can hear him now:

"Yo, man, they should take us off this flibbertigibbit island
today, man, they should bring that damn boat out here and let
us stay onshore overnight. Call George. I ain't spendin' a
minute I ain't got to out here."

Snow lies in a long drift inside the latticed east window, in
little drifts inside the north door, and falls lazily outside, gathering in the salt hay. We tend to the stove. Minus four degrees
of mercury, Fahrenheit, on an island such as this, is ferocious
cold, not because it is so cold, though it is, but because the
nearness of the sea allows some moisture to remain in the air,
and so lends the wind a razor edge, when there is wind.

But there is no wind now; all is still outside, all is frozen,
silent. In such cold, things shatter; the cold brings with it im-
mediacy; when I go out, perhaps to walk to the outhouse, and
hear the latch on the red door to the house click shut behind
me with a deadened ring, and hear the ground under my feet
squeak with the rime, the molecules in the stones so stilled in
their movement that even a footfall might cause them to shear
apart, the stone to break, then I sense that everything might
rupture suddenly, the island cracking down its center and capsizing into an iron-blue sea, the stones of the shore flung into
the air and raining down into the shallows, sinking into new
depths of dark sea steaming with the cold snow of the hills now
vanished and the pigs swimming in circles among the flotsam
of the house and fences and driftwood until they sank, too, the
snow resting gently on their foreheads and then melting as the
waters covered them.

It is that cold; the grass crackles and breaks under my boots,
and I can see that this might happen to my attachments to the

past, too, that in such cold they might bust, ligatures broken
into shards to vanish into the sea, leaving me this here, this
now, this walk up the gentle hill to the outhouse, the moan of
these hinges on the gray plank door with the first quarter moon
cut out of it, its thud muted by the frozen air as it closes behind
me, and the rasp of the coarse and stiff door lanyard moving
through my leather glove as I loop it around the cleat on the
door frame and throw a hitch on, then the rustle as my pant
buttons surrender to my fingers, the smooth sound of the fabric
of my long underwear as I slide them and my pants down my
legs, the quick inhalation as my ass hits the firelike cold of the
smooth wood seat, hoarfrost on the window and my good
brown boots resting on the worn plywood floor before me, my
toes growing numb as I look out at the tawn of the fields and
the white of the frozen bay, and, minutes later, the soft report
of my turd hitting the frozen mound ten feet beneath me, the
fumbling with numbed fingers with toilet paper that has somehow become wet and then frozen, and so shatters into white
flakes which litter the worn plywood floor and my boots, then
finding another roll by walking in half steps with pants round
ankles to the far end of the house where the bucket of lime sits
in the corner, wiping in a half stoop, looking down the hole to
where my offering steams atop the frozen dungheap in the
belly of the outhouse, replacing clothes, bumbling back out
into the cold of the day, and hearing again the whine of the
gravel under my boot soles as it struggles not to shatter. It is
that cold. Looking out on the vast white plain of the frozen sea
from the height of the island, it is the silence of the scene
which grips me. Everything, even the sea, has been stilled.

I S it working? Any of it? I have no hard evidence, but I know
that it is. I see it, day in, day out, an increase in their involvement in the community, in their depth of caring, somehow.
Sonny built shelves around the perimeter of the living room
downstairs last week, for the hell of it. They are healed by the

rhythms out here, by the steadiness of it all, the unrelenting beauty, the untiring decency that we the staff show each other. The other day I disagreed with Jeb about the bearing relative to north of a part of the island. In the end I allowed that maybe I was wrong, and we laughed about something his girlfriend had done, and then he walked away. Sonny watched all of this, then walked away shaking his head, saying, "I woulda decked 'im, no doubt," under his breath.

SATURDAY, January 15. We were stranded by ice on Friday, as the wind came up strongly from the northeast and pushed the ice even more strongly down the bay into the Elizabeths. All the holes were blocked solid, and while there was a narrow channel to the southwest, leading to open water south of Cuttyhunk, George didn't like the thought of going around Sow and Pigs, the reef southwest of Cuttyhunk, and another eight miles out of his way in treacherous waters. So he called a helicopter, at ten dollars a minute, which pulled us off in three trips.

The guys, of course, were overjoyed at this, many of them never having been in a plane, not to mention a helicopter, so there was much rejoicing, with imagined scenarios:

"I know," said Sonny. "Let's turn it into a helicoptuh gunship and go and blow the juvenile school right to hell." They all loved that ride.

I was in the last trip, the pilot a Vietnam vet, clean-cut, taciturn, and when we had revolutions, we lifted off hard, climbed straight up 75 feet, and then he moved the stick to the left and we slid crazily off over the cove, as if there were small-arms fire and flak to escape. I watched the knots dial to 120, as we slowly rattled the altimeter up to 300 feet. And the trip, somehow, was cheapened.

We were in a time warp; the journey which usually took an hour and a half in a heavy lobster boat, jostled by seas, was being compressed into a quarter of an hour. Ice in irregular gray plates moved below us, like random farmland seen from above, with the islands to the east, long and low-slung, themselves a patchwork of sandplain grassland and stands of hardwood. And those distant trees on the islands, in the luminous gray light of the afternoon, vibrated with a muted energy I couldn't place at first. They looked vaguely red, and it took me ten minutes to realize I was seeing the combined hue of millions of buds on hundreds of thousands of twigs of beech and oak and maple, each prepared to burst in three months' time, and already glowing dully. The trees were husbanding their energy, as were we, in expectation of spring, whose first sign came to me even on the hardest day of winter, in that muted red. Energy was seeping even out of the frozen earth.

We flew down the west coast of the islands, about a quarter mile out, and then slid in over Penzance Point and landed at the Woods Hole ballpark, the site of so many of my trials as a boy. Strange, to see a place like that from the air, see where the village boys used to play football every afternoon in the fall, where I used to see if being blocked into the frozen turf by 270-pound Jeff Macalester would hurt less than it had the day before. This had been the arena, and here we had run at each other, smashed into each other, thrown each other down, seen if we could take it. There was an unspoken agreement, that that was what it was about.

Tino Coughlin was the hardest one out there, not because of his size or his speed, but because he seemed to have the least to lose. He was a rangy Italian-Irish kid from another part of town, with a shock of dark hair and a mouth that took the steam out of you even after he'd walked away from the collision. "Fuckin' pussy," he'd say, as he looked down on you lying in the mud. He was six-two, with big, sharp elbows, and hands that came up fast to box if there was doubt about a play. It seemed, when he first came out with us, that he might be too fast to flash to anger, but after a week he understood our terms, was flattening and being flattened with the rest of us, knowing there would be no resentment of a good hit. That was all we wanted—to see if we could take a hit.

We'd square off, maybe six on a side, and I'd see if I could pull a new move on a kid I'd lined up opposite hundreds of times before. The ball would be hiked, and if I knocked my guy off the line, I'd maybe run an out to the right, get a pass thrown behind me, and then hear the footsteps, as I reached back for the ball, of Pete Swenson, whose feet made a whirr on the grass. I feared that whirr. He had shoulders made hard by winters of hockey, and he was so damned fast—he'd plant one in my back, and I knew I was paying, and then I was facedown in the mud, clutching the ball to my chest. Perfect.

I COULD see the outline of the diamond under the light dusting of snow as we hovered above the ballpark, and then as we vibrated gently down the snow was blown back in a sheet, revealing clay base paths where I had played my baseball as a kid, and where, thirty-five years before, my father had played shortstop for the All-Stars of the Cape League, this being one of the parks where they'd practice or play an occasional game. From what I know, he had a great arm—the kind which freezes a runner on the base path—and soft hands which drew the hard grounders up into his chest, to be stifled there. The tall grass beyond the outfield has probably advanced toward home since then, but I'd like to think it hasn't. I've reached it with a drive to left in a couple of softball games. I might have done better with a hardball, back then.

My father also came out once in a while to play ball with us neighborhood boys when we were six and seven and eight; I remember him pitching endlessly, softly, with a compact delivery, his arm at three quarters of vertical as it came over his head, index and middle finger gripping the ball in order to throw a looping curve, and our weak drives plopping into short right or center, driven by our late swings. That was when he was around a little, had given me perhaps enough to get to the next stage, to struggle on through junior high.

So we landed in this place, descended from the heavens,

and it was strange. A little ballpark with a chain-link backstop, deep left and center fields, a shallower right field, all backing onto a tangle of willow and red oak which give then onto the bottoms of the village, former marshland made stagnant when its cut to the sea was filled for road. A Ruthian shot would have fallen in the mire. This was the place. This was the shrine.

ONE guy I grew up with at that ballpark was close to his anger. At twelve years, he was blond, of average height, and good looking, with small features. But he was wound tighter than the rest of us. I remember him in a short-sleeved shirt, how his muscles were different than mine, more taut, bigger. And he could thump. When the rest of us would put our hands down and try to bull the other guy into a tree, or knock him down, Jeff would stand up straight and punish the other boy with his fists, hitting him square in the face or the gut. His neck would turn red, and then his face, and when you saw his blood rising you knew the fight was over, that he had won; it was as if a dark rage were percolating up through the earth to him, to his hands. It was time then to walk away.

He lived with his mother, who wore her hair in a tight gray-and-blonde braid. His father lived in a western state, and when I went to their house it was always very quiet. The little dog, a beagle, always sat in the corner, watching, and the house was stark, pristine in its cleanliness, almost hollow. I never stayed long—there was something hard and unspoken in that house I couldn't abide.

Jeff wasn't all stone. He had a good voice, and sometimes he sang on the bus on the way home from school, old Dylan songs that echoed off the lime green sheet metal of the interior of the nearly empty yellow bus, but there was that underlying anger there, which I knew of.

When we were twelve, we bought a bottle of whiskey from a boy named John Cooper. He was seventeen, but he looked older, and he could buy. He brought it to us, a fifth of Old

Granddad bourbon in a paper bag, behind the historical society building, a small, old, shingled place, near the post office. I
could smell the warmth of the sun in the old cedar shingles on
the walls as we leaned on them, that afternoon, waiting for
John.

When it came, the bottle felt heavy and warm in my hands,
and I could feel its warmth in my ribs through my backpack.
We pedaled it to the ballpark.

Behind the tennis courts at the ballpark there is a dry creek
bed, and we put the bottle in a hole in the bank there, and
went home.

A couple of days later we went back, after school, and
played catch for a while. I'd been thinking about that bottle, at
school, thinking about being discovered with it, about its
power, something I knew about that no one else did, except
Jeff. It lent focus to the world.

"You feel like a little nip?" he asked, holding the ball next to
his ear in his glove.

"What do you mean a 'nip'?"

"Like some of the old man, the Old Granddad? Don't you
know what a nip is?"

"Oh. Yeah. I've heard that. I just didn't hear what you said."

We went back there, into the tall grass behind the tennis
courts, and found the bottle in the bank. Jeff broke the seal,
spun the cap off the bottle with one finger, and held it out to
me. I took it with both hands, held it nervously for a few seconds, and then took a pull. It tasted like burning leaves going
down, and hit my stomach with a gravity I'd never felt before,
as if I'd eaten a stone.

Jeff then took a pull, and I watched it move down past his
Adam's apple, and I another, and he, and then we put the bottle in its bag, hid it in its hole, walked slowly back through the
tall grass to the short grass of the outfield.

A warmth spread through my body; we played catch for a
while longer, as the sun began to go down, and then he called
me a pussy.

"Throw the damn ball. You can throw it harder than that. Pussy."

I threw it hard. At his head.

"You throwin' at my head?" he said.

"You asked for it. Pussy."

"Let's go," he said, walking toward me and throwing down his glove, smiling. "I'll let you take your best shot in my gut, but after that we go."

He stood in front of me, arms at his sides, tensed his stomach, and nodded. I took my best shot. He winced, and then we leaned in, and started pounding away at each other. For the first time I felt that anger, that rage coming up from somewhere beneath me, rage for being alone, without a guide, without a father. And for a couple of minutes it was a draw—I blocked his good shots, and he mine—and then for the first time I was able to back him off, throw my shoulder into him, and swing away at his chest. I wanted to kill him, to see him die right there in front of me.

He pulled back, shocked, and then came at me, this time swinging at my head. His face was turning red. I blocked most of those shots with my forearms, landed one good blow above his right ear, and we went down in a heap. He came up with the headlock on me, I gave, and that was that. For me, the anger was gone.

We caught our breaths, locked eyes for a second, ambled back to the bikes as the sun went down, rode home, home to our mothers, who no doubt thought the red cheeks of our faces were from the chill wind and the ride.

And I remember watching the men in the town back then, the workingmen, who shouldered through the wind in old sweaters, who seemed to carry some assurance with them, some hardihood and masculinity that was basic to them. I wanted that, wanted to walk bowlegged in work boots like I belonged to the place and the way, like I was part of what went on there, in Woods Hole, as a man, with a hammer. Jeff and I were looking for that hardness, trying to beat it into each other,

kill each other if that's what it took. We knew no one else was
going to show us the way.

SHORTLY after touchdown, Sonny and Ned and I went
into town to get a movie at Eden Video in Falmouth, which
we would watch that evening at the onshore house. The conditions were that we wouldn't get anything predicated on violence or sex.

I walked into the place looking like I'd just walked off a
farm, which I had, having mucked the chicken shit out of the
little barn before leaving the tractor in there for the weekend. I
had on my Carhartt pants—ripped and patched and ripped
again—and heavy boots, and a hundred layers and a big old
work jacket—I would have gone straight to the bottom if the
copter had crapped out over the bay. The boys were in much
the same condition, and we must have looked a sight arguing
over movies.

"So what are we going to get?" said Sonny. "Are you going to
pick out a *Pink Panther* movie for us, or what?"

"Why don't you guys each pick out something you want to
see, and we'll draw straws, but nothing that's all violence and
sex, all right? It's got to have some redeeming features."

"Yo, I'm headed," said Sonny, and we split up. Five minutes
later I was standing in front of the Hitchcock section when
Sonny came up to me.

"Yo, Dan, I got this one and this one, man. I can't decide.
This one is a Van Damme, and I can't remember if I seen it or
not, and this one is a Seagal, which my boy Joey said was hot,
but I like Van Damme."

"What's that one called?"

"*Bloodsport.*"

"Sounds pretty violent to me . . ."

"Nah, it's cool, like, not too many people die and they always deserve it, you know, and there's, like there's no puppies
shredded or nothing."

"Uh, and what's the other one?" I said.

"It's called *Under Siege II.*"

"Uh-huh. Well, I've seen a Van Damme film, or part of one, and I gotta say I think we can find something with action that isn't just about killing and maiming—"

"No, these are fat, Dan, believe me, these are some good films, man. Hey, Ned, you like Van Damme, right?"

"Yeah, man, he's good," he said, coming over to us, "killin' those cocksuckers all over the place, *biff! bap! kunh!*" he said, as he shadowboxed with a video rack, his brown hair flying.

"No, but really, Dan, these are cool," said Sonny.

"Ned! Watch your language, man. Look, I can't let you guys get the most depraved stuff in the place. Go get a James Bond or something, or a drama. How about a classic like *North by Northwest.* It's a murder mystery with this beautiful woman, Eva Marie Saint—"

"Does she take it off?" asked Sonny.

"Well, that's part of the beauty, that you have to imag—"

"Does she give it up, Dan?"

"Well, she—"

"She don't. C'mon, man, let us see what we want to see, man, we been on the island for a frickin' month, man," said Sonny.

"I can't spring for the Van Damme or the Seagal. It's too much about violence and disregard for human life."

"C'mon, man, don't be a prick. We ain't lookin' to get re-doomed by the movie, we just want to chill."

"'Redeemed'—go get a James Bond film or a—how about Clint Eastwood—"

"Bond's a fag and Eastwood's a pussy, man, he's washed up, and you're a cocksucker. If it don't fit your narrow definition . . . You ain't gonna keep me from seeing anything I ain't already seen."

The manager, a heavy man with thin, greasy hair, was looking over at us uneasily now; the last expletive hadn't calmed him down any.

"Look, Sonny," I said, hissing at him across the eight films in the foreign section, "look at the position I'm in. I can't get you guys a film that's got the message that violence is all right, man. That's not what we're about on the island, and you know it."

As we spoke, big-breasted women in tight dresses and heavily muscled men watched us from posters that hung around the store.

"I know you're a cocksuckin' whore, that's what I know," he said, walking away. "I'll be in the car. Get what you want." He walked away. Somehow I knew that Sonny, despite his words, respected my decision.

"Ned, any suggestions?"

"Nah, man, get what you want. I'm straight."

When I got in the school's tired Plymouth minivan, which squatted in the rear like an old dog, Sonny regarded me stonily from the backseat. It occurred to me, that, according to his own estimates, Sonny could have hot-wired the car and been gone for ten minutes. In a strange way, I trusted him. He never pulled his punches. Ned slid into the passenger's seat, and we headed back through a light snow to Woods Hole.

"So what'd you get, Dan?" asked Ned.

"I got *The Unforgiven.*"

"What's it about?" he asked.

"It's a western, and it's about a washed-up gunslinger who gets convinced to round up some criminals just one more time for a reward. There's a lot of shooting and stuff, so you guys might like it, but there's a real strong message in there, too, about the senselessness of it all."

"So it's got a lot of shootin', huh?" said Ned.

"Yup."

"Good."

"But there's some thinking that goes on about it, too," I said.

"Oh, that don't matter to me. I just watch 'em," said Ned. "Hey, you seen *Natural Born Killers*, Sonny?"

"Yup."

"That was a fat movie, man. You remembah right before he wasted all of those dudes, he said to her, 'Let's make a little music, Coloradah?' That dude was funny, man."

"Fat film, yo," said Sonny from the back.

"Well," I began, "there was kind of a message in that film, too. Remember that TV announcer who was following them?"

"Yeah," said Ned.

"Well, he was in there to show you that it was the newspapers and TV shows that were building up the killers, that they were a big part of the blame—"

"That dude was a fag. I was glad when he bought it," said Sonny.

"Don't be a bigot, Sonny," I said.

"Suck my dick, and quit tryin' to be my mother."

"That cost you big—five bucks—along with another five bucks for what you said in the store. How can you expect me to respect you when you don't respect me?" I said, eyeing him in the mirror until he shifted his gaze. When I looked back, light snow eddied in the headlights and the dark tarmac unfurled ahead of us.

"Whatever," he sighed back. "What the fuck ever."

"I was glad when they shot him, too," said Ned. "So there's a lot of guns in this one, Dan? Like the old ones that you gotta pull the trigger every time?"

"Yeah, the old ones," I said. "They use the old guns in this one."

15

FRIDAY, January 27. I had Jerome and Reggie in school two days ago. The stove was inhaling quietly in the background, the day outside was gray, and both guys sat at the heavy oak table with their chins propped on their hands, looking up at me balefully. As a primer for some short essay writing, we discussed violence versus nonviolence, and whether we as a country should excuse the actions of criminals. They both said no.

"No way, man. You do the crime, you pay the time," was Jerome's answer.

So I asked if a person should ever be excused from violence.

"If you was being threatened, it would be okay to take it in your own hands," was Jerome's reply, and Reggie came in with, "I don't think violence is ever right, but if somebody gonna mess with you, expose you to harm, then you got to be able to defend yourself. Simple as that."

"When should a person be killed?" I asked.

Reggie said, "If he be threatening your life, then you got to use force, maybe deadly force."

Jerome said, "If he threaten you or rob you."

"Of how much would this robbery have to be?" I asked Jerome.

"A lot," he said.

We whittled down his conception. Nine hundred and ninety dollars stolen would call for only a beating, but one thousand dollars stolen would call for the thief to be killed, according to his code, which might have been invented just for the day. Perhaps the capital amount has gone up by now. I let him know that I had a different code. We'll discuss it again tomorrow.

"JESUS, I'm lonely," I wrote in my journal not long ago. This life is too damned long to go through without a woman, and I'm doing it. Part of the problem is that I spend half of my time on an island inhabited by criminal boys. Which I enjoy, in a sense, but it is hard to find a woman who understands the drive to teach in such a place. I think. Or is it hard to find anyone when I am either teaching or exhausted?

In either case I feel at the frail edge of isolation, an explorer marooned in the Arctic, locked in ice. I don't know if I need this, if my personal discovery here is so intense that I couldn't be with anyone, or if I am isolating myself out here, as if I were in a lab. I lie in bed in the night, listening to the quiet of the house, or to its creaking in the wind, and to the soft hiss of lamp flame next to my head. I lie in that narrow bed, feel the sea stretching out on every side of the island, feel the work of the day in my body, feel the lifting of stones or the swinging of the axe in my back and forearms, feel the long walk with firewood in my legs, and I feel a body that is growing older alone, untouched.

Perhaps this must be. Perhaps I am so hard at it, learning my own voice, that this single bed in this loft, with this kerosene lamp and this blue wool blanket and this streak of soot above my head, this is all I get. But I feel famished, hungry for contact. "People need human contact!" says Maxine in Tennessee Williams's *The Night of the Iguana*. How right she is.

But I wonder, could she understand what goes on out here? I went to dinner the other day at a friend's, and met a woman there. She was long and sinuous, with straight brown hair and a sculpted Eastern European face—Natassia Kinski in Polan-ski's *Tess* in my mind—and we talked about our work. She said she was an editor, and I explained that I was a teacher. I thought I saw her figuring my income in her mind as we spoke, but she asked about the boys, what they were like, and seemed interested. And she had this thing she did with her mouth, a kind of half smile, that was intriguing.

"How do they explain the things they've done?" she asked.

"Explain them?"

"Yeah, I mean, what excuses do they make?"

"Excuses? They don't make excuses. At least not at first. And for the most part I don't think it really occurs to them," I said.

"But they must think about it, they must have regrets . . ."

"Well, a lot of the time that's not how their minds work," I said.

"But how could you not have regrets about being in jail?"

"Well, I guess you would, if you thought you were the cause of it," I said.

"And they are, right?" she said, tucking some of her brown hair behind her right ear, and cocking her head at me. When she did that I could see her body shift under her sweater.

"Well, they are, but often they don't see it that way."

"You mean they blame their parents?"

"Well, sometimes," I said, "but these guys just don't get cause and effect a lot of the time, because they have grown up in such illogical homes. 'I'm good, so Mom beats me. I'm bad, so Mom beats me. I'm just quiet, so she doesn't beat me . . . then passes out. Then her boyfriend comes home and beats Mom, and comes after me. So I go tell my uncle, and he's drunk and turns me around and pulls down my pants and fon-dles my thing.' That is their experience. So, when they get to the island, they don't necessarily make the logical connection, or understand that what they do has consequences."

"But you're saying that they have no sense of 'if this, then that'?" she said.

"Yeah."

"Then they're unteachable," she said, showing me her

turned-up left palm and dropping her voice at the end as if she had won.

"No, they're just not living in the same universe as you and I. They come from a different place."

"But," she said, putting her wineglass up to her mouth and holding it there for a moment, her other arm hugging herself as she looked at the floor, then letting her dark eyes float back up to mine, "what can you do for someone who isn't even well-adjusted enough to think?"

"You send them outside where they get consistent responses from the island, and you respond consistently, too, and after a while they come around," I said, thinking that what I was really interested in wasn't even on the table, baby, and that I was tired of sparring.

"But they can't be without any concept of cause and effect, I mean, we all learn that along the line somewhere," she said.

"Well, I had a kid ask me the other night, 'What's that big white thing up there?' and I said, 'What big white thing?' and he said, 'That right there,' and pointed at the moon. I told him it was the moon, and he said 'What's the moon?' The boy had lived all of his life in the inner city. He'd had a different kind of upbringing. And he'd always thought it was a big streetlight, or searchlight. That's where these guys are coming from."

"You're bullshitting me. He didn't ask you what the moon was," she said, throwing her head back and laughing. She did have nice hair.

"He did."

"I don't believe you. You're teasing me."

"I'm too tired to tease you, and I wouldn't anyway," I said.

"Hey, Tom!" she called over to our host, turning away from me. As she did so, her sweater rose up a bit, showing where her pale blue shirt disappeared over her slender waist into her jeans. I envied that shirt. "Dan says he has students who haven't even heard of the moon, and I don't believe him."

"Oh, don't believe anything this guy says," said Tom, who was carrying a tray of crackers and cheese. "Here, try one of these. Can I get you another glass of wine?"

"Yeah, that would be nice," she said, and they drifted toward the kitchen.

"So what are you working on now?" Tom said to her, as he looked at her over the rim of a glass of gin. They were leaning on the kitchen counter.

"It's a travel book about some of the great country inns in Vermont."

"Good," he said. "Sounds like a good assignment. We all need country. I do. Need anyone to go with you on assignment?"

It was clear to me that in some ways my instincts had been dulled.

LATER, I walked home on the quiet streets, under the big elms and Norway maples, with the old incandescent streetlight sifting down through the branches, and thought about her, thought about my big bed in the cold cottage, how the moonlight would be coming through the latticed window and would spread itself there, on the mattress, and how that might have been her. Why wasn't she with me now, or at least her phone number a small glad scrawl on a scrap of napkin in my pocket? But I hadn't even asked her for it. I couldn't have. Because I couldn't have told her where I dwell.

I feel as if I am moving between two worlds; even though I am the same man, the same person I was, I'm not. I see these guys, how everything in them is understood in terms of what they saw as they grew up, what blows fell on them. They move through the world in a tangle of reactions, anger rising when a voice resembles the voice of the father who called them dirt, or when someone is hard to read, and it feels like it did before they got belted. They are victims, and I am in the netherworld between that way of seeing and a new way, where I might just see the world fresh each moment, and not through a scrim of my father's shoes lined up along the wall in a room that will always be silent.

16

FEBRUARY. The off week. I sit in my little house, yet again, and the day out is raw, just above freezing, and moist. It is the damp cold of the sea, the heavy wet air that comes off the bay and across the Hole and collides with the mainland a scant fifty yards from my door and then is shunted up across the slim beach through the leafless stems of the honeysuckle thickets and rosa rugosa, leaps the road and comes across my lawn like a gang of teenagers and then slams into the wall that lies just beyond my outstretched feet. It is a thin wall, and the floor is thin hardwood, and sits on a foundation of cement block which the wind whistles through, a wind which cuts.

I am sitting beneath four blankets in this big chair. It is a typical Monday after coming off the island. I haven't seen any-one yet, and I won't want to for two days. On the island I am on duty, with antennae up, and psychic energy draining from me, twenty-four hours a day for six days. The drainage doesn't stop when I'm asleep. Which means that once I am home I need four days to decompress, to stare at the wall, to listen to nothing. Screw companionship (at least it's something to screw). I just want to be alone. My boundaries, however, are becoming better defined, less easily pierced by an unexpected hit. My efficiency is improving, my recovery time dropping. I am more in the moment, less reactive out there, able to hear "whore" thrown my way and let it go for what it is—the jibe of a young man in pain.

But as I sit here, in this chair in this simple little home, what I'm remembering is the other house by the bay, in Woods Hole, where I was brought up from ages ten to eighteen, and the quiet of the winters there, the muted colors of gray sea and browned grass, when we shut down the house, lived in three heated rooms, and I split wood for the stove in the evenings within earshot of the waves. How pervasive the feeling there was of the power of the sea—as the sun fell into the waters at the end of day—and the death of a family.

My mother's sister would come around occasionally, looking for something. She would knock on the door, a big tragic woman in heels and a crooked dress, with her hair a slightly inorganic red, her nail polish chipped, her head held at an angle that told me she was both convinced of her stature in life and slightly drunk.

She would come in when I answered the door and rumble off into the wing where my grandfather had died, and come out with something somewhat valuable, a chess set or a vase, and say that her mother had promised this to her when she died and that she was taking it, as she pulled on a Pall Mall and left lipstick on the filter, and shook her head (as if she still had long hair) as she pulled the cigarette out of her mouth and inhaled, the smoke solid and visible in her mouth for an instant and then gone into her lungs, and her hair moving around on top of her head as if it had a life of its own.

I loved her, the stale smell of smoke that she left in the house, the gauzy sense of the 1940s and the right sort of people and old money that she carried with her, even though she drove a corroded Toyota Corolla. Aunt Pat, who left little piles of ashes on the floor.

And at ten years old, I had the vague sense that all of this was my fault—the absent father, the mother who felt keenly the hardness of raising a child alone, the family that had produced Aunt Pat and her sister Rebecca, who was so gorgeous, stunning and wonderful, who brought all the young men of Newton to their knees, so thoughtful and fragile, who in time couldn't be left alone because she might drink, or harm herself. How could this have happened to us, this family that I loved so much?

But perhaps there are other ways to remember all of that, to remake the memory, recall other details less wintry. In some of us, the mind recalls best what is painful, perhaps to have close at hand what to avoid in the future. Is this a survival trait, retained from when I was a rodent-like creature scrabbling around on the leaf-strewn forest floor, avoiding badgers? If this is the default pathway in the circuits of my emotional memory, I renounce it.

And the island is still with me. I am in mind of the lepers, what their experience must have been out there. Desolation, I imagine, and the end of things on a forgotten lump of land. They watched the sea endlessly, breaking on the rocky shore beneath the southern bluffs, ate their food, swathed their swollen feet, read. What did they make of it?

There was a doctor there, Frank Parker, and his wife, who dedicated their lives to those who died slowly on the little spit. There was no cure then, no way to halt the disease, as there is now. Parker could not have known whether he would contract the disease, or if his wife would.

I imagine them, sitting by a fire in a dark room after a day, the sea dark beyond darker land out the window. He would have tended to the eight or ten patients, as circulation to their feet or hands or ears slowly lessened, as the inevitable end neared, and she would have looked after supplies, ordering more gauze and more coal and more nails and more sheets and more butter and more soap and pine boards for a long box, and it all would have arrived on the weekly boat, a small schooner and, later, a little steamer, unloaded by men who wore gloves even in summer, who looked impatient to get away, who dropped the gloves in a bucket of kerosene as they walked onto the boat for the last time.

I see them sitting there, the Parkers, looking into the coals, the thrum of a tug distant across the bay, and the rhythm of the surf coming, as it does now, from the southern shore, and I wonder if they said anything, or if there was nothing to do but remain, arise in the morning, as the cock crew, light the fire again.

I AM thinking back on Wyatt, what he told me in the shop. We were alone in the high-ceilinged old building. It is a rough place, built by the school on a foundation that stood open, I imagine, for years after the leper colony's plant was dynamited. Its weathered beams, worn plywood floor, and scarred workbench are all peppered with nails pounded in and bent over by bored young men. It is a strangely quiet building, usually strewn with tools. The high ceilings absorb smaller sounds; in warmer months barn swallows peer down sagely from their wattle-and-daub nests.

We were sparring verbally as we worked. Wyatt was banging on a rough box being built for cassette tapes, and I on a tool box. He called me a bald-headed geek, and I probably called him an adolescent punk, or an eight-year-old, and we merrily traded insults for a few minutes.

And then, under his breath, he said, "Dan, I'm lost." Very softly.

I said, "What?"

"Nothing."

"What did you say?"

"Nothing."

"What did you say, Wyatt?"

"Nothing, you fuckin' bald-headed geek."

"Did you say 'I'm lost'?"

"No."

"I thought I heard you say that."

"Fuck you, man. I didn't say nothin'."

So we drifted into silence, and a few minutes later it was time to go.

I AM concerned about Wyatt, who outwardly is making strides, who seems to me to be getting closer to rounding the corner and seeing the real cause of his pain, whatever that is. I see him approaching it, but I don't see the healthy vulnerability that should go with it, the quickness to anger, or tears. He is isolating himself, and that speaks danger to me, for I see so much of myself in him.

SUNDAY, February 16. We had a rough time of it again on Friday. Thursday the ice had come down in spare gray ribbons from the northwest, reaching for us again across the dark blue waters of the bay from New Bedford. The guys were nervous, and we wondered among ourselves what would become of us. Would we be marooned for a time? I was in school with Jerome, working on reading and the five-point essay, which he grasped in record time, and wrote quite well, working on the views of women as held by the narrator of *Manchild in the Promised Land* and himself. So, he wrote of "hos and bitches," and of how one should treat a woman.

The day carried on cold and windy, with thick snow falling. There were five-foot drifts behind the barn and outhouse by evening, and Friday, our day to go home, began little better. The *Hill* set out at 7:15 A.M. from Woods Hole with the weekend crew aboard, tried to come down the bay, couldn't for the ice, tried to nose out into the Sound on the other side of the islands, couldn't there either. We all sat in the staff room huddled around the radio as Pop's warm voice barged through the static, or the latest weather report crackled thinly through, and as the wind bumped and clutched at the house. The boys "bugged" (jumped about nervously).

"Why you didn't take us off the island yesterday? You just want to be paid more money," said Jerome, who then started making a staccato sucking noise with his mouth that signaled discontent. Wyatt groaned. Jerome chimed in again.

"They need to call the chopper. That fool Jones don't know what he's doin' drivin' that boat. Where's George?"

"I better be back by one-thirty, or I'm goin' to miss the hos comin' out of school," added Reggie.

"You mean the respectable young women? You can see them later," I said.

"Nah, I got to see them *then*. I got some vested interests," he said, looking at me with fire in his eyes.

Eventually, around noon, in driving snow, the maroon hull of the *Patriot* hove into view—a fifty-foot steel boat that could break the ice—and promptly ran aground just south of the dock. She had arrived at low tide when there was only five feet of water there, but she managed to ease off again after some moments of panic. We were in town by two-thirty, after a slow trip during which we skirted the ice floes. Reggie missed the hos coming out of school.

FEBRUARY 22. Louis. It is his first day of real school here. He seems bored by life. Maybe I can light a fire underneath him. He is light-skinned, of Cape Verdean descent (there are many of Cape Verdean ancestry in southeastern Massachusetts), a narrow, loping, toes-turned-out, lackadaisical kid with an easy laugh. He does push-ups with his ass high in the air, just from the shoulders, the way a lot of guys do when they first get here.

After lunch, just uphill of the house, in a thin mist which made the house seem to float somewhere above earth, the tractor died. A bunch of squawking kids descended on it, with Kenny taking charge. As we stood around, warming our hands with our breaths, Ken would yell, "Give it a try, now!" to whoever was sitting at the wheel, and then he'd dandle the fuel shut-off, not knowing what he did, convinced this would titillate the god of the tractor. She'd cough, sputter, die again, the faithful old girl. He'd do it again. No luck. And again. No luck. Fuel filter. Had to be. I stopped him before her battery got too low.

And, when it became clear that Louis and Ken and I would be fixing the tractor, they both complained, wished they were building a chair with Jeb. So I had them draw straws. Ken won, left to work on the chair; Louis had the odious duty of staying with me to clean the filter.

"What the fug do we do?"

I let the language slide—we were outside, away from the house and Gail.

"Well the first thing we do is look at the thing for a minute, let it talk to us."

"What you mean talk to us? That thing ain't gonna talk to us."

"I mean get the big picture, see if there's anything we're missing."

"What the fug could we be missin'? The fuggin' thing won't staht."

"Watch your language. What I mean is . . . we'll get the tools. But I'm trying to show you how to approach something like this. A little slowly."

He looked at the sky for ten seconds, caught his breath. The kid had potential. Someone had taught him to count to ten when an asshole pissed him off.

"What do we need?" he said.

"We need the new filter. There's one in Jack's box upstairs. We need a Phillips-head screwdriver, an adjustable wrench, a three-eighths and a one-quarter-inch crescent wrench, clean fuel, and a couple of clean rags."

"So?" Louis said.

"So what?" I said.

"Go and get it," he said.

"No, *we'll* go get it," I said, seeing that every moment of the undertaking had to be laid out. And I saw as we went that Louis had probably never had a man show him how to do anything. So, he expected to do it wrong, expected to be shamed for it, because unknown territory is not filled with angels.

One tip-off to this was the pace at which he went, which was breakneck. Care is learned, not innate, I think. And he was scared. So we went, got our materials, resumed.

"All right," I said, "let's take off the filter housing and clean it up and put in the new filter."

"How do you expect me to do that?"

"Well, we'll work together. You unscrew it here . . . Whoa— other way. Yeah."

And so it went; we cleaned the housing, put in the new filter, bled the lines, got the thing running, he undoing everything too fast, I telling him to slow down, go slow, take your time, kid—exactly what no kid wants to hear—as he did everything up too fast, crossed the threads.

We got it going, and through luxurious mud hauled wood up to the house from the pier for an hour and a half, stacking four-foot lengths of white oak, tulip poplar, black cherry, and black locust in the old cart, with Louis driving too fast, managing somehow to turn the thing around at the pier, popping the clutch, *ba-dow!* I fined him for the mistreatment of the tractor, but not for his spirit, and explained this to him carefully in the evening by the big woodstove.

And I am worried about Ken. He looked at me as if I were a dog he'd like to kick when I stopped his tractor fixing. He doesn't speak to me anymore, just mumbles his replies. Why I don't know. Isolation of that sort is a bad sign.

17

MARCH 7. Out splitting wood yesterday with Wyatt, next to the winter garden thick with rye, I tried to explain the poem "Axe Handles" by Gary Snyder.

"Let me tell you about a poem, Wyatt."

"Fuck that, man."

"No, really," I said.

"No, really," he said. With a *whack* his axe split a thick log cleanly down the middle.

"Nice one," I said, with a nod to the log halves lying in the duff.

"Thank you," came back with a shit-eating grin.

"It's about how you make an axe handle."

"Cool. Get lost."

"It starts out with Snyder showing his son how to throw a hatchet so it will stick into a stump," I said.

"How far away?" he asked.

"Twenty-five feet."

"Guy's a pussy."

"Whatever. But while they're doing it, Kai remembers an old hatchet head without a handle in the shop, and gets it and says he wants it for his own."

"Who's Kai?"

"His kid."

"Oh. So he wants an axe handle. Who gives a shit?"

"You do."

"Why?"

"You'll see."

"What am I going to see?"

"Shut up a minute and listen."

He did, much to my surprise. I continued.

"So, Snyder goes and finds an old axe handle in the shop, and they start shaping it with the hatchet they'd been throwing . . . and they work on it together for a while."

"Uh-huh," he said, and whacked another log in two.

"Are you following this so far?"

"I dunno. It's about an old hatchet." With that he set another log up, whacked it in two, reached for another one.

"Well, where do you think the poet's going to find the pattern for the new handle?" I asked.

"Up his butt. I don't know."

"Think!" Amazingly, he did.

"Uhhhhh. Oh. Duhhhhhh. He's using a hatchet. He's got the pattern right there."

"Yeah!" (This was a rare victory for me.) "So then as Snyder shapes the new handle, he remembers an old phrase he first learned from Ezra Pound:

'When making an axe handle
the pattern is not far off.'

"See, that's just what you said," I said. At this he smiled.

"And he shows his kid this," I said. "Shows him what he's doing."

"He shows Kai?"

"Yeah."

As I replied, he was already bringing the axe down and through another log, a big one this time, and he exhaled as he brought the blade down; the log seemed to jump apart.

"Who is Ezra Pound?"

"He was a poet Snyder liked from earlier in the century. He was known for being a bit of an anti-Semite, but he was a good poet."

"You mean he was one of those guys who didn't like Jews?"

"He may have been a spigot, yes."

"Bigot, you bald-headed geek."

"So, you see anything else going on in the poem?"

"Like what?"

"Any other patterns?"

"No. I give up. Just finish so we can keep going."

"All right. Then Snyder remembers another poet who said the same thing, this Chinese writer Lu Ji from the fourth century, who said in an essay—"

"They made them write essays too?"

"Yeah."

"Poor bastards."

"Yeah. See, Lu Ji said, 'In making the handle of an axe by cutting wood with an axe the model is indeed near at hand.'

"So, just like you said, the pattern is right there." (Amazingly, he keeps listening.) "So, then Snyder talks about one of his own teachers, this guy Shih-hsiang Chen, who translated that and taught it to him, and Kai sees the pattern." At this, Wyatt looked at me, for a moment, and then turned to the log he had set on the stump, addressed it, smote it cleanly on the grain, then turned to me with his face like an open window.

"So, what is he saying?" I asked.

"A lot of guys knew how to make an axe."

"Well, yeah. But he's saying that things get passed down from man to man, generation to generation. So where'd Snyder get his information?"

"The heavy guy, the Pound guy."

"And where'd I get my information?"

"The Snyder dude who wrote the poem."

"And where'd you get your information?"

"Fuckin' Pie Inna Sky," he said with a smile that showed one chipped front tooth.

"From me, you twerp. Do you see how things get passed down from generation to generation, the good and the bad?"

"Yeah already. Can we split some wood now, Mr. Teacher?"

"It's up to you to decide what you want to accept, and what you want to pass on, Wyatt . . ." But he was already turned and going for more wood to split. Later, after lunch, when no one was around, I slipped a copy of the poem under his pillow.

LATER still, as we lifted weights in the basement, in the yellow light of the kerosene lamps, Wyatt wound up saying that he understood.

"I know what you mean, man. My dad used to teach me some axe, man. You know, an axe is a guitar. He could play, the blues, you know, and shit. He could fuckin' play. He had this beautiful Strat, an' he used to leave it at Buster's, and Buster said he was going to bring it over the other day, but I haven't seen it. But I'd like to play the blues."

He trailed off here, and we kept on with the weights.

I remember vividly the day when a boyfriend of my mother, Dave, showed me the right tension to which to tighten a spark plug. He put his hand on the wrench and my hand on the wrench, and said,

"Now I *want* you to *feel* how this *feels* when you tighten it."

And he torqued it, and I felt where he stopped. I didn't ever spend a lot of time with him, but something moved over in that moment, and a whole world of possibility became mine, in that I could then conceive of doing what he had done with his hands. It could have been painting, writing, sailing.

FRIDAY, March 19. Winter has us hemmed in. Six in the morning. As I write, the fire roars in the cook stove, and the sky begins to lighten over the cove, showing a low bank of clouds over the eastern horizon; hard weather coming in tomorrow or the next day.

Four days ago, just before breakfast, Ken decided to hurt me. I saw this in his eyes as he sat on the couch. I had asked Jeb about the big woodstove, how well it burned with the door open.

"How does that thing do with the door open, Jeb, does it burn well?"

"Not too well; the problem with burning it with the door open is creosote buildup up in the stack."

Ken, sitting in front of the stove with the door open, told me how he felt about that.

"I know how a fire fuckin' works, bitch. You want me to close the door, fuckin' ask me, fuckin' bitch."

"Chill, Ken. I didn't mean anything by it."

"Naw, fuckin' bitch . . ."

"Ken, I was just asking Jeb what he thought about the stove. No reflection on you."

"Fuckin' bitch, all I hear around here is whine, whine, whine."

"Hey, Ken, keep it up and it's gonna cost you, all right?"

"Let it, motherfucker," he said, standing up and walking toward me with his arms swinging loose at his sides, his head cocked to the right, and his eyes nailed to mine.

But I had already started out the door toward the volleyball court, saying over my shoulder,

"It just cost you, Ken. We'll talk about how much after the game." I could hear him following me.

Things felt dangerous, the way they sometimes do on a city street late at night. I was angry, and I wasn't sure what to do. Ken had been pushing us a lot recently. He was a big, scared six-year-old, really, but one not afraid to play with the minds around him, and to try to intimidate us into doing things his way. And the anger I felt over that began to come out. I could feel prickly energy moving through my shoulders and neck, and my jaw stiffening up, as I moved across the deck and started down the steps to the garden. He was close behind me, jawing. I was watching for the chair he might throw down, but that wasn't what he wanted.

"Yo, let's settle it now, motherfucker, let's go," he said. "I'm not afraid, Dan. The two of us, let's dance. Fuckin' make it right—right now!"

I got to the bottom of the steps. "Let it alone, Ken," I said, and walked away from him along the edge of the red snow fence that lines the garden, my back to him; I was listening hard for footsteps. My heart beat fast, I tasted adrenaline, sound became magnified, and there was a rushing in my ears. I was ready to throw down. Dave Masch's words came back to me: "Always, always let them have the last word."

I kept walking, feeling rage percolating through my chest. I worked my fingers, relaxed everything in case I had to drop him, which I didn't really know how to do. But it was clear to me: I would hit him in the face or I would hit him in the balls, as hard as I could. I counted my steps, listened to my breathing. Forty-two steps. I reached the far side of the volleyball court, and turned around.

Ken was standing next to Reggie, a bull next to a gazelle, on the other side, in the server's box, looking at the ground. He wouldn't look at me. He had offered himself, and I had refused. I didn't know who had surrendered. We had an uneventful game in the damp air of the gray morning, and then went in for scrambled eggs and bacon, oatmeal. I asked him after breakfast what he thought I ought to fine him, and he said, walking away, "Whatevuh you think is right." Two dollars. A half day's pay. What did it cost me? A number of hours wondering if I am up to this, if I can be hard enough and easy enough to give kids like Ken what they need.

M Y week off. Yesterday I went to Martha's Vineyard on the venerable ferry *Islander* to meet with an old friend, the writer John Hough, who twenty-five years before had written a book called *A Peck of Salt* about teaching in VISTA in the inner cities of Detroit and Chicago during the late sixties. His book had inspired me, in part, to the service I now undertook. The day was calm, and the old ferry leaned gently into the turns she made around the channel markers on the forty-five-minute ride.

I called John from the terminal on the island, and his voice came back, dour, a strong yet hesitant New England baritone. Hesitant, it turned out, because something had come up that afternoon, and he would have to spend it untangling family knots. He had to break our date, and I was on my own.

So, I walked the quiet dirt roads of the middle part of the island, in fickle rain, for most of the day, down lanes with graceful pin oaks leaning over the roadbed, thinking about how the middle part of the island, the sandplain, as recently as the late nineteenth century, was a commons, land held by the whole community. I thought about the time when there were community nets into which a person could fall psychologically and be caught, about how this was reflected even in the way the towns saw land, put some of it aside for everyone to use carefully, a central store of energy. You couldn't be disenfranchised, not completely, then.

As the light failed, I headed back to Vineyard Haven, trudging the mile and a half on the main road in my seaboots and yellow foulies, hitchhiking. No one picked me up—no wonder, I looked like an unfamiliar workingman, wandering, doing some of Woody Guthrie's "Hard Traveling." I caught the evening freight, and by the time we left the dock the rain had come on strong, and I stood in the lee of the superstructure, watching the drops roil the wake in long sheets.

Almost as soon as we were away, a small, thick man in dirty yellow foul-weather gear approached—a workingman, by the looks of him—wearing seaboots and with three days' growth on his face. He spoke:

"You work on the boat?"

"No. Just ridin'."

"Oh." He looked away, out at the sea.

"You know my cousin's the captain. I used to give him lobsters. Huge. You know, fuckin' hundred-years'-old lobsters."

The diesels picked up as we passed the breakwater, the two columns of hazy exhaust darkening the air astern.

"I gave him cod. I gave him fluke. I gave him—"

[He leaned in here, pursing his lips to cradle the words.]

Scrod haddock, and beautiful gray sole. I used to give him fuckin' everything."

As he said this I smelled the sharp vinegar of whiskey as it rose on his breath.

"I ask him, 'Could I have a free ride?' 'Cause my check come in and I gotta cash it. He says, 'I can't do a thing for ya.' How quickly people forget, you know?"

"Yeah."

A pause. He swayed on the light swell, hood tight around his head, making him look like a little boy with a mustache. I was afraid he'd stop telling, so I asked,

"Where're you headed?"

"New Bedford. I'm gonna cash my check, get fucked *up* tonight."

Pause.

"How's New Bedford these days?"

"Sucks. There's no boats fishin' out these days, no trips. I ain't had a trip for . . . foah months. Foah fuckin' months. What I'm supposed to do, huh? I can't even pay rent. That's why I'm livin' ovah here with my sister. I got three kids. I don't get my visiting rights. My old lady, you know. The cunt. That's how they are."

"Yeah," I said, not knowing what to say. Then after a pause, I asked.

"Not many fish these days for the boats, huh?"

"Oh there's fish, plenty fish. If you're willin' to fish the rocks; there's just too goddam many boats."

"Too many boats, huh?"

"Yeah. Too many. They don't leave nothin' for the rest of us."

With that he vanished inside, letting the heavy iron door slam behind him, and I was left to the quiet of the rain and the thrum of the diesels. We get a lot of kids from New Bedford.

* * *

THERE has been a transition out here. Alan, Ned, Sonny, and Cyrus have all moved into the onshore program, the halfway house in Woods Hole where they get school every day, and work in the afternoons in local businesses. Sonny commutes to Falmouth by bus, and works for an electrician. Ned works as a carpenter, Alan commutes to the Vineyard by ferry, and works for a boatbuilder, and Cyrus scoops ice cream. Somehow, I don't feel they are gone yet. I will see them at the end of each two-week cycle as I return home, and they come out to the island for a weekend. But they are all out of our lives, for the moment, poised to reenter the regular world, and we prepare for the next litter to arrive.

Still with us are Wyatt, Ken, Jerome, Louis, and Reggie.

I HAVE survived another shift. I sit in the chair here in my draftily endearing little cottage, feeling wind chasing through her, wishing to hell I had a woodstove. The town is utterly quiet—the weather is gray, and the streets are dark, greasy with rain. Have I done any good? I don't know. For hours I sit here in the chair. Later I will make mushroom-barley soup. Later still I will go for a five-mile run, every inch of which I know; since I was a boy I have known these roads. I finished *War and Peace* not long ago, after reading *Anna Karenina*. It has been that kind of winter. Long books, watching snow fall, snow gather. I have no real society here in this quiet town, and I am at home here.

I am back here, in this town which I have known so long, to find out what it means to be *in situ*, on my native soil. The place works on me. I walk out by the ocean every day, take in its colors, the deep cold blues of winter, the infinitude of browns and grays in the spartina grass of Sippewissett Marsh. And there is the always changing mouth of the marsh, where the channel cuts through the barrier beach, where the marsh breathes, a six-hour breath in and then a six-hour exhalation, the water warmed in the sun and flowing out to the blue bay in a broad green fan, and I breathe in the grayness of the winter streets, of the tree limbs stark against the sky. I am becoming conscious of my childhood, of how I learned to be back then, what I react to, what it is these guys need, and what I have to offer. I try to put together lesson plans, curricula, a coherent course, but am I getting to the core, to the essence of their disturbance? Each one is different, except that they all seem able instinctively to sabotage whatever I come up with. There are four new students on the island—a new era is come, and I wonder if I will do any better with them.

Bobby is a smart guy from Arlington, an emphatically Irish kid who finds strength in the clover, in some of the traditions of the Irish (as held by him)—the short temper, the given to drunkenness, green. He and I and the other new guys hung around the fire on a Saturday night after they'd been on-island a week. I asked him what he'd be doing if he weren't here. His ideal weekend went something like this:

"See, I'd buy the beahs on Friday night, we'd get cocked; Billy O'Connor'd buy the beahs on Saturday night, and we'd get cocked, and then we'd trip on Sunday. No consciousness allowed."

Big grin at this, and then an explanation:

"See, we come up together, me and Billy, in the projects. We fuckin' understand what we like, you know?"

He's a character. Tall, skinny, wiry, blond, sharp of feature, missing his upper front teeth. And he is smart, full of big words and intelligent conversation, and always, it seems, close to explosion.

Andrew is a goof from Lawrence, a seemingly happy-go-lucky fifteen-year-old with blond crewcut hair and a sleepy smile, who speaks as if his voice is emerging from beneath a blanket. He seems muffled, somehow, and my instinct is that he has been damaged, perhaps as a small child, perhaps just as a matter of course growing up in the projects. He is a husky kid, solidly built, and commands a respect that belies his manner. There must be some hidden sign of competence in battle that I'm not picking up. He also plays basketball beautifully, fluidly, a boy born to the court.

And he likes his gear. As we stood around the fire on Thursday night he wore a $400 sheepskin coat. I asked him why he'd brought it to a farm on an island.

"I didn't know it was going to be like this. I thought there'd be streets and stuff. So I brought it, figured I might as well wear it. I don't get many chances."

"Where'd you get the dough for it?"

"A sort of job. I could make three hundred a night, easy. I bought this coat in a night."

Three hundred. That's what I make a week, after taxes.

Drew, the third new guy, is from a rural town in the southwest of the state, which gives him an appreciation for the island some of the others lack. This is a strength in some ways, although I don't think he sees it. He is small, wiry, with a big mouth, another self-consciously Irish kid who is a terror back home but who can't hold a candle to the crimez of da city boyz, at least in his own mind. He talks about smoking pot, fighting, and riding three-wheelers, so far.

Josh, the fourth new fellow, is African-American, a quiet, good-looking, big kid from Dorchester. He didn't join us at the fire. I don't really know much about him.

The weather is moderating. Plovers have returned, scavenging outside the barn where feed is scattered for the chickens, along with red-winged blackbirds; simply seeing them return to forage in the winter rye in the garden is a deep, good feeling.

APRIL. Spring! We have lost Andrew the goof. It happened during my off week, the last week of March. One of the weekend staff lost her temper with him, scolded him, and he became upset. So he went for a walk to the pier, got a dory ready to row away. They caught him just as he put an anchor in the boat and started to push it out. When a kid tries to go, he is a threat to his own safety and that of any staff trying to save him. So the boat was called to take him off; he begged to stay, but the trust had been broken, so he was shipped. Once ashore, he was allowed to watch TV alone for a little while, and slipped out of the onshore house. Ten minutes later he was driving away in an oldsmobile Cutlass, stolen from a local. Hours later the car was in a junkyard outside Lawrence and Andrew was home, free until the next time. So it goes. I really liked the guy. We paid our neighbor for the car, which reduced the school's endowment to four manual typewriters and a couple of movie passes.

GETTING to know Bobby has been a delight, as the kid is alternately full of bull, and then a bright, intelligent presence, a boy fully able to be a boy. On Saturday we went for a walk in the rain, dressed in foul-weather gear, slogging around the island. We wound up on the north side below the ruins of the leper cottages, and although the wind had dropped from the gale of the day before, the waves still came on in a five-foot set, dark green and roaring in on the rocks, sending spray far back into the cellar holes of the cottages. The occasional giant rumbled in, too, holding its shape and energy far longer than the others, a long green ridge until it broke, losing its shape around Bobby, who stood waist deep in these seventh waves, screaming as if he'd lost himself.

I was worried he'd lose his foothold, slip down, whack his head, be pulled out to sea, but I couldn't get him to come in. He'd never seen anything like it; my calls to him to be careful were lost in the waves. I felt I'd be able to drag him out if he fell, so I left him, thinking perhaps he'd never been addressed by anything that took him for exactly who he was, didn't judge him, didn't do anything but be with him.

The waves didn't let up, and he came in, after forty-five minutes of breakers crashing around his waist, completely soaked, awash. Halfway home, as we walked the path along the top of the hay field, I showed him how to empty his boots, which made the going easier.

So it was too bad when last night, after being on edge all day, he called Jack a fat fuck, which prompted Jack to fine him, which prompted Bobby to say that if Jack wrote the fine into his blue (grade) book, he'd piss on it, which led Jack to say that if he pissed on it, he'd be thrown out of school. All of which came to pass.

And when I ambled to the pole this morning in the blear, I looked down at the sodden blue binder that lay in the damp sand, and was moved by what a transgression this had been. Bobby might not have understood its symbolism, but the words in that book—"up on time," "cooperation," "maturity," "honesty," "effort," "initiative," "care," "skill"—those words matter to us, and he'd pissed on them.

Could I have saved him? The boys come to us, savable, salvageable, and they do their dance and we do ours, and some of them seem to clutch the rope, and others to let go of it, to fall perceptibly into the abyss. And I watch them, helpless sometimes, often not knowing what to do. It is much like watching cars crash from a safe remove. It is harrowing, and I can't help but take it personally at times. I am to blame. I am not to blame. I am.

18

AN oppressiveness hangs over the place. Rain falls steadily, and beneath that sound, just beneath it, is a murmur of malevolence which we all feel. It's as if someone were whispering verses of hate in our ears. Josh will not speak, and this makes him seem larger than he is, which is large, and makes his darkness sinister. Something is throwing the guys off, something, and the staff all have a strange feeling about Josh, as if he is the one coordinating the group's disdain. I picture him huddling with the others, behind the barn, pointing his finger at one chest and then another, instructing each with what to do to break the harmony. But that is paranoia. There is nothing specific to point to, just general discontent, frayed tempers, tension.

KEN'S lip curled easily today, as I asked these guys to do their math—fractions for both him and Reggie—and history and writing and reading and journals. They struggled through, dotting i's, crossing t's. And then it ended.

"Why I gotta know about the French Revolution?" Ken shouted. "I don't care 'bout no French, frence, France. I ain't goin' over there. They could come over here and see me. I don't give a fuckin' shit 'bout no goddam French nothin'.'"

"Well, it's because that was a new idea when it happened. That was one of the first times a people rose up and threw off a government they didn't like, and it is important to know about that idea, and the troubles they ran into, so we can learn from history, so we can have the courage to—"

"But I don't give two shits about what the fuckin' French was doin'! That's old. That ain't me. I wanna know how to make some bills, go out and have a good time, know what I mean?"

"Yeah, I know Ken. Well, lemme just say that knowing this stuff is power, is having the power of knowledge—"

"This is bullshit. I got the powah, I got a nine [millimeter pistol] at home. That's fuckin' powah."

His mouth was round and wide as he shouted, and his head dipped from side to side with the rhythm of his speech. And he went on,

"Don't tell me. Powah ain't nothin' but. . . . I open doors with my nine, man. You ain't heard a word I was sayin'. I ain't doin' this shit, fuck this." Ken's back moving away up the path toward the house.

"That'll cost you, Ken."

"Fuck it," hurled back over his shoulder.

Always let them have . . . But he and I are in a bad way.

KEN'S voice: "Yo, I ain't even goin' to lie to you. I hate this place. Place is wacked, yo. Like, they always sayin' to you, nah nah, do it this way, see it this way. I ain't goin' to 'do it this way' if I don' want to, simple as that. If I feel like doin' one way, that's how I'm gonna do. They always tryin' to make you into somethin' you ain't, see. Like, I ain't goin' to college, and I sure ain't goin' to no medical school, nothin' like that, know what I'm sayin'? Let me be who I am. That ain't me. I am who I am, I come up one way, that's how it is.

"The way I see it, you're either a hood or a geek, you know? There's either way, two sides, and I wasn't made to be on the other side. I'd rather die, see.

"I mean, this place is better than lockup, sure; you get to go around, mess with the animals, get to build shit, get to be off on your own when you want to, like when there ain't work to do, go walkin' around the island, and I'm healthy, healthier than I was. Yo, and I ain't been restrained since I was, since nine months ago I ain't had nobody on my back, yo. That's gotta be a record. 'Cause I been workin' hard at that, I don't want to be behind bars rest of my life. No way.

"But see, when I was comin' up, yo, you don't understand, we had our ways, like, back in my neighborhood, we'd play games, like who could take the hardest hit, like we'd go around and take turns punchin' each other in the gut, and the first dude puked, he lost. But you couldn't hit the guy if he didn't know you was going to hit him, that is if you played by the rules. See, there's rules to everything. But, see, it was a losin' game, you could only really lose. But that was what we played, and windows. We'd pick a house, and we'd pick the smallest window, and the first dude put a rock in that, he won. Lot of rocks aroun', see, got to do somethin' with 'em.

"But, I really wasn't home much. There was eight of us, but we wasn't always sure who was in the family and who was a cousin or whatever, and there was just my mom, so it was a lot of confusion, like, and you had to fight for it, whatever it was, you had to be in there with your head, bangin' for it, which was good for me 'cause I know what it's like out here now. Either you take it, or you don't get it, right? Unless you're a staff. Then you give it away like it's a gift, like that's real. C'mon. That's a fairy tale, yo, that's a fuckin' lie is what it is."

BIRDS are coming home. Yesterday I saw my first osprey, which looked like a seagull until I looked. It was more stolid in flight—less buoyant on the wing—and had patches of white on the underside of its wing up under the shoulder. It should build a nest soon, if it has a mate. But what a bird. Any being who can make a living pursuing swift fierce bluefish in the cool waters of the bay, stalking, hovering, then stooping down to strike with talons in a great splash, then fly home with a four-pound flapping fish held beneath its chest—and from this grow feathers, live only in the tallest trees, and winter in Costa Rica—this is a rare being, a being of discernment.

I also saw snowy egrets, the long-legged virginal wading birds which, in the low umber light are a shock of white across the cove where they stalk crabs. "Why they call them snowy?" was the question from Drew, and I see in it, for all of its innocence, something sinister. These guys don't use adjectives like that, much less metaphors.

"Because they're white like snow, numb nuts," Wyatt chimed as we stood on the deck, and Drew saw. But where have we lost that quick leap from one quality to the next, where a word can become a vibration, a thing can become a color? The language as we know it is dying a little.

Drew and I also saw spotted sandpipers, winging low over the greening hillside, as we sat watching the sunset last night before dinner. It was a vermilion affair, with purple clouds streaking the horizon as Drew jawed about smokin' pot and bong hits and how he and his friend found a bag back in the woods and how stoned they had been, ad nauseam. I listened because this wasn't a war story, wasn't about his looking for me to approve the smoking. It was about his looking for someone to pay attention, to just listen. I disapproved mildly, when I could get a word in.

And then five curlews flew by and stole our attention. Suddenly, there was quiet. I heard the waves. Drew stopped yapping for the first time since we'd been sitting there. I kept my eyes on the horizon, waiting for more birds to silhouette themselves against it, trying to keep his eyes there. Still he didn't speak. The red of the horizon deepened, darkened. Finally, he sucked in a breath.

"Did you see those motherfuckers? Motherfuckers had bent beaks, man—they were bent. Totally bent. Like, bent down."

And they had been. Curlews in flight look strange, almost warped, as their eight-inch, narrow, downward-curving beaks cut through the wind in front of them.

They had flown silently, a flight of three, and then two more, losing altitude and turning east to follow the shore, silhouetted gliding above a gun-metal sea against the muted reds of the low night sky. Drew's eyes had followed them. And I think the boy was in those birds for a moment. He glided down to water's edge, landed with them there.

"Those weren't motherfuckers, Drew, they were curlews. They're wading birds."

"Waiting birds?" he asked.

"No no, Wading, like they wade around in the water, looking for food. Those beaks are for probing down into sand for worms and crustacea . . ."

"What's 'crustacea?'"

"It's little crabs and shellfish. And the curlews, they're just stopping in on their way from Guatemala to the Bay of Fundy, up in Maine, just to pick up a little gas on the way."

"Where'd they come from? Guat a what?"

"Central America, south of Mexico, a country called Guatemala."

"Guate-efin-mala, man," said Drew. "They get around, huh?"

"Yeah."

BIRDS, boys. John Hay, a local naturalist, writes from his home on Cape Cod of birds in his essay "Homing":

"To locate ourselves, we need to be located. If the warblers failed to arrive in May, how would we recognize our station between the continents?"

He goes on to speak of terns:

"Young sooty terns fledged in the Dry Tortugas off the southern tip of Florida migrated in their first autumn all the way across the South Atlantic to the Gulf of Guinea in Africa, which they had never seen before. Nor did they have the benefit of adult leadership, since the adults left their breeding grounds after nesting but appeared to go no farther than the Gulf of Mexico. The young did not fly directly. The route they took was apparently 20 percent longer than that which could be traced on a direct line across the Atlantic, and it was the most favorable one, facing them with less resistance from prevailing winds."

There is so much in the birds on the island. Why are these human children so damned different, not seeming to be able to develop independent of parents and elders? Sooty terns can, migrating to Africa by the best route on the information that is within their genes, and do fine, absolutely at home in their tern-ness.

The more I look at the boys here, the more I see that we, too, pass down this kind of homing information, but that the human being has evolved so that communication of large amounts of "genetic" information—information critical to the survival of the species—has been streamlined biologically. Rather than carrying it all on the strand of DNA at birth, a child or young person "learns" this information as he develops, learns it in the form of rituals and stories that encode the sense of place and the ability to "home," stores this floppy DNA in the memory in bytes of language, maybe as a blues, or stories told by elders that give a sense of origin.

And when the continuity of this line of inheritance is broken, things fall apart. Of course, stories continue to be told, but they are told by the boys to themselves, and so take on the demons that grow in the absence of the other, older stories; the young people's replacement stories are about violence, about the negative warrior energy that they feel must be theirs if they are to survive. Which is gangsta rap.

I'm trying to teach these boys how to home, and I don't know if anyone ever taught me.

* * *

AND the irony now, in this moment, as I write, is this: I see the boys clearly, see Wyatt, Ken, how the lack of something has wounded a part of them, perhaps mortally, and I see the god-damned birds riffing through the air beyond the deck, swallows, or terns, perfectly at home. I see where I fit as their teacher (the boys'), how I might see all of this chaotic schooling as the perfect lesson for me in dysfunction, and yet there is *still* a place in me, which I've known of since I was twenty, where there is a feeling of implosion, as if a small void at the center of my chest, a dark star there, might take my heart, absorb it, end it there. I am in trouble these days, when silence really reigns, and at times, recently, it feels that the only way to resist that strong force inward is to explode outward, get angry, rip a kid apart. I am scared of what I might do. *I* am not yet healed. I am watching myself.

19

WYATT'S sentence on the island came to an end last week, during my off week, and it fell to me to take him to court as the official Penikese rep, which I did, all the while wondering if I could tell him what he needed to hear.

I picked him up at home. His mother was at work. She was to meet us at court.

He was out the door of the small gray house as soon as I pulled up, bounding, jittery, dressed well enough in a clean pair of jeans and a canvas button-down shirt under a dark sweater, a neat red wool beret covering his now short dreads. I opened the door as he jogged to the car. His jaw looked sharper, I noted, and it occurred to me that he might be mistaken, at a distance, for a military man.

"What up, homes?" he said as he got in.

"Not much, man. This is it, then, the big finish, huh?"

"Yeah, man." He drummed on the dash with his hands. "I'm busted out. My boys finally busted my ass out."

"Shall we?" I said, trying to be grand.

"Let's go, dude. I can't wait." More frantic drumming on the dash. "I have a dream. Free at last, free at last, *thank God* almighty I'm free at last," he said, his dreads flying, palms pounding on the dash.

"Wyatt, watch the car there, man," I said, fearing for the old plastic.

"My man Martin. I get emotional when I'm talkin' about my man Martin."

"Yeah, well, imprison yourself in that seat belt."

"Oh, man."

So we headed out, down his small road to the larger road lined with scrubby pin oaks and pitch pines and Capes and half-Capes and Garrisons, at last to an old secondary highway.

I had thought a lot about what conversation we might have, on this ride. I was nervous. I doubted I could be strong enough to be a mentor to Wyatt over a long term, but I thought I might be able to pose some hard questions to him, serve him a little over the course of the day. I wanted to ask him about that conversation we'd had in the wood shop.

So, once we were five miles downstream, and he had stopped threatening to spontaneously combust, I posed the question.

"Wyatt, you remember that time when we were building things, just you and me, in the wood shop?"

"Nope."

"When you were building a cassette box, and I was building a tool box?"

"Nope."

"And you said you were lost."

"And I called you a punk motherfuckin' bald-headed geek?"

"Yeah."

"No, I don't remember none of that."

"Why did you say you were lost?"

"I didn't."

"C'mon, man, we both know you did."

"If I say I didn't, I *didn't*, man."

"What did you mean by that?"

A pause here. He looked out the side window, watched a marsh slipping by, still brown with winter colors, and the light from the window played over his fine features.

"I guess I meant that . . . I didn't know how to make a decision anymore, kinda like I didn't know who I was anymore."

"Do you know now?"

"What the fuck do you think?"

"I think maybe you know better, that you know a few things that you want."

"I do. I want to be home, be with my girl, have a normal kid's life, you know."

"But you said you didn't know who you were anymore. What did you mean by that?"

"It was like I didn't know where I fit in, you know? I useta be a bad-ass fuckup, and now I don't really want to be one as much."

"So you're out of luck for now—no new skin to wear."

Pause. Clam bars and drugstores sped by outside. Then he sucked in his breath, looked at me with his innocent blue eyes.

"How do you know who you want to be, man? I mean how do you do it?" he said, turning to me, his long fingers stretching to grab "it" somewhere in front of us on the highway.

This was a hard answer for me; I don't always know who I am, in the moment, struggle with this myself.

"Uh, I look for models. You know, role models like your man Martin there."

"I got news for you, Dan. You have a kind of skin differential there with Martin man. You aren't ever gonna look like him."

"Neither are you. You know that doesn't matter. And you know what I'm saying, right?"

"Yeah."

"So I try to make decisions sometimes the way I think people I respect might make them."

"Yeah."

"So you know what I mean."

"Yeah, but that's too far out there for me, man. That's like a out-of-body experience, man, like I saw on TV. That's not real."

"What would make it real?"

"Like living it, like the way we do on Penikese, like watchin' you and Jeb and Gail and Jack not be assholes, that's as close as I've gotten."

"But we're all thirty-plus and you're seventeen."

"All old shits, and I've still got juice."

I took a moment to gather my thoughts here, as motels closed for the winter moved past.

"Wyatt, you're trying to change all the assumptions you've made about life, seventeen years of assumptions. You think that happens overnight?"

"No. I guess." He thought about it for a minute, and then we were entering a rotary, beginning that strange New England circle-dance of cars.

"So how do you feel about leaving us?"

"Scared."

"You think you can remember what you learned on the island?"

At this he took off his hat, put it back on, looked out the window, pulled the car's cigarette lighter out and put it back in three times, then said,

"It's like there's two of me, the old bat out of hell, and the new one, who's calmer, sorta . . . and I never know who's gonna be in the driver's seat. But I gotta get calm guy more wheel time."

"But you feel scared about leaving the island?"

"Yeah."

"You know, you've grown up a lot."

"Yeah."

"You've got to find friends who aren't into baiting the cops."

"Yeah. I've gotta find me some geek friends. You know, thinking about it," (here, a whole part of Wyatt, which I had glimpsed before, began to talk) "I've learned so much on the island, and I love the place, you know, I really do. It's just that, get me off the place, and it seems sorta like none of it ever happened, and I'm right back where I was when I left home."

"What did you learn out there?"

"That I could work, that I could get along with others, that I wasn't stupid, that I could have a string of good days, shit like that."

"You're gonna be all right, Wyatt."

"You think so?" he said, looking back at me with the young eyes again.

"Yes. I know so," I said, lying.

He played with his hat in his lap for a minute or two, looking down at it fondly, lost in thought and turning it around, like a girl with a doll.

And then he asked could he turn on the radio, and I said yes, so he found a classic rock station and we were surrounded by the sounds of the Stones ("Waitin' on a Factory Girl") and Jimi Hendrix ("Spanish Castle Magic"), with Wyatt singing along or bumping the door with his fist in time, and commenting,

"Hendrix could play, yo, straight up play, yo," and, "Dude in the van there must be stoned, yo, look at him drifting around out there, the crackhead." Then, between songs, he said,

"You really think so?" Looking at me again with the young eyes.

"Yeah, I do, Wyatt. You're gonna be all right."

And then we were turning off the highway, and soon into the courthouse drive, where soon enough again the judge remanded Wyatt into the arms of his mother.

I drove home in the old Volvo, comfortable again alone, with the afternoon deepening and the window down, and the sun coming through the leafless trees along the roadside. And I felt again the emptiness, the lack of faith in myself, and tried to run back over the tape of our conversation in my head, hear there whether I'd done him any good. I think I had.

N O W , unexpectedly, Ken has been shifted onshore, having wangled the move a month ahead of his six-month schedule. He stocks shelves for a local market, and I breathe easier. I said good-bye to him on the dock, on a calm, pale-sky morning. He shook my hand lightly, with none of his strength, and wouldn't meet my eye. I couldn't get through to him. I see that I can't win them all. What effect did I have on him? Perhaps it was a help that I didn't fight him that day, perhaps some kind word I dropped his way got to him—I don't know. I think I'll never know.

20

O N E of the hard parts about working out here is that students disappear after six months, or a little longer. We have them in our lives, and then they go back to what they know. This is good and bad. Part of me feels that they should be with us longer, that the longer the magic of the island has to work on them, the better. This is so, and it is also so that they are young, and that six months is a long time to spend shut away on an island when one is sixteen; a kid needs to take what he has learned and try it out. Also, six months on Penikese is worth a year in another program. It is intense out here, there is no escape from the closeness of the "family," and the brevity of the program belies its deeper effects. Often, too, six months is the extent of their sentence. They are with us, partly our children and partly our nephews and younger brothers, and then they are gone.

Louis didn't return from his last weekend off; his whereabouts are unknown. This is hard to take. I get attached to these guys and the thought of doing them some good. What I remember now is how he spotted his grandfather the other day at the bus station in Woods Hole, standing next to his cab, with his arms crossed, talking to a friend. He was a reed-like man,

nattily dressed in brown slacks and a tan cardigan, with a line
of a mustache, and a brown fedora worn back on his head. He
looked like a jazz musician of the forties to me, relaxing at
midday, unaware of the coming of bebop. Louis knew it was
he, from pictures and from the name on the cab, but he
wouldn't go and say hello—he just stared across the lot at him
with wide eyes, the eyes of a child watching a movie he knows
will end sadly. The man was right there, moving his head
around, talking to his friend, with a blocky white ferry in the
background, and the harbor beyond.

M Y mother's father was a surgeon, a tall, spare man with a
strong jaw and a Harvard education. In pictures he gazes
fiercely at the camera: He is lean, hard, exacting, in a gray suit,
wearing wire-rim glasses, shoulders straight as if of steel. He
came out of South Dakota, was born and grew up there in the
sawdust and bustle of a butcher shop in Brookings, and then
he came east and left all that. He didn't speak of it. He went to
Harvard, became a doctor, served in the First World War, married my grandmother, was a man's man—shot skeet, fly-fished,
had a big house, played golf, healed people.

I am told he was much loved in the community, was
thought a warm and generous fellow. At home he bellowed,
shouted down, raged. All the time. Against what I don't know.

I do know a few things. His daughters were forbidden to
keep company with Catholics, which meant, I surmise, anyone not Protestant. Which I take to mean anyone who
couldn't get into the club. I mention this not as a dig at the
man, but as a commentary on his energies—exclusivity
grounded in anger. What effect this would have on a family—
this reaction with rage to any action seen as threatening his
status in the eyes of the church, the club, or the community—
I can only imagine. I see things in the home existing under a
veil of forced humor, projected gaiety, no one sure when the
next gale of bile would issue from the old man. From my un-

derstanding of his moods, I expect the old man was, among other things, an alcoholic.

Two of his daughters died young, their ends hastened by alcohol and drug abuse. His son died relatively young, of cancer. I never heard him speak of his feelings. My grandmother was a placid woman, when I knew her. In those years she didn't express much, at least not to me. I remember her smoking Parliament cigarettes in a big green chair while she watched *What's My Line,* and how she explained things to me at dinner, how it was to see her wrinkled face shape these words: "No, use the one with the smaller tines, dear. That's right." I recall how her pumps made her feet puff out along the top where the shoe ended, and I loved her sense of the whimsical, how she would clown failing to blow out a candle, her breath blown out the side of her mouth, and how she would dress a summer hat with a head of lettuce and wear it to a cocktail party. She died when I was ten. I've missed her for a long time now.

My father's father prosecuted famous men, like J. Robert Oppenheimer, and won the hearts of his law clerks when he became a judge. At his memorial service they came forth and spoke so highly of him. He, too, was an absent father, having left the home in Georgetown when my father was an infant. I recall his stentorian voice, made raspy by whiskey, cigars, and emphysema, and his pronouncements about Bull Run and Antietam, the rightness of the domino theory, Nixon's genius, and the wrongheadedness of JFK. I remember too how his nose was beak-like and red, how I wondered if mine would look like that someday, and the liquor in his house, the impression that he was often in a poor mood. I wish now that I'd had the chance to know these men, to understand the energy and intellect behind the medicine of one, the law of the other, and the bitterness that seemed to color both. Why the hell do we remember what we do, and how does it affect us?

My father's mother was a pillar of her community, a Ph.D. who taught high school English in my hometown for many years, and headed the League of Women Voters. She was a grand woman, much loved, who died prematurely when a vessel burst in the lining of her throat. I recall her love of language and her ferocious love of ideas, evident to me even as a boy when we would go to her house at cocktail hour, and she would have a bourbon, and I a ginger ale, and my mother a Scotch, and Grandmother would hold forth about *The Canterbury Tales* or Sir Toby in *Twelfth Night*, as she stood in the kitchen in a mote of sun, slightly stooped with age, peering through gray cat-eye frame glasses, smoking Lucky Strikes. I remember her the way you remember a film that moved you long ago: very special; flickery; disembodied. There are so many things to remember people for, and much of the time I choose to remember her for her years of teaching in the local high school, for the many times people have stopped me in the post office—older men and women in the town—and said, "You know, your grandmother was the best teacher I ever had," and for the real legacy of intellectual pursuit that has come down from her to (debatable fruition in) me. I miss her so much, what I might have learned at her knee if I'd had more time with her. They tell me that when she died, in the winter of my ninth year, there were twelve cases of bourbon in her basement. She was a single woman, living alone with a cat. I don't think the cat drank. One has to admire enthusiasm. And while there are many things to remember these people for, I choose here to look partially at the alcohol, a stream of which runs through the family.

It is a substance which in my experience isolates, often accompanies the condition of being emotionally unavailable, places a scrim between one and the world, even when checkbooks are balanced and the garbage taken out. So what? There is no crime in this; this is not accusation. This is some of my legacy. I say each of these ancestors of mine lacked an emotional conduit that would have allowed them to communicate well, would have allowed them to be emotionally present, open with the next generation; they didn't take one aside, and say, "This is who I am, what I dream of, what I lack, what I regret, what I am full of; I am strong, and I love you. Pass that on." They *seem* to have said, in a personal way . . . not much. And here I am, at the end of the limb. Resentment would be easy, a life structured around it easy, even in a subtle way. I don't write this for sympathy; that is a useless thing in the here and now, as suns set. I write it to establish a pathology. Each of these guys out here copes with the same, copes with the possibility of living, somehow, in reaction to the past. And man is it a trap.

I N the face of my obsession with ideas, the boys constantly bring me back to earth: After math and history (we're working on World War II) and English were done today, I had a long discussion in school with Josh and Jerome about swallows.

"Where the swallows comin' from?" said Josh.

"They're coming up from down south," I said.

"What, like Mississippi? Like down where my people come up from?" he asked.

"Yeah, and from Florida, and maybe even further south, like Costa Rica," I said.

"Where that at?" asked Jerome.

"That's south of Mexico, in Central America," I replied, and showed him on the map.

"You be buggin', man, that little bird ain't flied all the way from Costa Rica," said Jerome. "He ain't got enough fuel to do that."

"Well, you're right. They stop and eat along the way, and they eat while they fly."

"What you mean they eat while they fly? What they eat?" he asked.

"They eat insects right out of the air," I said. "Flies and mosquitoes and gnats and things."

"That's why they be swoopin' around like that. They munchin' out, man," said Josh, pleased. "You seen them swoopin', Jerome? They like a Harrier jet, man, with variable pitch wings, man, they like a Phantom, swoopin' around."

"Why they comin' up from Cosa Rica?" asked Jerome.

"They go down there for the winter, while it's cold up here and warm down there, and then they come back up here when it warms up."

"They be down there on vacation, huh?" said Jerome.

"They feed themselves down there, too," I said.

"How they know the way back?" asked Josh.

"We don't know that, but it has something to do with them being able to sense the earth's magnetic field. You remember us talking about that in school?"

"Yup. Man, those be some smart little birds, comin' along all that way," said Josh, his admiration for them obvious in his eyes.

"And they mate on the wing, too," I said.

"What you mean, in the air?" said Josh.

"Yeah. In the air."

"You mean when they be flyin' right with each other, one up and one down?" asked Jerome.

"Yeah."

"Nah. They ain't got enough time up there," he said.

"They don't need much," I said.

"Shoot, I be needin' more time than that, man," said Josh. "That ain't nothin' but a few seconds. That just a taste. I be needin' more time than that. I thought maybe I'd come back as a swallow, but that ain't right."

"Well, maybe they spend more time on it in the nest," I said.

"Yeah." He brightened at this thought. "That could be. I hope so, 'cause next time around I'm comin' back as a swallow, man, 'cause they be doin' mad tricks up there in the air."

Josh is fascinated by the rabbits and the pigs, too. He seems to have a rapport with them that is beyond any of ours. And I don't think he is the manipulator we thought he might be.

The other day he lay in the grass as the piglets, having escaped through a hole in the fence, mobbed him, eight little four-wheel-drive vehicles with curly tails, all trying to stand on top of his chest. He loved it, and they him. Another time, I found him sitting on the floor in the high-ceilinged wood shop, looking up at the barn swallows swooping around. They seemed to regard him as one of them, flying close enough around his head for him to have touched them, had he wanted. The falcons and the falconer.

What a healing this must be for him, and I have a hard time seeing where I fit in this, which, I see more and more, is fine. If I can hold the space for him, and let the island do its work, all will be well. But the ego suffers in this scenario. I am not the savior.

My thoughts, as I watch the young animals grow, turn always to the boys, how dependent they seem, in comparison, on the foregoing generations.

A FRIEND called me the other day, a producer for National Public Radio. He wanted to do a piece on the dreams of the homeless, and asked me if I would do the interviews on the streets of Boston. I said yes. On three successive weekends I went out, looking for street people, with a tape deck slung over one shoulder. The weather was hard, with fitful rain, and a raw wind coming off the Charles.

They were everywhere. The population that I usually see as little as I can seemed to inhabit every corner, and I saw the sinews of their community for the first time, as people I interviewed said hello to others tramping by, or took some unknown sign from a sister across the street that it was time to move on, that danger approached.

I talked to many—women, men, old, young, black, white— and then I went into shelters, and then transitional homes, and talked to some who were getting off the streets, who were looking back at years spent under overpasses, rooting through trash cans. One man, Jan, became representative for me of what I saw out there, seeming to hold clearly the landscape of a typical street person. He was a huge man, dark brown, the manager of a floor in a secondhand clothing store run by the

shelter. He was soft-spoken, almost bashful, and sat on the edge
of a stool that creaked with his weight, with his fingers linked
in his lap. He said he was forty. He could very easily have broken me in half. This is how it went:

"Can you point to one thing that landed you on the street?"

Jan: "Yeah, I think it was a few things. Drugs and alcohol being a couple of them, along with a bad marriage that I went
through. It was very hard on me, you know. I thought marriage
was supposed to be forever—that's how I was raised—and it
didn't end up that way, you know. I went through a lot of emotional problems, too, that brought me to drinking more liquor
and brought me to doing various drugs, and that helped me to
end up homeless."

I liked Jan. I admired his courage. He was personable, and
he was uncomfortable, spoke with evident effort, as if the
words were heavy stones he had to roll out of his mouth; and
yet he spoke.

"Did you ever think you would end up homeless?"

"Actually, no. 'Cause I came from a pretty good family, you
know, as far as morals go. My mother was very religious, and it
wasn't that rough coming up, even though I came from a project, because my mother still taught me the values of life that
you had to live by. It was a little bit hard bein' brought up by a
single parent, 'cause my father had died when I was nine years
old, and we had to struggle through that, but that's the only
real struggle I remember when I was a kid, besides that when I
was in school it was hard for me to learn. I think I was having
mental blackouts in elementary school because of my father's
death, and I also had a sister who died when I was young, she
was six years old, burned severely in a fire, and she only lived
for two weeks after the fire, and that really hit me real hard.
She was real close with me, you know, and I can remember
having good times with her, and then they disappeared; and
then I would just sit in school and wonder why these things
happened, because it was within three months two people who
were very important to me had died in my life. I thought

maybe it was me, if I got close to people maybe that was what would happen to them.

"You know, these are things I'm finding out about today. I really never knew that stuff was always on my mind, always right under the surface. But uh, other than that I really didn't have a rough life. I grew up with a good bunch of people. My neighborhood wasn't that bad, like it is today."

He paused here, and thought, and the old black rotary phone on the desk rang—a real bell inside it, ringing—and the sound of racks of clothes being rolled along the worn wooden floor came from the big room outside the office where we sat.

In Jan I saw clearly elements common to all who talked with me in the homeless community. He had suffered wounds of loss, both of family and relationship, and had sought to ease the pain with substances. Times were hard, jobs hard to find, but he was on the street for other reasons, too; there were wounds he couldn't heal but by going down into the low country, hitting bottom.

I watch these boys. I watch myself.

J O S H ' S sister died not long ago. His father died a year ago. He told me through a sly smile yesterday that he hated me as he and Jerome and I shoveled compost, heavy eel grass, and chicken and pig manure from one wooden bin to the other. The whole while we discussed why we were doing it.

"Why we got to turn this dirty dirt into that bin? We ain't going to use it," said Jerome.

"Yes we are, we're going to use it on the garden this summer, and we've got to turn it so it'll decompose better."

"What you mean 'decompose better'? asked Jerome. "It smell like it's decomposin' just fine right the way it is."

"That's 'cause it isn't getting enough oxygen—that's why it smells so bad, so that's why we've got to turn it, to give it some air," I said.

"We ain't got to do this. You just makin' us so that we'll have to do the worst job," said Jerome.

"This isn't the worst job. The worst job is digging out under the outhouse after a year of you guys. But this job, this is one of my favorites, because it's putting money in the bank. You look at the squash we grow this summer. It'll grow 'cause of this compost."

"So? I hate squash," said Jerome. "Squash sucks. Oooh, look at Bunsen. He after some ass now," he said, pointing at the big boar in the pig yard twenty yards away. "Look out, Melissa, he gonna stick it in you."

So we paused a while and watched the pigs play out the ritual behind the gray fences, as Bunsen sniffed and mounted Melissa, then Sparky, and failed in each attempt as they stood it for a moment and then slid him off their backs, prancing away and kicking up their dainty trotters. The ancient tragicomedy unfolded, and Jerome narrated the event, telling us of the details of pig anatomy he'd learned from the book *How They Do It*, which sits, dog-eared, on the bookshelf in the kitchen.

"He got a corkscrew dick, man. I read about it in that book. Look at it. It's like a corkscrew. That's nasty, man. He eyein' Melissa now. Look, he sizin' her up. But she ain't havin' it. She gonna fake right and go left. Watch this. Yup, there she go. She's too slick for him, she don't be wanting him up in there. That's all he be thinking about, too. That's all he care about, nasty old pig. Look at that beady eye, man. He just thinkin' about bump and grine."

"What were you and the guys talking about last night?" I asked Jerome.

"When?"

"Up in the loft."

He thought for a moment. "Girls."

"Oh," I said.

We went back to work.

"I know what you be thinking," he said, "but we ain't like Bunsen, man, we got some respect for the hos. He ain't got none."

And then we were back to pitchforking for a good hour and

a half, and the pile of manure and eel grass moved slowly from one bin to the next. With twenty minutes left before quitting, we worked on the garden wall, and got something done before five, as Nashawena began to glow red across the dark bay, and the swallows began their evening flight. It had been a good day, and even though Jerome and Josh wouldn't let on, I could see my words of praise for their work sinking in.

"You guys worked hard today at that pitchforking. I don't know if I've seen anybody work that hard out here, at least not that I remember."

Their shoulders got a little squarer as we walked to the house.

And I liked that Josh hated me. At least I mattered to him. That is a progress of some kind.

YESTERDAY evening, fierce little Drew and I watched the sun go down from the far side of the hill. We sat in the grass there, just beyond the old brick cisterns standing open to the sky, while the gulls cried and wheeled around, jockeying for nesting sites. After a while, Drew said,

"I'm thinking about putting holes in my condom so my girl gets pregnant."

"What the hell for?" I blurted.

"I don't know."

I was angry.

"That's about as thoughtless an act as I can think of. You would do that without telling her, without any intention of being a good parent?" I asked.

"Yeah."

"Why?"

"Because. Because . . . I could make it happen."

"Drew, if I ever hear you did that, I'll know that we completely failed with you, that there's nothing between your mind and Bunsen's."

"Hey I ain't a damn pig, man."

"You're talking like one. You have to go through the world considering your actions, the effects they'll have on others."

"Why?"

"Because if you don't you'll never get out from under what brought you here, man."

"The cops brought me here."

"You broke the windows, you torched the car, you did all of that."

"Because I was angry."

"Why were you angry?"

He was silent here for a moment, and I heard the waves coming onto the rocks down to our left; they had curved around the reef Sow and Pigs to the southwest, and then curved further around Cuttyhunk, and now had run the mile down onto Penikese.

"I don't know."

"So because of being angry, why you don't know, you would start a whole new life and not care about it at all? Think how angry *that* kid would be when he was your age."

"All right, man, I won't do it."

"Thank God."

"Prob'ly."

MIDNIGHT. The seas are rougher tonight—I can hear them spending themselves on South Point, and a damp, raw wind blows south up the bay, moans in the eaves of the house. It is a rare wind that moans so, and it causes the lamp to gutter by my elbow, as if there were a presence in the room. Heavy clouds pass in front of the moon, which hangs outside the window.

Jack lies sack-like on the bunk across from me, asleep on his stomach, as he fell there around ten, exhausted. Gail snores softly behind the half wall that marks her space, and what I can see of Jeb are his feet, which hang off his bunk across the way; the rest of him is submerged in a miasma of blanket and sheet.

It's on nights like this that I sometimes roam, after the boys are asleep, go out and walk the island, try to feel it as it was before us. If I walk out past the outhouse and along the stone wall that marks the top of the meadow, feeling the path with my feet, seeing the land only as dark shades around me, I find myself in mind of lepers.

What must it have felt like, to be assured only of death on a poor island, to sit in a cottage, one's feet too large to fit in shoes any longer, one's face misshapen, and to look out at the sea, only the sea, and the wind-bent grass, the blond boulders along the shore, to gaze on that for a while, and then bend again to a book or a shawl knitted for no one, wait for the sun to go down?

It's strange how time seems to melt away, water receding on an ebb tide, when the light is low, and when it is night. When I roam, the blackberry bushes and tall grass round out the hills, so that seen against the night sky they have their ancient shape, are what they were.

Why would I not, having walked the circuit around the island in the night, return instead to a Mayhew farmhouse, or a Gifford farmhouse, stepping through a litter of sheep down in grass for the night, and over a stile, to the door of a low Cape home of weathered shingles with nets to be mended in a pile outside, an old dory as a flowerbed along the south side? I would go in, perhaps, to a great room with a large stone hearth opposite the door; a black dog would doze on the stone by the dying fire, around which rough empty chairs would be gathered; a narrow stair would lead on the right to two low-eaved rooms upstairs where the farmer and the mother would sleep, and the sister and the brothers; the stairs would creak as I climbed them, the dog stir in his dream, and in the rooms above I would see the unshaven farmer on his back, breathing with his mouth open, his wife curled along his side, her head on his shoulder, her wind-roughened face peaceful with sleep, and in the room wound rugs on the floor and a spinning wheel under the one small window.

And in the other room the children, two boys and a girl,

teenagers, one of the boys with a book on his chest where it had fallen, a guttered candle out in its holder on the floor, the other stirring in a dream of taking a seal with his father out by Gulls last fall, the struggle, and the girl, her hair in two braids, dreaming of a ship under full sail, and her on it, bound away from this island for Paris, London, anywhere.

But I return to this house full of sleeping boys and men and one sleeping woman, the latch on the red door clicking behind me.

21

MAY 3. In the evening, the calm was broken. The newest guy on the island is Burt. With his hair cut close to the skull, a strong chin, deep-set eyes, and a wiry frame, he resembles a boyish Paul Newman, although his mouth running with a Boston accent sets him apart, making him endearing and tension-raising all at once.

"Fuck that" is his favorite phrase, which he trots out in response to nearly any request. Exchanges seem to begin with something like, "Burt, would you pass the salt?" pass through "Burt, clean up the language or it'll cost you," and finish too often with his "Take all a' my money you fuckin' dyke, I don't give a shit."

Both of his parents are in jail, have been since he was seven or so. As far as I can figure, he lives in South Boston near his grandparents and several other relatives. He talks often of his brother, who is older and lives somewhere near Burt, on his own. Or so says Burt. For all I know, the brother may not even exist. Burt came to us through the Department of Social Services, which means that he has committed no crime. We are, in effect, his foster home.

And last night, as a result of I don't know what slight, Burt stood in the kitchen by the cook stove, rocked back on his heels, and told some of the guys the following:

"Yo, you all better wise the fuck up, 'cause if you don't stop giving me crap, I'm going to call up my bro', and he's a skinhead, and he'll come out here with his boys and kill all a y'all, yo. I'm fed up with this shit. There won't be a person left standing on this island when he's done, not even a green blade of grass," and so on.

Well, we staff all rolled our eyes at each other, and wondered how this one would play out. Needless to say, the threat didn't go over well with the other guys, especially the black guys, who don't much like the skinheads.

Jack arranged that the warring parties would meet in the basement after dinner. When the food had been cleared away, we all thumped down the wooden stairs on his cue, and in the half-light, with lanterns flickering on the rough old stones of the foundation, barbells lying idle at the far end of the room, the sauna door gaping open, and the beach-stone gravel rustling underfoot, Henry (the other new fellow) began a soliloquy, speaking in quiet tones to Burt.

Henry is tall, thin, a dark-brown guy with an immense Afro, making him seem even taller and narrower than he is; a streetwise kid who lives in a section of Boston full of gangs and crack, which, he says, perhaps just for effect, that he has dealt.

"Now, the way I feel, and I think I am speaking here for Josh and Reggie, and everybody, really, is that I don't see you as being a racist, and I think we should just keep this thing on the island, Burt. Now, 'cause I don't know nothing about your brother and his friends, but we are here, and I don't have no problem with you, and I won't, Burt, until you demonstrate to me that you are a racist."

As he spoke, Henry held his long brown hands out toward Burt, palms turned up, and then toward us, as if he were cradling his ideas there.

"So, what I'm sayin'," he went on, "is that we don't have no problem with you, and we won't go on giving you shit, Burt, but we don't like racists, and it seems like it would be better for everyone concerned to just chill on all this, and let's settle our problems peaceably, and among ourselves, and not start talking about outside forces, 'cause as soon as we bring that race thing in where it don't need to be, things get *all* tangled up."

As he said this, Henry's eyes were wide, animated, and he turned them on Burt.

So everyone looked at Burt.

Burt looked back, then looked at his shoes, swiped at the gravel underfoot with his right foot, and then said, quietly,

"Cool," and smiled, and the tension broke like rain falling on a humid day. I expected a third-grade teacher to call out "Snack time" any minute, so innocent did everyone seem in that moment. Then Drew said,

"C'mon, let's play some fuckin' cards," and the blush was off.

"Watch your language," I said, and we thumped upstairs. Burt seemed happy. In a moment of frustration he'd gone too far, and it was clear he didn't really want to coordinate an off-island assault of Penikese by skinheads. Henry had known that, and he let Burt know without humbling him. I like that kid. He'll make a diplomat.

Later, while Drew and I played cribbage at the big table, and Josh and Burt wrote letters upstairs in the glow of lanterns, Henry, Reggie, and Jerome danced to a languorous R&B tune, "Brother, Brother," which eased out of the radio. They swayed slowly in the corner of the main room, trees in the wind, their eyes closed, as Marvin Gaye's gentle tenor filled the house.

I AM beginning to see what much of this teaching is about: It is about sitting with the child, lending him my presence, giving him witness, and caring for his soul, even if it's only for the few days that he's on the island. It is this constancy that lends me credence, that establishes trust, that gives power to my ministrations, such as they are. Clever words, theories, texts don't cut it. Time spent listening does, with these guys.

And as I feel my time here grow shorter, there are a few boys on whom I feel my experience will turn. Wyatt is one, even though he's gone, and Ken, though he's gone as well. I will remember them a long while, how hard it seemed to go with them. Burt, I see, is another, and so is Drew. They all matter to me, but these four seemed to hear what I have to say more loudly than the rest. Which is not to say they follow my wishes any more closely. Somehow, though, they are the ones closest to my soul, and it is with them that I wrestle most with the question of whether I can handle them, can find the notes they need to hear to move on. Is this hubris? Man, I don't know.

MAY. It is a strange and wondrous thing, to realize that when one of them, out of the blue, calls me a douche bag, I have such choice in how I react. I can feel the anger that rises in me, and let it take me over, or I can feel the anger, and let it go, and respond after a breath or two, after I've taken time to understand where the anger is coming from on their part—and on my own.

When I am able to witness a boy, just see him clearly, as a young man in pain, without judging him, my childhood looks different too. Suddenly, long days alone are no longer colored with bitterness, no longer a wound to nurture and protect. Rather, they become who I am, and if I am to love who I have become, I must love them too—they have made me what I am. In these moments of clarity gratitude is born. But it is a wrestling match with the old ways for me, every day.

Yesterday I offered to give Burt a hand with the lobster pots he was mending down in the wood shop, and he told me to "Get lost." Just like that. "Okay," I said, and something like, "There are polite ways of saying you'd like to be alone," and then I left, saying to myself, "See it for what it is, don't judge." I repeat that to myself. Cultivate the witness—I say that to myself sometimes, too. Sounds hokey, but it helps.

And the beauty of the place seems to stand out when I just look—the round dark shadows of the pigs stark on the snow in sunlight, and the fan of the waves as they bend around Tubbs and sweep into the cove in long curved rows.

Oh, and this note: During my off week Jerome went home, finished his time here. He is back at his old school. I'll miss him.

O N Thursday morning Drew and Henry and I painted a dory, a twelve-foot flat-bottomed pulling boat descended from the deep and seaworthy dories of the old fishing schooners. On Wednesday we had gone and lifted it out of the dewy, high grass where it lay, behind the boat shop, overturned against winter gales. We loaded it into the weather-beaten wagon behind the tractor, coasted down the hill past the outhouse and house, and hauled it into the wood shop, where we began to prepare it for paint, scraping off the old where it would come, and then epoxying a couple of holes where half frames had ripped off the inner hull. Sun spilled in the open doors. Henry was quiet, thinking about something, and Drew seemed content to talk about bongs and three-wheelers.

"You ever ride a three-wheeler, Dan?"

"Can't say that I have."

"They're great. Best damn thing to do. Better than sex. Get yerself a big fattie and smoke it—that's what me and my boy Caleb would do, get us a big fattie and smoke it out in the woods and then fire up our three-wheelers and just scream around all day, like through the bogs, get mud right up over the seat. We'd always get 'em stuck and then have to pull one out with the other, mud everywhere, and we're just laughin' the whole time. We should get us some three-wheelers out here, you'd love it."

"Sounds like fun, Drew. But we already talked about how I feel about drugs and machines being mixed like that . . . Hey, get that peely place under the gunwale there."

"Where?"

"Right there. Right in front of you."

"I don't see no place."

"There."

"You get it, you crackhead. I ain't gettin' that. You ever three-wheel, Henry . . . ?"

Then on Thursday afternoon we painted. Sunlight yellow on the hull, green gunwales, gray interior, and red trim. She looked smart, in a Caribbean way. But Drew, the little Irish demon, ignored my requests that he take care as he painted. The whole brush went in the paint, the whole hand, and then he painted all of the clothes he was wearing yellow on the front. He was a yellow man.

"Drew, what the hell? I asked you to take care with the paint, and you're yellow all over, man. You know that stuff is toxic. And we're out here to do the job right, not to make a mockery of it."

"I ain't mockerin' nothin'. This is how I paint, man. I paint everything. Look. The boat got painted, didn't it? The boat changed color. What's your problem, man? Chill out, bro. I didn't hurt no one."

"It's the principle of the thing, Drew. Check your care scores out tomorrow."

He laughed. Skinny Henry just shook his head, knowing better than I when to observe, mind his tongue. I have come to love his easy way with people. And within myself I admired Drew's sense of rebellion, which, though destructive, is still a shout of life, of resistance, and the most powerful presence in the boy's energy.

The next morning, as he sat at the long table, he stared at the zero in the blue book in the column under "care" for a long while. Then he stole glances at me, wondering with his eyes if I still liked him, still shared the camaraderie built so many days after work, watching the sun drop into the bay. I didn't offer him anything either way. He can think about it.

M Y father's old boat: *Capella*. She was almost a Herreshoff. She was what someone, in seeking to copy the classic fifteen-foot day sailer, with its beautiful slim lines and full sheer, had come up with in his backyard. When we sailed her, people mistook her for a Herreshoff, and she sailed almost as well, too. But she was a foot longer, and somehow, this was fitting. She knocked at the door of the club, but she was her own girl, a class of her own, and couldn't ever have hoped to get in.

What I remember is where she rested in Bucky Barlow's boatyard one winter into spring, sat on the back lot in her cradle, in the tall grass and vetch, hard up against a stand of cedar trees. I was seven. That winter my mother and I had moved to the Cape, and in the spring my father began to get the old boat ready. He lived somewhere else in town that year, before he moved away again. I don't remember where. He and I would go out to the boat some afternoons, in an old Jeep Wagoneer he had, and work on her.

One job that took some time was getting the old seam compound out of the seams between the cedar planks of her hull, and putting in new, which we did with putty knives. My father showed me how, spreading the dark-red compound over the seam so that the seam was filled, then scraping off the excess, which left a rough band of dark red over each seam, dark stripes contrasting with the dusty red of the faded bottom paint on the rest of the hull. I didn't understand, so he explained.

"See, when we're done, we'll paint the bottom with bottom paint, and then the rest of her with different paint, and then when the boat goes in the water, her planks will swell like sponges when they get wet, and the gaps between them will narrow, sealing out the water."

As he said this he held two big fingers out in front of him, and gradually brought them together so that they touched on the word "narrow," and I saw.

"See," he said, "the seam compound is a gasket—it fills the empty spaces."

My father's hair was still dark then, and he had those big ballplayer's hands, or those of a farmer. And with them, with improbable grace, he spread seam compound with a putty knife, or

leaned on a brace and bit, holding it with his left hand and turning it slowly with his right to drill a hole into the hull of the boat.
And then he would change bits for a larger one, and make a
countersink for the head of the screw, and drive a new bronze
screw there, through the cedar plank and into the white-oak
frame beyond. He would keep the screwdriver blade on the
screw head while he turned it. I couldn't do that yet, but I saw
that it could be done. One forearm twisted, showing the sinews
there, and the hand of the same arm clenched the screwdriver,
while the other hand clamped onto the coaming of the boat. He
would work his jaw back and forth as he did this, and exhale
when the screw was in, and then look at me and say, "There."

"Refastenin'," he called this, and when he said it he sounded
like Barlow, the man who owned the place, who walked around
in an oily green jumpsuit and a green cap, unshaven, his stomach round against the fabric, who said things like,

"Well, I suppose you could do it that way."

I liked Barlow and his friends, who stood around the potbellied stove in the big boat shed, stood in piles of fragrant wood
shavings with their arms folded on their chests, saying, "Yup,"
and nodding to the fire.

And I liked seeing those screws going into the wood, seeing
how it was done.

Y E S T E R D A Y, in a cool drizzle, as the drops gathered
gemlike on the stems of ryegrass and vetch in the meadow, I
spent the afternoon getting rocks for the garden wall with Burt,
who seized the chance to be a punk.

"Burt, does it register with you when I say it's not okay to
ruin things?" I said as I walked a few paces behind the slowly
turning black tires of the green tractor.

The tires spun in the mud as he popped the clutch and
gunned the engine, skidding the tractor around a curve, then
stopped and grinned at me over his shoulder. Here was a test. I
began to watch.

"Knock it off, man. That tractor doesn't belong to you. It's everyone's, and you've got to respect that."

This time he dropped the tractor into high gear and popped the clutch, jolting the chassis and skidding ahead, then looked back with a smirk.

So I caught up with him, told him I wanted to tell him a joke about "a man and a naked woman on a tractor—no, really," got him to stop the tractor to listen, hauled him off the tractor by the lapels of his coat, and drove it back myself. Which was accompanied by some choice language as he danced along beside me, throwing his face toward the sky, loosing volleys of cuss.

"What the fuck, man. What're you doing? I didn't *do* nothin'. Why'd you pull me offa there, man? You're an asshole, Dan. Just a asshole."

"Listen to me, Burt. This is why you're here, man, 'cause you won't listen."

"Fuck you, man. Everybody drives like that. That's how you're supposed to drive, man. That's how my dad useta drive. Everybody does. You're a fuckin' asshole."

Always let them have the last word.

After we came in, I had a few moments in the staff room as I put on dry clothes, and I realized that I had just pulled a boy bodily off the tractor. And shook him a little. His eyes had made little jiggly circles. I had had good reason—I feared for his safety, and for the tractor—but that wasn't something I would have done some months ago. I am more in this skin than I was. And Burt looked at me with a little more respect, I think, at dinner, although it might have been my imagination.

THIS skin. Can I be conscious of it, untie it and step out of it the way a shape-shifter would step out of the skin of a bear, walk into the world as a free man, seeing through my eyes alone?

From where does the skin come? The two parents, or the

four grandparents? Or further back? What are the conditions of my upbringing? I never knew my mother's father, but I got his energies, somehow. He raged, they say, outwardly, screamed in the house, controlled those around him with his anger. I rage inwardly, seethe, run eight miles to let it out like air from a tire, then take care of others, do them no favors in this, forget about what matters to me, about where I dwell.

I have his uniform from the Great War. It is a medical officer's uniform: a khaki jacket, with a broad leather belt and shoulder strap, which flares over jodhpurs, pants broad in the thigh and tapering once past the knee to fit into tall leather boots.

It is a uniform from the age of horse. I found it in the basement when I was fifteen and put it on. It fit like a glove. I imagined I was he, cursing the Hun, tearing the coat off to dress for surgery in a tent in a muddy field in France, sawing off the shrapnel-chewed arms of boys from Ipswich and Chicago and Mobile. Perhaps that was where the rage was born—when he saw the frailty of life in the presence of cordite.

Or perhaps it came from some time in his youth, a father who shouted him down, stamped him underfoot, told him he'd never make a doctor, threw him down in the sawdust on the shop floor and told him to quit his goddamned dreaming and face up to being a butcher; what made him think he was better than that anyway?

And the other grandfather, my father's father, raised in Vermont, the son of a judge who became a judge in Washington. Why did he marry the woman he did, and why did he leave her scarcely two years later, absent himself from that family, in time disinherit the son and the grandson, saying nothing?

And my mother's mother, where was she when her husband raged? How did she survive? By cowering in the linen closet? By pretending it just wasn't so? Who knit this skin, and how do I peel it off, exposing the older, wiser, more ancient and somehow playful self whose presence I feel in some moments of silence?

The other day I went and found that uniform again, in a box in the basement of my mother's home. It smelled of must and camphor. I tried to put the jacket on; years of shoveling, splitting wood, chin-ups on the island, had made my shoulders too large for the old fabric.

22

I SAT across the table from Gail this morning at 7:10, facing the cook stove. Jeb was to my right across from Jack. The blue books, seven of them, lay in an eccentric pile at our center. A few salt crystals littered the dark planks of the tabletop. Two thick china mugs and two scarred plastic mugs sat in a rough group next to the sugar bowl, which was big and glass with a hinged metal lid. Some kid had liberated it from a diner years ago and brought it back to the island as a present. He'd passed generosity with that. I hoped he'd come to honesty further along in the curriculum.

Jack stared down into *East of Eden*. Gail looked out the window. Jeb sketched on a napkin the joining of a keelson to a stem, and I listened to coffee drip down into the pot, which sat on the stove and ticked quietly with the heat as the big kettles of water for dishes steamed; the wood in the stove sighed as its sap burned. We sat. Occasionally a bench creaked as someone shifted their weight.

When the coffee stopped dripping Gail rose—before I could—and grabbed the pot, poured four mugs full, and moved one toward each of us. Jack grabbed the can of condensed milk from behind him. None of us took sugar. He knew that. "Think about Larry far a minit," he said.

We all knew we had to cast a vote that morning which might be the end of a kid.

Larry had come to us three weeks before, chubby, five-ten, Boston Irish and a storyteller, with eyes that bugged out just with the pressure of being. He seemed always to be looking for listening in our eyes, to his story, his joke, his "take."

"My take is that Jackie-O is working us all for his own gain," he had said the day before as he, Drew, Henry, and I walked down to launch *Smoke* and check the pots, "by which I mean that if we perform good on everything he proposes, then his chips go up, by which I mean we all gotta look out for each other, guys." Then he searched our faces for signs of allegiance, or shared ill-will. He was, it seemed to me, a kid congenitally without allies.

Two weeks ago, on the other shift, on a quiet night, the last staff member up had made a final round of checks. On a whim he'd checked the cellar, and found the woodpile there smoldering. Someone had doused it with kerosene, lit it, and gone to bed, no doubt ready to jump out a window when the flames rose. Or had he even thought that far?

Frank, a new boy, on-island for less than eighteen hours, confessed to the crime in the morning. He said he'd been told if he burned the house down, we could all go home. Apparently his was a gesture of generosity, with an eye toward team-building. There were lobbyists in our midst, and the whole thing had the odor of Larry.

Our shift had arrived the next day, and before we could accuse him of anything, Larry had approached each of us individually to deny any involvement.

"Why would I be involved in anything as low and inconsiderate as that?" he quizzed us, unbidden, eyes bulging. "I'd be jeopardizing my place here, and my overall rehabilitation, right? I'm glad you see that, Dan. Very glad. In fact, it's a relief to me that you see that, Dan."

Then, yesterday, as Jack, Jeb, and I sat at the table after lunch, Larry slithered up.

"Hey J's. Jack and Jeb, get it? J's? Hey I was wonderin', I

havta sweep upstairs and do you guys want me to sweep the staff room, too, 'cause it'd be no trouble. I might as well. Would that be all right with you guys? Want me to take your book back up with me, Jeb?"

"Yeah, sure, Larry, knock yourself out," said Jack. Jeb handed him the book.

We'd listened as he swept directly over our heads, the plywood floor like the skin of a drum, and then moved stealthily to the unlocked strongbox next to Jack's bed, from which (we soon found out) he took two packs of Gail's cigarettes, the hasp ringing softly as he lowered the lid, and continued to sweep. A few minutes later he was coming down the stairs with his full dustpan, whistling "The Battle Hymn of the Republic." Jack took the lead.

"Larr, thanks for the sweepin'."

"No problem. No problem at all," he said, emptying the pan into the barrel by the serving table. There was a long silence as Larry put his broom in the corner.

"You have anything to tell me?"

"Like?"

"Like? Like anything you want to get off your chest?"

"No. I feel good, Jack. Thumbs up for asking, though."

"So when I go up and check the strongbox, nothing will be missing?"

"What do you mean?"

Jack stood up and walked right at Larry.

"Like all the cigarettes will be there, Larry? Or will I find some gone?"

He swept past Larry, and was halfway up the stairs when Larry was transformed, gesturing, pointing, looking from face to face.

"Okay, fellas," he said. "The jig is *up*. You guys are the *greatest*. You got me. I give. Well done. I am *impressed*. An excellent exercise. I tested you, and we're square. No hard feelings. I just slipped a couple packs under a pillow up there to see how long it would be till you noticed. And you guys pass with *flying* colors. Beautiful. I love it. I love games like that."

"Larry . . ." said Jack, coming down the stairs.

"And I'm glad you see I was going to tell you before it got out of hand, 'cause—"

"Larry. Enough."

"But you gotta understand that I—"

"Larry, outside," said Jack, holding the door open, and they stepped out onto the deck where we could see Jack listening to the air leak out of Larry's head.

Jeb looked at me for a moment, then shook his head. "Kid's psycho," he said.

So, we sat quietly at the table for a few minutes this morning, the coffee dilating the vessels in our brains, silently weighing Larry's fate.

Then Gail spoke up. Unlike us, she always looked together in the morning, her brown hair brushed and clean, eyes bright. She'd taken a shower and had had a smoke on the deck before any of us had stirred.

"Okay if I get this started?" she said. Jack nodded.

"If he washes out, what happens to him?"

"He goes back to jail," said Jeb, whose hair shone with three days of hard work and no shower.

"We know that?" said Gail.

"We know that for sure," said Jack. The dry grass on his sweater from yesterday's wood hauling made it look as if he'd slept well at the bottom of his burrow.

"So," she went on, "we think he might have given Frank the idea of burning down the house, we know he just tried to get Henry kicked out with the cigs under his pillow, and since he's been here everybody's missing something. Now, the guys have been patient, but pretty soon the mood's going to deteriorate. I can feel it."

"Agreed," said Jeb.

"What am I supposed to say to George?" said Jack, playing devil's advocate. "Larry's making everyone cranky, so he's a goner?"

"No, no," said Jeb, thoughtfully. "It gets dangerous when the scene deteriorates out here, Jack, you know that. And I think he's the catalyst."

"There is someone with light fingers out here," I said.

"We can't say for sure it's him," said Jack, looking back at me steadily. We sat there in silence for a moment, and then Jack said, "Whadda you think, Gail?"

"I can't stand the lad. I don't begrudge him, but I don't trust him. I say get him out of here."

"Jeb?"

"Glib guy's gotta go."

"Dan?"

"I think he's a risk. Not worth keeping out here. He's dragging down too many guys, including me because I can't sleep with him out here. They're not quite smart enough to nail him. Yet. But I do think we're liable if—"

"Gotcha," said Jack, grasping my point. "Okay. I agree. The fire puts me over the top. He goes. We don't tell him to pack until half an hour before the boat arrives, capiche? Let him think he's still one of the pack, so he doesn't try to kneecap all of us. Shall we do the blue books?"

Thus ended our deliberations. After ten minutes of grading boat building, school, and table manners, we were done. "Wake 'em," said Jack on the stroke of seven-thirty, and Jeb was gone up the stairs to make the first pass. I would follow in five minutes.

While this wasn't the end of the line for Larry, we all knew this was another nail in his lid. We took that seriously. But we'd talked about it, all considered him to be unpredictable, and felt the presence of a malevolence in the house, albeit a stealthy one.

And I want to know (whether the kid was part of trying to burn the house down or not) who failed him when he was young. What sorts of heartbreak and violence were the landscape of his childhood? At some point, the onus shifts to the kid. But at what point? He left that afternoon, when the boat, making a special mid-week run for him, came and eased our minds.

* * *

1 1 : 3 5 P . M . As the sea stretches darkly away outside the big picture window, moths attack the kerosene lamps on the big dining table, fuzzy kamikazes desiring the flames, bouncing off the glass globes. I wonder what the impact does to their eyes, and am reminded of Alan, trying to kill himself with acid and dope. Would it feel good to burn out? It is Saturday night, first night of the shift. Already I am tired.

Burt saw his parents last weekend, both his mother, who is near leaving jail after being convicted of something he wouldn't tell me about, and his father, who is in for another two years for the same crime. They are divorced and in separate prisons. His mother got a day-long furlough, and they went together to see his father.

I went another round with Burt a week ago. At ten one night I found him out on the deck, rolling a cigarette with tobacco taken from discarded butts, which is something the guys are apt to do toward the end of the week, when they are out of cigarettes. This is not okay on the island, because it's hard to know what winds up in a rollie. So I told him to throw it away. He, knowing the rules, refused, and Jack came down hard. Burt reacted by telling us all to fuck ourselves, throwing his blue book in the trash, and storming out into the night. After a few minutes I went after him to make sure he wouldn't throw himself into the sea.

It was a dark night, with no moon, and the Leach's storm petrels (the island is their southernmost nesting site in the world) were making their alien-like trills from nests deep in the stone walls that ramble around the house.

I'd walked twenty yards toward the chicken coop when Burt emerged from behind the pole. He'd been waiting for me. I asked him what was up, he said he was heading out to the big rock, so we started walking that way. He wouldn't speak beyond that.

The "rock" is a huge glacial erratic, a lump of granite spit out by one of the tongues of the Laurentian ice that withdrew from the area about ten thousand years ago. It rises twenty feet above the surface of the island, and it has a presence we all feel. It is where boys go to sit, looking northwest over the bay, when they are distraught.

We sat there in silence for quite a while, watching the dim silhouettes of the tugs and barges shambling up and down the shipping lane, moving between us and the distant sulfurous arc of the New Bedford shoreline. I explained how navigation lights work.

"You see the green lights out there?"

"Yeah," he said, forgetting to be sullen for a moment.

"Those are the ones on the starboard sides of the boats."

"The right sides?"

"Yeah. So whenever you see a green light, you know you're seeing the right side of a boat, and the red lights are on the left side. There's never any doubt there."

Silence.

"So do you know what you're looking at if you can see both red and green? Then you know the boat's coming right at you, that it'll run you down if you don't move."

"DSS can suck my cock. They won't let me live with my grandmother, they won't let me live where I'm supposed to be, and they are screwing everything up, totally—they can just suck my cock."

I let the night take up the statement for a moment, then said:

"Do you think leaving the island is going to help anything?"

"I don't care. I don't give two shits. Fuck 'em all. Fuck Jack, fuck DSS, fuck this island, fuck it all. I'm leavin' tomorrow, I'm packin', and I'm leavin', and I don't care what anybody says, I'll be on the boat."

"They say it's gonna blow thirty-five tomorrow—I don't think they'll run a boat."

"I don't care. I'll row home. My brother and I, we'll just fuckin' go, we'll just get the fuck out of here, that's all. I don't owe them nothin', the damn DSS, come into your house—"

He turned to me here, and addressed me.

"How would you like it, them telling you they know how everything is, telling you how you're going to live, how they're going to just take it all over, that you have no say. Fuck them, they think they're fuckin' gods or something, like they know what goes on in my family. I been living in my family all my life, and they tell me they know what's right for me and my family? They decide how we live, when we can see each other, how long we can stay in the same room, how we should feel about each other? Why don't they come live in it if they know so much?"

"Well, you know they're just trying to do their jobs, and they don't get paid much, and they're not bad people—"

"That makes it okay? That they don't get paid much? It would be better it they got paid a lot to fuck up my family?"

"No. I'm just saying they're doing what they can—"

"They should be shot for what they did to my family."

"Look, I'm not saying what they did was right. I'm saying that those people mean well, and that they don't have the resources to do all they'd like to—a lot of them have a caseload way above what allows them to really be involved with a family the way they should."

"So they fuck them up. So they just go ahead and make decisions like they know what they are doing when they don't."

"Maybe they are a problem, Burt, but look at it this way, man: Okay, so they came in and screwed things up. And maybe there were some problems in your family before that. But how are you going to see all of that?"

"I'm going to see it as them deserving a good beatin'."

"How can you see yourself as existing outside of all of that?"

(In the pauses in our talk we could hear gulls moving in the tall grass along the bluff edge, calling out in warning or perhaps just conversation.)

"I can't. I'm part of that. What the fuck do you mean?"

"I mean, imagine you came down from the stars into your family, and chose them because of what they would teach you about life on earth, what if all of this is just part of your education, how does it make you feel then?"

"What the fuck are you talking about?"

"The possibility you don't have to be a victim to all of this."

"Right now I ain't a victim of nothin' but Jack's fucked-up justice, and I ain't gonna take it anymore."

"Look, Burt, you know you can't roll your own on the island, and Jack is tired of you acting like a spoiled brat around him."

"Well he's gotta understand what I'm up against, and how frickin' hard it is to mellow out when you can't even get a smoke around here . . ."

Eventually, after much wearying conversation, in which I tried to nudge him back to a more conciliatory place, we headed back, feeling our way along the foot-hardened path toward the dim lamplight in the house a quarter mile away. In the dark, you can feel when you've left the path because the turf underfoot is suddenly soft. Another step and you're in the blackberries, stumbling as they rake your legs. A distant tug thrummed, and the waves gave themselves onto the isthmus with a rhythmic chirr.

And in the morning, a change had come. Burt got up before any of the others, found a check in the bucket outside the door to the deck, smoked it, and sat in its haze on the deck for a few minutes, then came in and made a bumbling apology to Jack. He was marginally repentant. He fished his blue book out of the trash, and took it to Jack, who filled in the low scores. The thing seemed to have blown over.

YESTERDAY, Burt and I went for a row in one of the dories. I thought it might be a good chance for us to talk one-on-one. It was gray out, and still, with the blues of the sea thinning into narrow tongues and carrying onto the russet sand of the beach, resting quiet in the pools among the black rocks where tangles of sargassum lay. In this quiet we carried the dory down to the water, our boots scraping in the sand there, got a pair of oars and an extra oar in case from the old shed, and an anchor.

"We don't need a fuckin' anchor," he said, when I asked him to grab it.

Unfortunately for Burt, I'm particular about how boats are rigged, for I've worked at sea, seen people hurt for their negligence, and have run a sailing school, where no one ever got hurt. It's easy to get in trouble out there.

"Yeah, we do. Always take an anchor. No matter how far you go."

"Fuck that."

"We're taking it or we're not going. A guy I grew up with drowned three months ago right off Martha's Vineyard when the boat he was on flipped. I respect these waters, and if I lose my oars, I don't want to wind up in the middle of the sound."

"We don't need a fuckin' anchor to go around the cove."

"We take it, and life vests, or we sit on the beach."

"Aw, fuckinshit, man," he said as he picked up the anchor, and a life vest, and headed for the boat.

We loaded her and eased her into the water. Burt asked that I row to begin with, which I did, and as soon as we cleared the dock, he started rocking the boat. I asked him to stop, and he refused. I started heading in. So he threw our spare oar in the water, became a child throwing a tantrum. I swore at him, began to row to get it. As soon as I had shipped oars to grab the spare, he seized one of those and hurled it overboard. I got angry. So did he. I told him he was mutinous and that I might have to whack him. He said, "Go for it." The water was cold. I didn't want to risk capsizing. Never make a threat you can't keep.

So I swore never to go afloat with him again, and somehow managed to get us in. But not before three or four more oars swam. The kid is a puzzle, but I see a pattern. He gets attention from me when he screws around. I am perhaps the parent figure with whom he can act out. I am also the state, against whom he can rage. The challenge, then, is how to escape this pattern, without having to leave the job.

Burt doesn't trust his father, who is in jail, has been since he was seven, doesn't trust his mother, who is in jail, has been since he was eight, doesn't trust the state, which in his mind is an impersonal staff of family destroyers, and he barely trusts the island to be impersonal. When he encounters a guy like me, eager to try out all of these roles of mentor, surrogate father, trusted teacher, of course his eventual need is to test that trust, to rebel against his need to believe in the truth of his elders' motivations. So he throws the oars out of the boat, does his best to enrage me.

And the strange thing with Burt is that he bears such a striking resemblance to a portrait I have of my father, taken when he was fourteen or so. Burt is a little older, filled out, harder, yet the deep almond eyes and the softness in the face, the strong chin, the abrupt and handsome nose are all there. In Burt I see the boy my father was, and I know, in spite of myself, that I am trying to save that kid, trying to ease his way through the hurt, trying, somehow, to get through to myself.

JUNE 3. I was in the garden today, looking out over the cove, with Sam, yet another new kid. He is big, quiet, strong, brown-skinned, from Dorchester. He wears his hair in a natural, which is coming back into vogue, and his face is part child, part man. He must outweigh me by forty pounds. He is in for possession of an illegal firearm, and for dealing.

We spent the morning preparing beds, moving loads of prime, over-wintered compost—pig manure, chicken manure, and eel grass—to the garden in the wheelbarrow, then turning it into the beds we'd raised. Sam hardly said a word, just worked hard and steadily, manhandling the barrow with his big arms, which have cords of muscle running down them. I was a little unnerved by the ease of it all.

Stan, the wiry new kid from Gloucester with pale gray eyes and shaggy blond hair, was also part of our group of three. He flitted around like a sparrow, taking a wheelbarrow to get a load of compost and winding up mumbling to the chickens at the coop, then disappearing over the hill. If we sent him in search of ocean, I think he'd return with a handful of sand and no sign of water. He is with us for assault and malicious destruction of property.

I've had a couple of rambling talks with him that have ended with his drifting off into a reverie, then wandering out the door or up to his area. He doesn't seem to understand attention. I wonder if he's ever been shown any. He did let me know that sometimes he has flashbacks; suddenly he's reviewing in his mind a movie of a violent episode he's been through. When his mind goes, his body wanders around. He never knows where he'll be when he tunes back in to the world. He wouldn't tell me what he flashes back to.

All the while Sam worked and Stan wandered, the child swallows were beginning, attempting little flights—ungainly fledglings wobbling through air—from the nest under the deck to the garden fence, there to yaw crazily for a moment, then fluttering back home, their ebony backs and forked tails glistening in the sun. They remind me of jazz musicians vamping out into the unknown, then returning to the tune, except that they've barely learned the tune. How many shades of home there are. After fattening around here for the summer, they'll head to Costa Rica in the fall.

After lunch, we planted: gourds, zucchini, yellow squash, acorn squash, summer squash, giant pumpkins, cucumber, spaghetti squash—a plethora—Sam and I. He'd never done it before, and he asked,

"How they gonna grow? They ain't alive."

"Sure they are."

"Nah. They all dried out."

"Right, but as soon as the water hits them, they'll start to germinate."

"German what?"

"Germinate. That means grow."

"Say 'grow,' then. How they know to do that?"

"Say, that's a good question. They must have some intelligence, right?"

"So they sleepin' right now?"

"Yeah, it's just as if they are asleep right now, and as soon as the water lets them know it's time to wake up, they'll start to grow."

"What they gonna eat?"

"Right inside the seed there is enough food to get them started to where they can sprout, and then once their stem is above ground, it can start getting energy from the sun."

"Each one of these will grow into a big plant?"

"Well, if we're lucky."

We made mounds for each type, and then Sam went around to each mound and, leaning over, with a precious cargo of seeds cradled in one big hand, planted the small sleeping lives with his other hand as carefully as if he were laying babes down to rest, covering each with a handful of soil.

Later, Stan told me his flashbacks are of a friend being killed. He won't tell me how.

And now, I am jerked from my gardening reveries as big Sam, who planted those seeds with such care, looks up from his journal and offers that his best friend Lemiko went out on Halloween, stabbed a fellow who was trying to rob him, and is now in Concord for murder. Then he goes back to his writing.

23

JUNE 5. The note in the *Cape Cod Times* says that Wyatt who used to pummel the punching bag in the basement, who was so wired with energy that he could barely sit still, who just wanted to return to his girl, our Wyatt, was arrested and charged with breaking and entering with intent to commit a misdemeanor. This means, we think, some serious time for him, as he's seventeen now. He'll be in with the big boys. Damn.

Also, we hear that Jerome, fun-loving, chess-playing, staring out the window of the staff room wishing for the helicopter Jerome, our Jerome, was picked up and charged with possession of a stolen panel truck. His story was that a friend lent it to him, and told him that it was rented. The cops didn't buy it.

And I, I am walking around feeling like someone kicked me in the gut. This is the first time for me, the first time hearing that any of the guys who I spent six months cajoling through school and work, that any of *my* boys, was back in lockup. Have I failed? I don't know.

Also, Josh failed to return from his last weekend. Which means he's AWOL, chillin' at someone's crib, which means that if he returns, he'll have to start all over.

* * *

I WENT down to spend some time with Wyatt at the court-house in Barnstable, as he waited his turn before the judge. I got there around 9 A.M., and found him in the high-ceilinged waiting room, which echoed with my footsteps. He sat forward, elbows on knees, and watched his sneakers. He wore a black cotton jacket over a sweater, jeans, black sneakers. His face was gray, and his eyes dull. He looked tired.

"Hey Wyatt."

"S'up, you bald-headed geek?"

"How you doin'? You want to go get a cup of coffee? You have time?"

"Yeah, I got like, hours, they said."

"Let's go."

We went across the New England main street there, to a breakfast joint called the Anchorage, and found a table.

"What'll you have? You get any breakfast?"

"Coffee and a omelet and toast and home fries and a muffin'd be great."

"You got it."

"Thanks, man."

Soon the waitress appeared, a sleepy-eyed young woman with her brown hair up in a bun. We agreed wordlessly that she was attractive.

The food arrived. I watched Wyatt load his coffee with two creams and three sugars, watched him engulf the food, amoeba-like, waited until he was mostly done to ask him,

"So how are you doing with all this?"

"I'm fucked, man. They're saying three to six months in Brockton Y, and that's minimum. My mom just keeps cryin'. It just sucks."

"You're frigged, huh?"

"Yup. One screwed pup." As he said this he grimaced.

"Well, it's been nice knowing you." I waited for a beat, then said,

"But I don't buy it."

"C'mon, man, these guys aren't playin'. I'm goin' down." He said this with a little hope in his eyes, hope that I knew an angle he didn't.

"Yeah, you're going down. But how you go is in your hands. You know what I mean?"

"No."

"How you see it—it's in your hands. Whether you look hard at it or not, learn from the experience or not."

"What am I supposed to learn, not to fuck with the cops?"

"Yeah. But c'mon, Wyatt, you know what I'm getting at," I said, as the waitress traipsed over with more coffee.

"More for you guys?" she said.

"Please," said Wyatt, and I the same, as I rejoiced inwardly at his manners, and then we followed her retreat together with our eyes, and I said,

"Take a good look."

"I know. There's none of that where I'm going."

"So, you can look at the other guys in there—"

"Wait a frickin' minute, man."

"Not like that. I mean look at them and try to understand how they got there, what went wrong for them. Study them. See what I'm saying?"

"Crimes got them there."

"What's underneath that?"

"Underneath?"

"What happened to them when they were little, what is their history?"

"You get biffed for putting your nose—"

"Just listen, Wyatt, just observe. Their stories will come out. See if you can find a pattern there."

"Why?"

I could feel my heart quicken.

"Well, you have a choice, man. Either you don't understand why you're in there, and you wind up there again, or you understand your story because you understand theirs, and you learn."

"Learn what?"

"Why you screw up like this."

"Because I'm a fuckup."

"No. You are not a fuckup."

"Because you are a bald-headed geek."

"Because many things. Observe what you can in there."

"Does this go back to the axe-handle bullshit?"

"Straight back."

"There's no axes in prison, man."

"You've got it tough, Wyatt, because you— Are you listening?" He had started to push his fingertip through a pile of sugar he'd made on the table.

"Listening."

"You have to make your own handle, man. That's the hard thing."

"Why is it like that?"

"Who is dead?"

"What do you mean?"

"Who's dead?"

"My dad. John Lennon. I don't fuckin' know."

"Your dad. And I'm not your dad."

"Sometimes I wish you were. 'Cause then I could call you a punk bald-headed mother-lover all-a the time."

Pause. I shifted in my seat, caught a glimpse of the waitress wiping down a table.

"How's your girlfriend?" I asked.

"Sad."

"Is she going to wait for you?"

"So she says."

"So you're set. Do your time, figure out something about what's making you act out, and get out and begin your life."

"Yo, my mom says I'm just like my dad."

"You're not, and you're not like your mother, either. You're you."

"Yeah, fucking crazy me."

But he seemed more upbeat, his head hanging not quite so low.

"You are what *you* decide to be, what *you* decide to accept."

"I accept that you're a frickin retahd, man. Hey, how about another muffin?"

"You heard me, right?"

He looked me in the eye.

"Yup."

We got the attractive waitress to return, and then killed another half an hour talking about the old Mustang Wyatt was going to fix up when he got out. And then we went back over to the courthouse. I noted as we walked that Wyatt was now as tall as me. I asked him one more time what he was going to do in lockup.

"Observe," he said, with a big shit-eating grin. I gave him a hug, shook his hand, and walked away.

They sent him down for four months. I got his address in lockup before I left.

THEN, on Thursday, two weeks ago, I took Stan the wanderer to the Leominster courthouse during my off week, took him to a stately brick building on a tree-lined street in a town that looks like the American ideal. We drove in the old blue Volvo wagon. He wore his best, a Dodgers shirt and a pair of red jeans, and said hardly a word the whole way up, answering my questions with monosyllables.

"How are you?"

"Okay."

"Are you nervous?"

"Yeah."

"How come?"

"Dunno."

He was up on charges of ten thousand dollars' damage done to his high school (windows he'd broken), as well as assault— the result of a misunderstanding with his archery instructor at school.

I asked him about the windows.

"How did that happen?"

He shrugged, and with a blank face, as he watched the empty road in front of us, said, "I threw rocks through them."

"Why?"

"Dunno," he said, looking out the side window.

"What about the assault? What happened there?" I asked.

"One arrow didn't go toward the target."

"Did you mean to shoot it at the guy?"

"I was shooting it at the school, but he was in between."

"Oh."

"I drilled the school," he said, looking at me for a moment, then looking back out the window. I understood that if he had wanted to, he would have drilled the man.

I N the courthouse we stood in the polished and high-ceilinged hallway as a crowd of young defendants milled around, their ball caps awry, little gang-banger wanna-bes, with their pants baggy and falling off their hips, their shoulders rolling as they walked, talking about "glocks" and "nines" (guns), and, "What I'm a do when I get out, man. Yo, I'll just be chillin' yo, when I get out. Can't nobody touch me when I'm out, yo," sounding like radio repeating stations, just passing on what they've taken off the airwaves.

I stood and talked with Stan's mother, a slight, gray, sway-backed and long-haired woman missing a front tooth—about forty-three—and her husband, who is not Stan's father, who looked like an Allman Brothers roadie. He was six-four, stooped, with a big gut, long skinny arms, a skull on his gray T-shirt, and a Jack Daniel's "Field Tester" hat over his long gray hair. He kicked in an occasional guttural comment, like, "Kid don't even know how to behave."

He talked right at me, but if I seemed distracted he'd turn away and finish his sentence to the wall—an eloquent state-ment of the quality of his disaffection. He is perhaps so used to feeling the victim or beholden to someone for attention that he suffered my inattention, inadvertent though it was, without insult, just speaking to the bricks as if what he had to say wasn't important enough to insist on the eyes of the college boy in the tie and chinos.

At one point Stan's caseworker, a bouncy young guy with neatly cut blond hair and wire-rim glasses, came out to tell us we'd be on in about half an hour, and then pulled me aside and said, "You gotta see this."

We walked through a doorway into another small hallway, at the far end of which a family was gathered around a young man in manacles. He told me the kid had just been "sent down to the big house" for a year for robbery, and had been surrounded by relatives after the sentencing as if he had just graduated from high school.

We stood and watched the scene for a moment. "You did it man, you're in," was the comment from an uncle or older brother, a big, friendly-looking man in a leather coat, just before he hugged the boy, and there was much back-slapping and laughing. Strange, to think that going to prison could constitute a rite of passage, an entry into a way of life that is sought after. Even that kid is less alone than Stan.

During our hearing, minutes after it began, it came as a surprise to both me and Stan to hear what his mother had to say, although I don't think much surprises Stan anymore.

"Are you sure you want to relinquish custody to the state, Mrs. Boling?" the judge asked her as she stood at the defendant's table. She hadn't mentioned this to Stan or me during the hours we stood chatting in the hall of the courthouse.

"Yeah. There's no way I can control him, and he don't mind me any longer at all, so there's nothing more for me to do, really."

"You don't want him to have a place in your home?" he asked, blinking down at her.

"No sir, I don't."

Among other things, this meant Stan wouldn't be able to go home to Gloucester the next weekend, the only time in a year he and his girlfriend might be able to get together. She had a

home pass from her placement in Pittsfield, but now Stan had
nowhere to go. He was not happy. Which meant he stared out
the window, his big eyes empty, reflecting blue sky.

The judge let the ball roll, looking out over his half glasses
and droning to Stan in a tired voice peppered with the broad
a's of the region.

"Very well. Son, do well in your current placement, that
Penikese school, and the time there will count for the six
months you've been sentenced to. I don't know what can be
done about your weekends, since you no longer have a home
at which to spend them."

Stan's mother stood next to him as the judge said this. She
stared straight ahead. She never touched Stan.

"Do you wish to comment, Counsel?" the judge asked
Stan's court-appointed lawyer.

"I move to continue, Your Honor," she said.

"Very good," he said, and the gavel fell, and we were done.

Stan stood silent in his Dodgers shirt. He had been orphaned
so suddenly. I turned to ask his caseworker something, and
Stan's parents were gone when I turned back around. Then, after a few words, his lawyer was walking down the hall away from
us, too, her black skirt tight and high across her ass, somehow
sexless and professional. The click of her black high heels on
the polished floor died as she rounded a corner and vanished.
We were alone. I looked at Stan. He looked at the floor.

We had lunch at a burger joint in Bourne on the way back,
and after I assured him that we would work hard to find him a
place in Gloucester for the coming weekend, he opened up a
bit. I asked him about his flashbacks, and he told me the origin
of some of them—an uncle, killed as he argued with a man in
a supermarket parking lot, slashed in the throat with a shard of
a grape juice bottle. He died as Stan watched, life ebbing onto
the tarmac before the ambulance arrived. Other tales, of two
friends who had died before his eyes, one caught in a crossfire,
one hit by a car, came out.

And he said that in the flashbacks he lost consciousness as

he remembered a particularly violent incident, finding himself fifteen minutes later in another place, having reexperienced the scene. He said they left him weak. I asked him if he'd read anything about the Vietnam War. "A little," he said. We fell into a silence that lasted most of the way home, my old Volvo humming at sixty, the flowers on the median rocking in our wake. This time, I didn't know what to say.

S T A N ran the other day. He was on the mainland in Woods Hole for an afternoon, after being denied his weekend home. We had nowhere to send him. He asked Laurie (the person on duty) if he could take her bike for a spin. She said sure, and he hasn't been seen since. He's got five dollars in his pocket and a girlfriend in a treatment center in Pittsfield. Ten to one, he's headed for her, riding down a sun-baked highway breakdown lane strewn with broken bottles and shards of semi tires, grasses leaning in the wake of the passing cars. A rolling stone.

M O R E on Stan. Apparently, he rode for ten or fifteen miles, then convinced a fellow at a Mercedes-Benz dealership to let him take a car for a test drive. (Right on, man.) He drove the car to Pittsfield, and I like to think of him with the windows down and the radio up, a fifteen-year-old able to sweet-talk himself into a ride on a sunny day. The police picked him up eventually, but I don't think they charged him with anything but breaking his probation and driving without a license. They can't charge him for borrowing a car, or misleading a car salesman.

I don't know if he found his girlfriend before they found him, but that's how I see it when I imagine it, the two of them in the Mercedes, driving down a back road, stopping next to a stream, lying down in the sun on its banks, the sound of the water on the rocks, trying to find some sweetness in this life, in each other.

24

A F E W years ago, when the bars still held some romance for me, some promise of undiscovered country, the Captain Kidd was the kind of bar I liked. But I'm speaking of the Kidd I knew when I was a boy.

Then, it seemed at home in Woods Hole, with Eel Pond at its back, the little main street running along in front of it, and no pretensions to "wonderful chowder" or soothing the middle class. Strung along the bar you saw all kinds of working Americans—ordinary seamen, bikers, carpenters, fishermen, hippies, mothers, scientists. Motorcycles were outside, maybe four or five big, low bikes on any given afternoon, the door was propped open if it was warm, and a couple of local dogs lay outside the door, just for the company. Once in a while somebody was thrown out the doorway.

I only *saw* this happen once. A local biker/carpenter—a thirty-year-old guy about six feet tall, in a leather jacket—was thrown out one warm October afternoon in 1975. As I watched from behind the banister on the steps of the Community Hall (across the street from the bar, next-door to the firehouse), he stumbled into the street, fell on a hip, swore back into the dark doorway, pulled himself up onto his bike, kicked it alive, roared around in a tight U-turn, and ran into a scientist walking his bicycle out of the lot behind the firehouse. I could tell he was a scientist because he was bald, wore glasses and too-short pants, and walked like his sex was in his brain.

At impact, the biker laid his cycle down, couldn't stand it up because it was too heavy, cursed the scientist, and in full view of the darkened doorway, took a swing at the man, whose front bicycle wheel was now a whorl. The dogs picked their heads up off their paws. As the biker's right fist moved toward the man's left temple, the scientist threw up his left arm, blocked the punch, and nailed the biker in the jaw with his right. The biker went down. I heard groans from the bar. Along with cheers. Suddenly I considered a career in science.

The scientist walked away with his ruined front wheel in the air, shaking his head. The biker, swearing and shaky, hauled himself up from all fours, righted the bike, kick-started it, and roared off up the hill. I never saw him again. The dogs, chins again on paws, flopped their ears against flies buzzing around in the sun.

That street had grit then, and the decency to let something like that . . . just go at that. I miss the place, the relative simplicity of 1975. But that time is gone. Now, someone would sue, or draw a gun, and now I wonder what happened to the biker when he was a kid to make him a drunk and a belligerent. Back then he was just a cowboy who lost the draw, and the scientist a man secretly delighted to sacrifice a bicycle wheel to his own legend.

This was brought back to me by a recent visit to said bar. I had just come off a placid shift in which Jack Morrison's place had been temporarily taken by a Vineyarder named Ben Higson. In Jack's absence, Jeb was shift leader, taking the weight of father's blame while Gail and Ben and I soldiered on.

All had gone well until Tuesday morning, when Burt (once again) was convinced by old feelings to wreck himself on the reef of Ben's consistent behavior. Ben, a forty-year-old, solidly-built tug-captain, about five-ten, who'd gone to Haverford and then decided that he needed the sea under him part of every week, stared softly out at Burt from behind a great black beard as Burt serenaded him from his seat at the table, where he was reading a *National Geographic*.

"What do you mean I still gotta clean out the washing machine? I fixed it."

"Well—" began Ben, not fast enough.

"I put the new rawed in it, and greased the rockah arm, and plugged the bottom an' all."

(We had a hand-driven, island-built contraption that we proudly called "the washing machine.")

"Yeah."

"So I fixed it. I shouldn't hafta clean it too."

"But you were the last guy to use it. It's full of dirty, soapy water," Ben witnessed, his crow's-feet deepening, blue eyes clear as he looked calmly back at the boy.

"So what?"

"So, like anybody else, you still have to leave the machine clean. That's only fair."

"But I fixed it."

"And we appreciate that, Burt. We really do. But that doesn't mean you get to make moah werk for the rest of us."

"But I fixed it. I shouldn't have to—"

"Burt—," said Ben, and then the flood gates opened.

"You're a fuckin' douche bag, just like the rest of them, Ben. Didn't take you five days to start lookin' like a db to me, think you know everything. Fuck you."

"Burt, that'll cost you," I said from the couch on the other side of the big chimney.

"Fuck you. Why don't you let Ben fight his own battles?"

"Ben?" I said.

"That'll cost you, Burt," he said quietly, leaning with his hands on the serving table.

"Another douche bag," Burt said as he turned and vanished onto the deck, the door thudding shut behind him.

The wind blew hard later that night, moaning through the

house, and it seemed to take the matter with it. Burt was fined a couple of dollars, and cleaned out the laundry machine the next morning. The week ended uneventfully, and on Friday morning we clambered onto the *Hill* and rode home. Jeb slept in the fo'c'sle, curled around his tool box on a bunk; Gail smoked, sitting on a pile of junk lumber on the stern. Ben and I read the local papers and chatted with George about the weather and lobster prices, as the islands filed by to starboard.

And when we were in, unloaded, the *Hill*'s lines made fast and she quiet in her slip, just before we all split, Ben asked if I'd be up for a beer at the Kidd, just across the street.

"I've got a half hour before my boat, and I've got something t'ask you," he said. I said sure.

We crossed the street, streaked gray with salt, and as we pushed open the heavy green door of the bar, the smell was of stale beer and old wood floorboards. A small group sat at the far end, underneath a hockey game on the TV.

We ordered a couple of drafts, and while Ben gathered his thoughts I took in the fading wall murals of ships and sailors, the life rings from long-departed vessels, that hung among the images, the bottles stacked in rows behind the bar, and the two clean-cut young bartenders, who wore polo players on their left breasts, whose image alone probably repelled any ham-handed bikers who happened to wander in.

"What I want to run by you is Burt," said Ben, after the drafts had come. "He's been on my mind, because I thought he and I hit it off, so the whole thing kinda threw me." I could see in his blue eyes that it hurt him when the kid had pushed him away so hard.

Ben, we'd all decided, was a good man. He'd worked a couple of times on the other shift in the last month or so, and I'd found him to be solid, slow to anger, predictable in the way that stable people are, and independent—willing to find a project and see it through. He'd been reconditioning an old marine railway on the south shore of the cove, and the boys seemed to like working with him.

"What threw you about it?" I asked.

"We'd been working together well, and he seemed like he'd taken to me, and would listen to me, and then, all of a sudden I'm a douche bag, and he wouldn't look at me the rest of the week."

I looked down the bar. Directly under the Bruins, who were killing a penalty, sat two young women, talking. Each had a beer, and brown hair that hung down her back; each wore a wool sweater and jeans; each had a leanness of jaw and neck that told me she was lithe, not yet more apt to sit than move. I was distracted. Ben could tell, and was polite. I, ever the maroon, knew also that when I came in here, there they were, every time, the same two, on the same stools, sirens on a reef. To be avoided, especially in a fog. I jerked myself back.

"I mean, it's not *so* disturbing to me," he was saying, "but I'd like to understand it."

I wasn't sure how to respond, but I had a thought or two.

"I think what's going on here is he likes you. And he likes you enough so that's a threat to him."

"What do you mean?"

"He's used to *everybody* he likes disappearing and disappointing him. So he's beating you to the punch. If he alienates you first, then he's in control of the hurt, not you. In a sense he's complimenting you, in that if he really didn't like you, he wouldn't say anything to you. He's afraid to like you, because it's too risky. Because on some level he feels like you're going to abandon him, too."

Ben looked down the bar, mulling this. The Eagles sang about a girl driving a flatbed ford, and one of the girls strode by on her way to the bathroom. A scene repeatable (like good science) in ten thousand barrooms across the country.

"That seems right," said Ben after a moment, reassured. "He's lost a lot of people?"

"Both parents. Grandparents. His whole family's scattered. He's on Penikese, where kids come and go. Who knows how hard his growing up was. You can't take it personally."

"Yeah," he said.

"It's pretty hard not to, though," I said.

"Yeah."

This seemed to set Ben at ease, so we chatted about projects on the island, finished our beers, and said so long, parting ways outside the barroom door as I reflected on the fact that I had never come close to being a biker or a scientist.

25

I GO to Vermont for six weeks in the summer as I have for the past four summers, working on a master's degree in English. The campus is high in the mountains, as high as you can get in the old and worn granite hills there and still find space for three hundred people to congregate around Shakespeare or Whitman, the Brontës, Langston Hughes.

Since I began to teach at Penikese, the work in graduate school has seemed immaterial at times, lacking real worth in the face of pulling delinquent youth out of the mire, though I always knew there was worth in story, in tales of common humanity.

Still, I had a hard time with the ease of it all, the life arranged—classes at such and such, meals between, rooms furnished and fresh paint and quiet halls and bills paid. There was an otherworldly air about it, as if I were living somehow in avoidance of the real problems.

Then I came upon Beowulf. I was living in an old farmhouse, down a mountain road from the main campus of old inn and barns and houses, all painted a muted yellow and trimmed in green and sitting at ease in the mountains, and I had chosen a class in the oldest story in the English canon. I didn't know why. Partly it was because the professor seemed fierce, and partly it was because the age of the thing intrigued me, but largely I didn't know why I'd chosen the old poem.

I was reading in that old house, in what had been the parlor, sitting in an armchair by an open window on a cool gray summer day. The sugar maple in the yard stood quiet, and few cars passed. As I read a recognition began to form. This was a story about abandoned youth. Moreover, it was the oldest written story in the English canon *and* it was about abandoned youth. The more I read, the better it got, and revealed more of why boys are delinquent than any other text I've found.

I ask you to transport yourselves, as I did, sitting in the armchair in that old farmhouse in Vermont, to a windblown and desolate land, Denmark in the eighth century, a land of ferocious tribes still dwelling in the pale light of polytheism. When you die there, you die. There is no afterlife, and what matters is creating a good memory of your name, if you are a man, by being brave and strong in life.

We are in the kingdom of Hrothgar, a hard little fiefdom where law is decreed by the mightiest and enforced by his thanes (knights), who wear heavy and foul-smelling armor and from whose belts dangle iron swords with which they, from time to time, avenge the deaths of their cousins and brothers at the hands of neighboring tribes who in turn seek revenge, from time to time, for the killing of their cousins and brothers.

This is their business, and of course making sure that things are well at home—that the wife and kids are okay, sheep sheared, goats milked, cabbage planted, and of course then there is the mead to be drunk each night at the mead hall, where they often carry on far into the night and then fall asleep in their cups.

Into this pastoral comes a monster. His name is Grendel, and he lives in the mere, wanders the barren waste of the moors and the heathery hills, trods goat tracks and the high paths of the forgotten. He is huge and awful and strong beyond measure and reeks of swamp and rot and has great snaggly teeth that escape his enormous mouth, hair like eel grass and great bulging veiny eyes which roll in his head, which hangs at an angle. Grendel is a good fellow, but his has been a hard lot. He is the son of a monstrous mother (an actual monster), and of Cain—he is the son of a broken home. He's been around for a while, and his assignment has been to live with Mum and wish that he had friends. And he's fed up.

Recently he's been roaming, feeling lonely and looking for company, and what he often sees on his jaunts are the assembled thanes in the mead hall, roaring with good cheer, celebrating their brotherhood and skill in battle. But he is not invited. So, one night, as the thanes lie sleeping off a bender, he steals into the mead hall and in a riot of gore tears apart and devours thirty of the brave knights and then retreats back to his horrible lair, where his mother presumably asks him where he's been, to which he presumably replies "out" and rumbles off to his messy room. The next night he goes out and eats even more, and then carries on with this random terror for twelve winters.

Well, pity King Hrothgar. We are told that the "Scylding King/endured in torment all possible cares/the fullest agony . . ." as a result of being helpless before the monster these twelve long years. Delinquent boys *are* a pain in the ass. Then, into Denmark, from across the "whale road," arrives a great boat with fifteen battle-tried men from the kingdom of Hygelac. At their head is Beowulf, and he has come to meet the monster and best him how he can. Now, Beowulf is a big fellow, has the strength of thirty men in his grip, but he is not yet fully initiated into manhood: He needs a monster to stand down in the worst way. There is talk and more talk, and then they decide to lay a trap.

Beowulf and a crew of thanes go down to the mead hall and bunk for the night, hoping that the monster will come again. He does, but only one thane ends up in chunks in his maw before Beowulf seizes the battle claw of Grendel, and the struggle is on. They wreck the place, and finally, after a titanic struggle,

Grendel's arm is torn off at the shoulder, and he runs away across the moors, mortally wounded. There is much rejoicing at this, a great feast, the thanes fall happily asleep in their cups that night, and along comes Grendel's mother (who is only slightly less lethal than her son), and she in revenge makes off with another hapless thane, whom she devours once back at the bottom of the mere.

Beowulf, like any good hero, sees that the job isn't done, so the next day he goes to the mere, dives to the bottom, and, finding Grendel's mum, beheads her after another titanic struggle. So the monster is dead. The story could end there, but it isn't so simple, just like on Penikese.

Grendel, we find if we look at the text, is a very human guy. It says there that "The great monster in the outer darkness/suffered fierce pain for each new day/he heard happy laughter loud in the hall/the thrum of the harp, melodious chant/clear song of the scop."

He is lonely. But, fatherless child, demi-monster, and castaway of the moors, he cannot be part of the club. So, his solution is that of the outlaw. He strikes at the establishment, trying in anger "savage and reckless" to shame and punish those who would not embrace him. This was, we are told, "great torture for the lord of the Scyldings/a breaking of spirit. The wise men would sit/high-ranking, in council, considered all plans/what might be done by the bravest men/against the onslaught. Little it helped them."

Grendel is a classic juvi. He is from a broken home, his mother is poorly socialized, and he is an outcast. He would love it if there were a gang of friends like himself to run with around the moors, maybe steal an oxcart or two, eat the oxen. Then he'd have a troop (*gedryht* in the Old English) of his own. That might change things entirely for him, but he has no gang. So he throws rocks through the windows of the high school, and beats up the honor students and wrecks cars on lawns and you know the rest, although he takes it a little farther.

The thing about Geatish society (of which the Scyldings and
Beowulf are part) is that if you are a man, you want to be part of
the warrior troop, the *gedryht,* because then you know where
you belong. You want to have an heirloom sword dangling at
your belt, some blade that belonged to some long-dead ancestor,
you want to have a rep for being fearless and nutty-strong in battle, and you want to have a leader to serve unto the death. *Best* is
to be honored by your leader by his giving to you of an heirloom
sword. Then you know you're a made man. That is where you
find security and the possibility of making a name for yourself.
Conversely, when this position is threatened, you become murderous, as your psychic security is being threatened.

So, "peace" between peoples is had when neighboring
tribes feel either disorganized enough or fearful enough of
each other not to attack, which is to say, rarely. More often
they remember past slights and incursions and leap to revenge
them, which is fine (in a sort of twisted way) because the real
psychic "peace" that the men desire is found by them in the
security of being part of a troop, knowing where one fits into
the team, not in true peace.

Beowulf recognizes this dynamic of endless internecine
tribal rumbles, and when he returns home he tells his king,
Hygelac, that he thinks things will be okay in Hrothgar's kingdom for a while, but only for a while. And then he tells this
story:

> Then, at the beer fest, an old fighter speaks,
> who sees that ring-hilt, remembers it all,
> the spear-death of men—has a fierce heart—
> begins in cold sorrow to search out a youngster
> in the depths of his heart, to test his resolve,
> strike blade-spark in kin, and he says these words:
> "Can you my comrade, now recognize the sword
> which your father bore in the final battle
> under grim war-mask for the last time,
> that precious iron, when the Danes killed him,

controlled the field, when Withergyld fell
in our heroes' crash at Scylding hands?
Now some son or other of your father's killers
walks in this hall, here, in his pride;
exults in his finery, boasts of his slayings,
carries that treasure that is rightfully yours."
He continually whets the young man's mind
with cruel words, until a day comes
when the lady's retainer, for his father's killing
sleeps bloody bearded, hacked by a sword . . .

and the whole bloody spree continues, ad infinitum.

So, Geatish society turns on men being secure in their place in the hierarchy of their society, and on what they do when they feel that their honor, dignity, security, or needed role is threatened. When their role is threatened, things get ugly. By extension, when a man in Geatish society feels that there never was a role for him to fulfill, a similar murderous rage rises in him; so Grendel eats the thanes who will not include him in their *gedryht*.

I finished this crazed and thick and gory old tale in the front room of that old farmhouse in Vermont one evening in August, trying to make sense of it while the wind moved through the leaves of the old sugar maple in the yard outside. Suddenly the plot as it lay in my mind was accelerated, the way one can drive down a road in one's mind, seeing the whole extent of it in seconds. In a rush I saw that Grendel was the classic outcast, his pedigree as pure as could be, reaching back to the West's original outcast (Cain) and that he was exhibiting the same behaviors I had observed in my charges on Penikese. There is exhilaration in finding what one knows to be true expressed in the words of another.

But what of Beowulf? Who was he? I looked further into his history, and found in the text that he had been an orphan as well, that his father had been banished from Hygelac's kingdom when Beowulf was but a boy, and that Beowulf had not been expected to amount to much. He had been part of the royal court, but marginally so. He was an outcast, fatherless, with no chance of becoming king or receiving an heirloom sword unless he did something truly impressive. His defeat of Grendel was this, and upon returning home, he was given an heirloom sword by Hygelac, and later, after some time, succeeded him, and ruled for fifty years of peaceful time, so much did his enemies respect his strength and so well did he play them off against one another.

Why hadn't Beowulf taken the destructive path of Grendel? Well, he had a better chance of making it in the established world—he was human. But I think it goes deeper than that. Here is a paradigm shift in how to see the story: Any story can be seen as a sort of dream which one person relates to another. Jung felt that characters in dreams are just parts of the persona of the person who dreams them. If this is so, then Beowulf and Grendel can be seen as parts of one personality, parts who war with each other, one of whom must actually die for the other to live. And that makes sense. Cain and Abel were "brothers," but don't they really represent a range of possibility for how to see one's relationship to a father? Or to a metaphorical father such as society? And can't they also be seen as two ways of responding to fate, or god, or God? If the real question is psychic security, what if Beowulf is an example of a choice that a soul can make, the choice to see a hard lot—orphanhood or abandonment—as a hardship, but not as a judgment of one as worthless? This is getting at the core of the problem.

I see Grendels every day on Penikese, and at war with them, Beowulfs, all packed into the same adolescent bodies, each boy searching half-crazed for a sense of belonging, a sense of not being adrift in an insane and metaphysical sea. One could say that finding a sense of place and role in a hierarchy of society is illusion, in the end, but the lack of such a sense is, in my estimation, what drives these boys to violence. They feel adrift, untethered to society or the natural world, and without hope of finding initiation, or the elders who would usher them into the psychological safety of a group, of a tribe.

And, whether I know the origin of youthful violence or not, the looming question to me on Penikese has been whether I have heart enough to act as an elder to a young man. This is still not clear to me — whether, lacking a father, I can ever grow into one.

26

SEPTEMBER 1. I have been away for a summer of grad school, and now am back at Penikese for a second year. I am now a master of English, but just what that means eludes me. And in my two months away the cast has changed almost entirely. I feel empty, somehow, as if what there was of a family for me here has fragmented. Wyatt, of course, is gone, in jail now, and Jerome, Sonny, Cyrus, Ken, Ned, James, Reggie, Alan, Mose. They were my students and I theirs, as I learned what to take as a real threat, when to be scared, how to hear the jibes, and how to see those years of growing.

Now, as I mix with this new group, listen to their insecurity and fear coming out in obscenity and trash talk, I hear it for what it is. And my past looks different, as if it were a film that has much less to do with who I am than it did, a film which I can choose to be inspired by, or educated by, but which has no power over me which I do not lend it. Or I like to think this.

I stroll through the days here with confidence I didn't have last year; I have earned my stripes from the JDs.

The cast now is Henry, Burt, Josh (returned after some months AWOL), Drew, Sam (all of whom were here before), and Will and Cal. My question is what these two new boys have for me, and I am waiting, perhaps too eagerly, for their lessons. Will is a Native-American, half-Caucasian boy, lightly built, who is with us for an undetermined crime. He won't tell us what it is, and none of us cares to squeeze it out of him. They know onshore. He is not a real threat, but he is a follower, needing approval, and might be convinced to do something by one of the others.

Cal is a well-built sixteen-year-old, with long brown hair pulled back in a ponytail. His self-possession is clear as soon as he walks into the room, and he seems to look on the rest of the guys as so many children. He is with us for attempted murder, having hurt a boy in Cambridge who he says was attacking and meant to kill him. I buy it. He plays none of the bullying games that guys like Ken delighted in, and carries himself with an assurance not threatening or cocky, but which says, If you come here, I will respond. He asks only for his space. He is the undisputed alpha male out here now, and rules benevolently.

J O S H (who returned a month ago, and had to begin the program again, after running with a gang and living at his friends' crib for the better part of the summer) and Burt and I wrote haikus in school today, after doing math and English and history and science, during our last forty-five minutes. The guys were against it until I began one, explaining the motivation behind it—the wish to capture the essence of something in few words— and then began grilling them about the essence of this place.

"What you mean five-seven-five beats a line? Nobody talk like that, nobody talk in beats."

"It's like rap, Josh. It has a pattern, like rap, which the guys who write these know about, and they all agree to go by the pattern in order to write the same way, like always using the same kind of ball no matter where you play basketball, so they know where they stand with each other."

"What for? I don't give a shit about no pattern. I just want to say what I want to say, and that's all. I don't need to put it in a hikku."

"It's 'haiku.'"

"Whatever. Who gives a shit?"

"Burt? How do you feel about it?"

"Bullshit, man. I'm wit Josh."

"All right, I'll write it down, and you guys dictate." They did.

SCHOOL HAIKU #1

Haiku sucks, this sucks.
I got somethin' in my fuckin' eye, man.
It sucks, you don't learn nuttin'.
—*Burt and Josh*

SCHOOL HAIKU #2

This thing's givin' me
A cock-fucking headache, man.
And Burt's hat is fucked.
—*Josh and Burt*

Which pretty much communicates the essence of haiku with Burt and Josh. But they began to understand haiku better, so then it was time to take on the next best thing, the outhouse, and then lobstering.

OUTHOUSE HAIKU #1

I pull my pants down,
A cold breeze hits my ass. I
look at chickens fuckin', shit, leave.
—*Josh and Burt*

OUTHOUSE HAIKU #2

I smoke a cigarette
While I shit. Flick my ashes
Down the hole next to me.

—*Burt and Josh*

LOBSTERING HAIKU #1

Lobstering sucks, man.
Rotten fish bait fuckin' stinks.
I row *Brooke* back home.

—*Burt and Josh*

SEPTEMBER 22. The weather is turning slowly, with swallows passing overhead in fluttering myriads, heading again for Florida, Costa Rica, wherever the living is good. I wonder what is left down there of the good life. The staghorn sumac leaves turn a brilliant red, along with those of the rosa rugosa, and the grass loses its green. The sea, too, looks more blue, deeper. The zooplankton and phytoplankton are no longer blooming, and so the green of the waters fades.

Yesterday, in the morning, I got a surprise. In the usual lull after breakfast before we all head to work, Burt grabbed three rolls of toilet paper and announced,

"Yo, I'm headed to the outhouse."

I was sitting at the long dining table, thumbing through a *National Geographic*.

"Burt, man," I said, "I was up there right before breakfast. There are already two up there. Just take one roll, okay?"

He turned to me, standing by the front door, holding the three rolls, and said, with conviction, "Shut up, you fuckin' whore."

Something a long way down inside me snapped.

I stood up fast, pushing the bench back with my knees; it yelped as it slid across the floor. In my mind I saw my left arm feinting up to draw his attention as my right shoulder turned toward him, driving my right fist through space to break his nose. I was as close as I can come to that without doing it. I almost took the three steps that would have led to that, or perhaps just putting him through the door; I can see him now, lying dazed among pieces of shattered red board on the grass outside.

Burt looked at me when I stood up, knowing he'd gone too far. His eyes were wide, and he was back on his heels, ready to turn and put a piece of furniture between us.

I looked at him hard for a long moment, then averted my eyes, sat back down. After a few seconds he hurried out, and I tried to breathe. In. Out.

Like a stream, the jibes have worn away the stone bed of my patience. I have lost some of my stamina. I am no longer safe out here. I think, responsibly, I can make it for another six months. Which is what I will tell Laurie, in the office. This was unexpected, and I am perplexed with myself. Why am I not beyond this now? It cost Burt one dollar.

OCTOBER 1. Two days ago Jack, Josh, Henry, Burt, Cal, Drew, and I rowed to Cuttyhunk in *Smoke*, the long, black pulling boat. It was an easy pull over there, with a following wind and fresh arms moving us. We had three sets of oars pulling. I manned the forward oars, where I could steer; at the center thwart the guys switched off, each taking one of the long sweeps; Jack and one of the guys rowed at the stern station, each with a long sweep. One guy sat in the stern and "chilled." Jack sang sea chanties and the guys smoked cigarettes, wore bandannas and tattered clothing, and generally looked like privateers.

We landed on the rocky beach of the channel leading into Cuttyhunk's harbor, about a mile as the crow flies from where we started, and after setting out an anchor and pissing nearby, began walking the island, which is perhaps five miles around. We took the narrow dirt road that winds around her southern flank, first meandering among low summer houses with rose-bushes and white pickets out front, and then up through the dense thickets of scrub oak and staghorn sumac that alternate with natural grasslands in the outback of the island.

Cuttyhunk is a world of its own; there, everyone knows everyone and their business, and the mainland is held at bay. And you feel this as you walk the island, as if the trees had eyes in them, or the deer were eavesdropping—pretending not to look at you, but really watching you, and saying something like, "Hmmmph. That one sure walks funny." Indeed, the deer of the island were a hot topic as we walked; most of the guys had never seen one in the wild. Cal was adamant, and spoke in a fake Italian accent piled on top of his southeastern New England accent, because that's what he liked to do sometimes:

"I ain't a-gonna see one. I know it. Evybody else always a-sees one, and I nevuh do, and it a-pisses me off, 'cause it's-a like they a-voidin' me or a-somethin'." We all reassured him that he would see one; he remained unconvinced.

We made the south end of the island around noon, and ate our lunch in the shadow of the old stone tower there, built on a tiny island in a salt marsh in honor of Bartholomew Gosnold, the first English explorer in the region. The boys found an old skiff, and floated around in it, paddling with remnants of an oar, Huck Finns for a half an hour. And then Cal and Burt went out to the little isle, which is perhaps fifty feet by fifty feet, thick with scrub oak and honeysuckle, climbed the tower, hung about on an old rope, and then came down.

Suddenly there was a crashing and three big, terrified does, having risen from their hiding, galloped once around the tower and then leapt right off into the deep water on the far side of the little island, swam twenty feet, and, gaining sand covered by a foot of water, galloped breakneck down the marsh with silver spray kicking up from their hooves. Cal stood awestruck by the tower, his mouth hanging open. The Italian accent was gone.

"They almost ran me ovuh!" he said. "They fuckin' almost ran me fuckin' ovuh. I can't believe it! Crazy! That was great! I seen a deer. First time, and I seen three deers." At this he fell to his knees and looking upward, yelled, "Jesus, I'm-a comin' to you!," jumped off the island in his clothes, swam the twenty feet to the shallows, and ran off down the marsh after the deer, still yelling, and growing fainter, "I seen some-a deers, I seen some-a deers," with his hands waving over his head.

So it was a good day for Cal. When he returned half an hour later, we hiked back to the boat, and then shoved off the beach into a lively westerly.

When we were halfway home, having rowed for half an hour, most of the crew (all except Cal, who was too thankful to offer solidarity) went on strike, refusing to row any further into the steady wind and chop that had set up while we hiked.

"Yo," said Burt, "I ain't rowin' anymore. My back hurts, and my hands hurt."

"Yeah, fuck this shit, yo. I'm goin' to sleep. Wake me up when we're back," said Drew, and wrapped himself around the anchor in the bow.

"Yo, I'd like to know what you guys were thinking when you asked us to come over here, yo. What do you think we are, machines? We got feelings, yo, and bodies that wear down," said Will.

Five young voices said, "Yeah, man," at once.

"We were thinking you might like to get off of the island and see something new and have a picnic, is what we were thinking, but I guess it wasn't appreciated, was it Dan?" said Jack, and the boat fell silent, lost way, and turned broadside to the seas, which began to push us away from Penikese. About a minute later, Henry made the connection.

"Hey, wait a minute, we goin' backwards man. That's cold, yo. Put out the anchor, dog, throw it over till the wind change."

"Too deep for that here. It won't hold till we're just off Nashawena," said Jack.

"You guys arranged it this way, didn't you, knowing we'd have to row back into the wind?" said Will.

"Yup, we dialed up the wind this morning, one-nine-hun-dred-ill wind," said Jack.

"Yo, that's cold, yo. You guys can row the rest of the way. I'm on strike," said Drew.

"Yeah, we're on strike," said Will.

"Oh, we can't move this boat alone, just me and Dan. It's too heavy. We'll just sleep under rocks on Nashawena, when we wash up there late-ah this evening," said Jack, leaning back in the stern, and smiling at me. Again silence fell. Five min-utes later four oarsmen volunteered to row, and we slogged our way back upwind to the rhythmic creak of oars on thole pins and the occasional curse of a boy as he caught a crab. We fi-nally made the cove around five o'clock.

Since that day, I have noticed a change in Cal. He is more open to the world around him, smiles more easily, and has be-gun to draw—landscapes, portraits of us, and fantastic crea-tures that are half caterpillar, half horse, such as one would find in *Alice in Wonderland*. He has talent. "I haven't drawn since I was twelve," he told me the other day. The deer have set something free in him.

W E have a new boy: David, of Somerville. A Puerto Rican kid, damned smart, and a good athlete, who likes to sling around big words. He is not particularly big, or well built, but he has a solid presence, and he is quiet. He listens, which sets him apart. He is quick in school, flying through his algebra and history, and he seems to respect us, what we're trying to do. He dresses neatly, with a new baseball hat worn all the time. He plays chess with Jeb, the way Jerome used to, and he seems to take pride in working hard. We all like him a lot, and if he can stay away from an older brother who sounds like a bad in-fluence back in Somerville, maybe he'll be one who makes it.

But I remember what George said about the chameleon.

*   *   *

THIS morning, with David, I poured the concrete cap on the outer foundation wall of a greenhouse. It looks roughly flat, which is all we can ask for—relative flatness, that gravity should marginally assert itself out here. He worked hard on it, back behind the school where Cyrus had wrassled with Thoreau the year before as the steeplebush and yarrow went to seed; he mixed the concrete well, wearing his spotless ball cap, using his big words, telling me,

"I don't know about this, Dan, I never attempted nothin' with concrete like this befoah. I am highly skeptical."

NOVEMBER 2. A week ago, during his weekend home, David the good, of the clean baseball cap and the self-control, of the chess played with Jeb, was arrested at a crack house in Boston, and taken downtown by police. For some reason, they didn't charge him. He was released, and came back to Woods Hole a day later with three or four hundred dollars in his pocket. At 3 A.M. he and Drew (my bird-watching foul-mouthed little brother, onshore for the evening after arriving on a late bus from a home pass) hit the road, stuffing their beds with pillows the way fugitives do in the movies. They are who knows where. Rich? Dead? Turning tricks? We have no idea. Life is full of surprises.

NOVEMBER 4. Last night I sat at the fire with Will, the half–Native-American boy who seems to have a "v" for victim carved in his forehead. Cal has given me his teaching on inspiration, and the wild; Last night, I think Will began his teaching. We were grilling steaks for dinner, and watching the evening come on, the glow of the sunset still in the air, seeping over the hill. We talked about what makes a boy take the wrong path. Digging around in the coals with a stick, Will rambled:

"For me, I think it's a lot about I never had nobody to show me the right way. I always had to deal with my mom and her boyfriends, you know, always weird shit going on, so I never had a chance. But I just want to get a job, and go to school, you know, man. That's all I want, to go to high school, have a normal life. It isn't that much to ask, you know, but I don't seem to have that thing, that whatever it is that some guys have, you know, that little boost. I mean, where do you get that little boost, Dan?"

I hadn't expected him to ask me. I didn't say anything for a long moment, then ventured, "I don't know, man, you just have to have faith that it will come."

"I been having faith, and I'm fed up with having faith, man. I want the boost, man, I want some of that sweetness. When's it gonna come?" he said, looking up at me. This sounds concocted, but it happened. I remember how the firelight played on his face.

"I don't know," I said, "but it's got to come from inside," and I let the evening take up the words. He went on digging in the coals.

I felt like telling him, "I don't know, Will. You're asking the wrong guy." But how do you tell a kid that it's possible to ace college, grad school, teaching jobs, to feel that boost, and still not really know what lies at the core of yourself, still not really know from where that sweet little boost comes.

27

H E N R Y ' S voice: "Yo, I don't know really what to say. I'm
from Boston. It's bad up there, yo, but I ain't sayin' I want to
leave there or nothin', 'cause, like, it's what I know, and that's
where my people are at, but I ain't gonna lie. It's dangerous,
and shit be happenin'.

"They always sayin' here, like, 'You can get ahead,' you
know, 'Keep your nose clean and you could go to college,' you
know, stuff like that, and I know that's true, but it's hard when
you just tryin' to get over, you know, when you just tryin' to
stay safe and have a little money, you know, to do things, because it isn't like there's a lot of options, and, to tell you the
truth, I don't feel bad dealin', 'cause I ain't twistin' their arms
to buy nothin' from me, you know. I ain't twistin' nobody's
arm. I'm just a entrepeneur, like Mr. Iacocca, pure and sweet.

"They always sayin' here that I'm bein' part of the 'chain of
negative energy,' or some shit like that, and I know what they
be sayin', but it's like, what are my options? I don't have no
money for college, it's a good chance I'm gonna be lookin' at
you from the grave in a couple of years, and I need some loot
every time I walk out the door. You can't do *nothin'* in the city
without some loot, man, nothin'. Can't even go to a movie. So,

what I'm gonna do, go flip burgers at Mickey D's? Now, I may not have much respect for myself, but I got more than that, a lot more than that.

"But this place is wack, in some ways. They be treatin' us good out here, with respect and all that, and I'm learning a lot of stuff, like how to take care of animals and how to make a boat—shit like that—and I'm keepin' up with my studies, but man, it ain't like I'm gonna be usin' this stuff in my life. Like I ain't gonna be heatin' my house with wood, and I ain't gonna be catchin' my own lobsters and quahogs, you know. But I don't mind knowin' those things, and there's a lot of time to think out here, and that's good, and I don't have to be watching my back all the time, you know. I like that.

"But I miss the bi . . . the girls, man. I miss them bad, like I feel like my life is passing me by out here, like this is time I can't make up, and . . . I guess I'd feel that anywhere they put me, but you know that's tough, to be missin' some sweet thing I mighta run into otherwise. Damn, man, that's the hardest thing. And not goin' to the crib, man, to hang with my boys, 'cause we tight. But I miss the girls bad, real bad, like I be havin' nightmares where I wake up and I'm an old man, all rickety and shit, and they all still young.

"Do I know my father? I know who he is, I know where he stay, but that's about all I know. He ain't doin' so well, you know.

"Do I go out strapped? Well, let me put it this way. I don't feel safe out there. Like, because I ain't a big guy, and I ain't a small guy. I'm just a guy, but with a strap, man, I could be as big as anyone else, right? Mine could run as fast as anyone else's. I mean, it's the damn westerns out there, you know? Little dudes be takin' out big dudes, David and Goliath and all that, so I'll just say that without the power you feel vulnerable, right? I mean, it's the same thing they got goin' over in the Middle East, man, you know that back and forth thing. But strapped, at least a fellow got the benefit of the doubt with him, see what I'm sayin'? But I don't like all that. It shouldn't have to be like that. But to be general, no I don't walk around with a strap. No I don't."

DECEMBER 4. I played cribbage with Will last night at the long table. We played late, after the other guys had gone up, and it was a quiet night out, quiet enough to hear the hiss of the kerosene burning in the old lamps and the peal of the bell buoy over by Canapitsit. Will told me, in halting phrases, as we played the simple old game, of his mother's depression, and of her boyfriend who drinks vodka like it's water, right out of the bottle.

"He's big. I mean this guy's big. Wide. And he just sucks it down like it's water, like it's spring water, man. I can't mess with him.

"Yo, but I decked him one night about a month before I got here, 'cause he was so on my case about shit, and he was threatenin' my moms, and I just lost it and hit him on the eye, and he fell over, and then he got up and came after me, so I booked out the front, and he wiped out on the porch behind me, couldn't hardly walk, so I went to my boy's house, and it was all right. I figured he'd kill me in the morning, but he didn't say a word. Didn't remember none of it. Just limped around."

We turned in, after a last round, at about ten-thirty. Will preened in front of the mirror by the big stainless-steel sink for a few minutes, lost in dreams of being a cinema star in the yellow light of the lantern on the little shelf there, and then clunked upstairs. I went out on the deck, where it was moonless, quiet. Just the sound of the water coming faintly into the cove, and the stars hanging quietly overhead, the dark sea stretching away. What do I say to him?

"See, Will, there's this monster inside you named Grendel who has the strength of twenty men. He's the part of you who judges you as bad, and you just have to kill him, and then things will be fine." Do I say that? Maybe I say nothing, listen hard.

I see that I am not going to "win" at this in the way to which I am accustomed. None of my students is going to win essay or poetry contests or be transformed before my eyes, none of them is going to be a casually reformed young man who will call and visit me after graduating. I will never see any of them again. Probably. And if I do, that will be good and perhaps it will be easy and natural, a young man and his one-time mentor recalling a past life. But the reality is that I will say good-bye to these boys soon, having done what I could, and much of that good-bye will be without closure, will be my exiting in the middle of a meal, in the middle of a day, in the midst of the family discussion, in the midst of a scene. I also see no failure in this. I have done what I could here, and that is all I can ask of myself. *Some* of the time I see no failure in this.

SCHOOL with Cal and Will. The north wind is up, surf is booming on the isthmus, and the sky is gray and low, which tells me the weather is going to do something strange. My thoughts are on the greenhouse, and what we can accomplish today. Things are framed, and the rafters are up. All is ready for glass. That's what we'll do—clean the glass. But when I look out there I can't help but think of David, who helped me pour that cement cap on the greenhouse foundation, on a wet day a month ago, standing with a shovel propped on his boot, doubting our cement expertise, and Drew, who helped dig out the foundation, and who laid the first course in the front wall the day I smashed my finger under a big blond piece of granite. The finger was truly flattened at the tip, mashed into a pulp of torn flesh, and faithful little Drew, Jackal-Boy, walked with me to the house in silence as big drops of blood ran down my hand and splatted on the ground. Minutes before he'd sworn at me, but he gave me his quiet support, then, for fifteen minutes, until we'd gone back to work.

David was finally nailed last week with twenty-six bags of coke in his pocket. He went down for six months. Drew was scooped up a day earlier for the same. I don't know how many bags he had on him. I see him sitting morosely on the edge of a bench in a cell, hat askew, staring down into his hands, wondering which big mother will want to rub his shoulders next. I know they'd both rather be out here. It is hard to watch them screw up.

DECEMBER 22. My time here grows short. Yesterday evening, toward the end of work, Burt and Will and I went over to Tubbs to watch the sun go down. I had an idea that if we looked from there, across the cove and toward the high hill, we might find that the sun set close to two pointed stones embedded on the southwest side of the hill, where they offer their sharp silhouettes when the sun is low behind them.

It took ten minutes to get there, and as we hiked the rounded fist-sized stones of the isthmus and then up the fifty-foot rise of Tubbs, we could see it would be close, that the only way to see an alignment would be from a large exposed boulder on the northern edge of Tubbs. We sat in the tall grass there, and waited for the disc to descend.

"How the fuck is the sun going to wind up between those rocks, Dan, and what if it do?" said Burt. "It don't matter. We could go anywhere's so it would line up right."

"I already told you that this is the shortest day of the year, and that this was a sacred day for native people for a long time, right?"

"Yeah. So?"

"So, the Native Americans used to set up calendars using the sun and the stars, and they did it right over in Woods Hole, and all over New England."

"So?"

"So I have a hunch they might have done it here. In Woods Hole, they set up a row of stones so if you looked along it on December twenty-first, the sun would set over a standing stone on the far shore and then reflect on the harbor in a line, if it was calm that day."

"So?"

"So there's a building blocking it now, but I think they might have done the same here."

"So?"

"So we're going to watch."

"You are one weird-ass dude, Dan," said Will.

We stretched out in the tall grass to wait. It wasn't long. Within ten minutes the molten disc had nestled down between the two pointed stones, a quarter of a mile away, and then slipped quietly into the hill. On a calm day a brilliant line of sunlight would have reflected on the cove's surface. We might have been the first humans to record the winter solstice in this way, on this island, for four hundred years. I told them this. Will was quiet on the way back to the house, and Burt walked on ahead of us, saying he needed to think.

FEBRUARY will be my last full-time month out here. I have decided I can't give any more than I have, and what I have is exhausted. I told the school in September I'd stay six months more, and I'll be true to my word—I'll get them through the hardest months of winter, and then I take back my emotional life. It will be hard to walk away.

JANUARY 12. With the new year comes the last new student I'll see. Rafe is a big, articulate, light-brown kid with a funny way of clipping his words, as if he doesn't want to give up too much of himself. He is from different parts than most of these guys. He is from a nearly asphyxiated mill town in the Berkshires, way up in the northwest corner of the state, an Appalachian burg with crime and poverty and hopelessness, but with little of the energy that one feels in the inner city, which is at least still inner. I'm not sure what his lesson will be for me, but I have a pretty good idea.

I had a meandering talk with him the other night over cribbage at the long table. He told me of never having met his father, how angry that makes him. I told him of never really having one around, how angry that made me, makes me still, sometimes, although less and less. He was surprised.

"What, you never had a father?"

"Well, I did, I mean I know him, but he was hardly around when I needed him, you know. I'd see him once in a while."

"How much?"

"It depended. When I was small, maybe every couple months I'd get a glimpse of him, and then when I was older, well, about the same."

"He loves you?"

"He was hardly around, man. I think he loves me the way you can like that."

"I heard that."

He stared at his cards. I could hear the soft hiss of the kerosene lamps to our left and right.

"What about you?" I asked.

"Never met the man."

"That's hard."

"Someone told me that was him in the distance, once," he said, looking me in the eye, "but I couldn't get close."

"How'd you feel?"

"Pissed me off." Then he said, quietly, "That's why I feel like goin' out and kickin' the shit out of someone sometimes."

"Me, too."

"You used to get in fights?"

"Well . . ."

"You used to fight, huh? I can see it. You kicked some shit, all dieseled up."

"No, no. I haven't been in a fight since I was fourteen."

"What!"

"Maybe that's bad, 'cause I didn't let it out, but I could always see that the poor guy standing in front of me wasn't what was making me angry."

"I never see that in time."

"Start to."

"Yeah."

"But I hear you, man," I said.

"That's fucked up, Dan man."

"What?"

"That you know what I'm talking about."

"Yeah, I know."

He whispered this with a sly smile. "And you're a fuckin' white boy, man."

"Don't tell anyone. Turn your hand over."

"Why?"

"Turn it over," I said.

"Yeah, we're both white some ways," he said.

We talked on; he hinted that he had let his anger get the best of him, but he didn't say how. I didn't press him. But I could tell that there was a bit of wonder there that a white guy and he could be talking about fathers together. That is a bit of surprise we all have to get over.

Last night Rafe and I had another late game of cribbage at the long old dinner table, with the kerosene lanterns hissing quietly, and the occasional toll of the bell buoy in Cannapitsit coming faintly across the calm waters. He had built up a healthy lead by the time I asked him why he was on Penikese, and what that had to do with his anger, and suddenly he was all right with telling me.

"I fucked this dude *up*, man," he said quietly. "That's why."

"How?"

"With a crowbar. I mean, I'm not kidding. I hurt him."

I could see that it pained him to say this—he had looked me in the eye as he said it, and then he looked away. He wasn't proud of it, and he wasn't backing away from it, either. Which took courage.

"How did it go down?"

"I was just out walkin' with a friend of mine, on a side street, and these two dudes who I knew—they were a little older— they came up in a car, and one of them started callin' me nigger this and nigger that, and something just snapped. I opened the door and pulled the driver guy out of the car and threw him down, and his friend came around at me with a crowbar, so I punched him down and took the crowbar and the first dude was getting up by then, coming at me, so I knocked his teeth out with the bar. Knocked 'em right out."

"Did you plan any of this?"

"No. It just happened. Just like that. So I got picked up."

"What'd they call it?"

"Aggravated assault with a deadly weapon."

"Would you do it again?"

"I don't know." He was quiet for a minute, and we played out a hand, the pegs clicking on the varnished board as we counted our points. Then, he said,

"It's hard to hear that word like that."

"Yeah."

We played another half a hand.

"You know what?" I said.

"What?"

"You're going to hear it again."

"I know."

"Yeah. So what are you gonna do?"

"Defend myself, demand respect."

"What if it's a question of not fighting there so you can win elsewhere? How're you going to have that control?"

"I'm not."

"Well, you better, or you'll wind up back in jail. What if you didn't just react, what if you thought about how low the person using the epithet really was?"

"What's a 'epithet'?"

"A word used the way 'nigger' was there."

"Oh."

This was the point where I usually lost them.

"What if you could see so clearly that the person dissing you was just dissing himself, that he really couldn't touch you with it, that only you had that kind of control over yourself, that nobody could threaten your dignity with just a word? What then?"

"I don't know."

"Think about it."

"It's hard to be thinking calmly at a time like that."

"Yeah, I know."

He proceeded to thrash me in cribbage, and stood over me as I did the forty pushups we had on the game. He was smiling when I stood up, breathing a little hard. "See, Dan. That was control, man. I beat your ass with control."

T H E greenhouse is about done. Burt and I worked the past couple of days on it. It was strange. He had gotten in a near-fight with Will, which I broke up one evening. In the heat of the moment I told him he'd just ruined my last week on the is- land, and he took it to heart, and has been trying, I think, to make it up to me by helping with the greenhouse. He's doing good work, although today he won't speak to me as anything other than the goof, in a high, tinny, lisping voice, unless we're speaking of a bevel or a miter. Then he's Burt again, for a mo- ment. He is a funny, funny kid. He is teaching that today.

We framed the west doorway yesterday, and got the door in place. The damned thing heats up, by god. How about that? And perhaps Burt will build one for himself one day.

F E B R U A R Y 1 5 . I am saying good-bye to the island, for now. In all likelihood, I'll be back to work a weekend or two, but I am beginning to detach.

I took a walk around her, early yesterday morning, before dawn. It was nearly dark when I began a clockwise circumnav- igation, walking down past the eight apple trees, down the still green path past the schoolhouse, and then down onto the cove beach. The call of that loon, from the morning Wyatt called me a punk mammerjammer, came back to me, as I laced my way past the lone dory lying on the sand and then on through the boulders of the beach. I thought I heard the high whistle of oystercatchers winging over, but it's the wrong season for them. Must have been an echo.

Then I ambled out to South Point, where there's a little pond, on the shore of which sits a great lump of Roxbury conglomerate, a "puddingstone," a jambalaya of pebbles and stones embedded in petrified mud, another remnant of the Ice Age. I said so long to the rock, where I hid clues to scavenger hunts so many times ("I know wheah that is—it's that weird-ass rock out on south . . ." I could hear Ned, the wild-looking metalhead, saying).

The surf came onto the shore there, and I turned west and north, having run out of land, and walked the western shore under the bluffs, topped with leaning grass and the stems of the dark blackberry thickets. Vacant gull nests—discarded pie plates of hay—dotted the high beach. Glancing up, I thought I caught the silhouette of a dark head and shoulders moving against the hillside, leaning, almost as if driving a plow, but of course everyone was still in bed, and my imagination being what it is. . . . Perhaps it was the land's recollection of John Slocum in 1796, or Silas Gifford in 1821, or one of his sons, cutting the sod for winter wheat.

I kept on, the bluffs losing height, then giving way to the plain at the north end of the island where the leper cottages lie in ruins. The surf came on roaring, with spindrift blown off the waves clinging foamy to the grass in dim light; old lobster buoys, washed up, rested in the lee of foundation stones. Squinting, I could almost see the outline of the old cottage frames above the open cellar holes. The name plate of a forgotten fishing vessel—*Eva Mae*—lay faded in the dead grass alongside the old laundry building.

I thought of Archie Johnson, the teenage leper who kept a ham radio in his bedroom there, in the second cottage, and of his mother who stayed with him until he died, not knowing if she would be allowed to leave again. She was. And of Iwa, the Japanese leper who lived in seclusion in his own cottage nestled back in the bluffs, a parrot his only companion, his feet wrapped in white bandages as they swelled. The bird would have been awakening on its perch now, in the half-light. The old man received visitors graciously, it was said, serving them green tea from an iron pot.

I climbed to the little cemetery Sonny had first shown me, the fence freshly painted green now, the sixteen graves marked with dim numbers, keyed to their owner's names on a stone at the entrance. The sea washed below. I walked on, back down to the beach, and kept on, along the isthmus where Alan and I had gathered so many rounded stones, had stranded the tractor, had faced ignominy, and where I had seen the great owl the winter before with Ned on the banks of the shallow pond there. All those images still alive. The sea came on the beach in a five-foot set, its sound filling the air, stones clacking as the waves receded.

And I walked on, set out around Tubbs, the Alaska of the island. Nothing out there but a sweeping vista of tall grass and tern nesting sites awaiting their keepers homing in again. And a seal carcass, still disintegrating a year after Wyatt and I had come upon it, the eye sockets upturned and open to the sky. Had it seen its essential self there, before the eyes glazed? Had Iwa, counting the waves?

I rambled along the southern shore of Tubbs, and the house came into view across the cove, with those sharp stones above it on the hill, black against the lightening sky. A lantern still glinted in the kitchen window, and somebody was up, smoking on the deck. What would he make of me, on the far shore, a dark figure walking in the dim morning light? I would disappear at the far end of the beach, behind the boulders there. What did I look like? The ghost of a fisherman, stranded, forever walking the shore to a house no longer standing?

I walked on, gained the isthmus and its rounded cobbles, took the wagon track back through the hay field with that rambling stone wall along its spine, passed the rocky pig yard. The pigs, still piled on top of one another in their hut, watched me and raised their ears as I passed. Seeing I carried no bucket, their long-lashed eyes closed again.

And then I climbed the steps to the deck, sat down on the bench next to Burt, who was sitting with his arms crossed, looking out over the cove.

"I wondered who the fuck that was over theah."

"Man, Burt, no swearing before breakfast, all right?"

"Word up, bru-thah."

I shall say my good-byes.

Epilogue

THE year and a half of full-time work at Penikese was field study for me, immersion in a culture of dysfunction of which I thought I had no ken, and there are a few stones I tripped on that I have to write of here.

It hadn't occurred to me, when I began at Penikese, that it might be possible through disciplined looking, disciplined awareness, to separate a self from its past, from its upbringing, not in a way which disallows knowledge and traits and tradition, but which allows a person to fully inhabit himself, no longer to be victim to his/her past. This is at once such a simple thought and one which proves endlessly complicated; it was so clearly shown me by the boys, each of whom dwelled in his own house of anger, mistrust, disappointment, misapprehension and melancholy, and each of whom so clearly had a larger and brighter self than that built by those finite details of an early life. Each thought himself condemned by those early years, and the question forever will be how to convince them otherwise.

What I saw so much in them, too, was self-judgment, almost a rising tide of judgmental water, which rose within each to fill any space not filled by good feeling. The rule in this seems to be that when they look within, wherever these boys see neutral territory—territory neither condemned nor labeled "sacred" by a trusted elder—they call this land bad, evil, damned, negative. By default. They judge themselves, they expect the worst. Why? This is a calculus I can't explain, but know, like gravity, to be true. Accept it.

Often, now, I find myself speaking among people of living on the island, of teaching the boys, of confronting their anger, their hurt, their sense of loss and of being lost. Over a beer in a backyard a man or woman will tell me how well I have done, how good it was of me to go there to the island, to break bread with and try how I could to help these boys move on. And they listen to my telling of the story of Beowulf, or to a description of a day there. They nod, take a swipe at the grass with one foot, tell me again how good it was of me to go. And I see that it is so. But I see too one of the deep truths of such service— that it's I who have been taught by the boys, that it is their anger, their bitterness, their attention to the lessons of abandonment to which I owe the greatest debt.

What can you do? Get with a troubled young man; pay him attention; convince him that he is sacred within; help him see the Grendel who tramps through his veins; help him see his parents for what they are—flawed humans to be understood, forgiven, loved; show him the possibility of seeing, rather than standing in judgment; teach him to laugh and love. Expect to achieve none of this. Do it anyway.

DOES THE SCHOOL WORK?

Yes. I believe so. There are still not hard numbers to show this, and that is one of the difficulties of running a school on a shoe-string—you don't have staff psychologists or sociologists tagging along. My gut tells me it works. The one study we have (mentioned in my conversation with Cadwalader on the boat on the way to the island) indicates that we do well. And then there are letters like this, which arrived one day, addressed to Pops, near the time when I left:

I write this to you back at Penikese to let you know that the school really does have its affect.

I finished there in 1979, and every day I see how the place has meant changes for me. When I'm in a hard time I was always able to sit back and figure out something better.

The thing is, when I went back from the island, it made me angry, because that was the end of the family on the island. I was O.K. when I got back for a while, and then using the drugs got me right back into the old me. I had no respect for nobody, and then you know what? I'm back in prison.

What happened was, I knew this guy next door was beating up on his kids, and I knew it wasn't right. But then one night I could hear his little daughter and little son crying, and me and a buddy were drunk, and we decided we'd take care of the problem.

Well, he didn't die, thank god, and I served 3 years in jail for that, and I see now it was something I should have let the public handle.

After I got out, I started thinking about the island, things I took in there. So I started down a whole new road. I live good now, I'm married eleven years, and I have the three best kids. I have my own house, and people can't even believe I'm the same guy I used to be in their town. I am doing well, and every day is easier.

What I can tell you is this: to the boys on the island, there's a lot of things out there for you, and many lessons which you can take and use how you need them.

Your friend,
Bill (age 32)